Enterprise learning in action

For over a decade the education and employment systems of western industrialized countries have had to adapt to the changes brought about by the post-industrial age. The recession of the early 1990s has led the education and business communities increasingly to look for ways to co-operate in preparing young people and unemployed workers for a new social and economic order.

Enterprise learning in action draws on case studies in community and enterprise learning from around the world to show how young people and the unemployed can be taught the enterprise skills which will enable them to survive in an uncertain world. Dale E. Shuttleworth looks in particular at how this can be done outside the formal school system and within the community in ways which are responsive to the particular needs of each locality. His message is overall one of great optimism for a future in which those who are at present rejected by the system can become active and valued contributors. *Enterprise learning in action* will appeal to all students and researchers from primary through to adult education and to those in local economic development.

Dale E. Shuttleworth is Superintendent of Community Services for the Board of Education of the City of York, Ontario. He has over thirty years experience as a community educator and is the author of more than ninety published articles.

Educational management series
Edited by Cyril Poster

Managing Evaluation in Education
Kath Aspinwall, Tim Simkins, John F. Wilkinson and M. John McAuley

Education for the Twenty-first Century
Hedley Beare and Richard Slaughter

Parents and Schools: Customers, Managers or Partners?
Edited by Pamela Munn

Education 16 – 19: In Transition
Eric MacFarlane

Opting for Self-management
Brent Davies and Lesley Anderson

Managing External Relations in Schools
Edited by Nick Foskett

School-based Management and School Effectiveness
Edited by Clive Dimmock

Enterprise learning in action

Education and economic renewal for the twenty-first century

Dale E. Shuttleworth

London and New York

First published in 1993
by Routledge
11 New Fetter Lane, London EC4P 4EE

Simultaneously published in the USA and Canada
by Routledge
29 West 35th Street, New York, NY 10001

© 1993 Dale E. Shuttleworth

Typeset in Times by LaserScript Limited, Mitcham, Surrey
Printed and bound in Great Britain by
Biddles Ltd, Guildford and King's Lynn

British Library Cataloguing in Publication Data

A catalogue record for this book is available from the British Library.
ISBN 0–415–06859-2

Library of Congress Cataloging in Publication Data has been applied for.

I read and I forget,
I see and I remember,
I do and I understand.
    (Confucius)

A long time ago came a man on a track
Walking thirty miles with a sack on his back
And he put down his load where he thought it was best
And he made a home in the wilderness
He built a cabin and a winter store
And he ploughed up the ground by the cold lakeshore
And the other travellers came riding down the track
And they never went further and they never went back
Then came the churches and then came the schools
Then came the lawyers then came the rules
Then came the trains and the trucks with their loads
And the dirty old track was the telegraph road

Then came the mines – then came the ore
Then there was the hard times then there was a war
Telegraph sang a song about the world outside
Telegraph road got so deep and so wide
Like a rolling river . . .

And my radio says tonight it's gonna freeze
People driving home from the factories
There's six lanes of traffic
Three lanes moving slow . . .

I used to like to go to work but they shut it down
I've got a right to go to work but there's no work to be found
Yes and they say we're going to have to pay what's owed
We're going to have to reap from some seed that's been sowed
And the birds go up on the wires and the telegraph poles
They can always run away from this rain and this cold
You can hear them singing out their telegraph code
All the way down the telegraph road.
            (dIRE sTRAITS, Telegraph Road, 1983)

Success has a thousand parents . . .
Failure is an orphan.
        (Shuttleworth, 1992)

Contents

Tables

Preface

On December 18, 1991 General Motors shocked the world when it announced a massive industrial retrenchment that would reduce its workforce by 71,000 over the next four years. Twenty-one plants would be closed and office and managerial staff reduced by 20,000. This is not only the world's largest company but the planet's 20th largest economic unit, with a Gross National Product larger than Finland, Denmark, Norway and Saudi Arabia.

This is the corporation celebrated in William Whyte Jr.'s 1956 classic *The Organization Man*, which describes people who not only work for "The Organization" but "belong" to it as well. "They are the ones of our middle class who have left home, spiritually as well as physically, to take the vows of organization life, and it is they who are the mind and soul of our great self-perpetuating institutions" (Whyte, 1956).

How the economy has changed in 35 years! No longer can we depend upon multinational corporate security to guarantee "the job for life." In the recession of the 1990s we are seeing plant closures throwing "The Organization Man" out onto the street, where he may never again find ongoing employment. It isn't just the semi-skilled blue-collar worker who faces this fate. The well-educated white-collar employee has also seen his dream of employment security turn to despair and disillusionment.

We have reached the end of an era for most western nations in which spiraling prosperity has been replaced by a sense of dread about the future. The post-industrial age has arrived. Whom do we blame for the hollow dream? How can we protect our standard of living as we reach for the twenty-first century?

These are the questions and concerns I will be addressing in this book while exploring the relationships between education and the world of work. As the influences of the industrial age diminish, we are desperate to know how to prepare our youth and displaced workers for the new social and economic order. The 1970s and 1980s were a time of experimentation as we began to move outward from our protective institutions into a world of uncertain employment. What have we learned from these experiences to prepare us for what has been characterized as the "knowledge society," the "information age" or the "post-industrial era"?

My own awakening to these new realities has been very much a journey of discovery. As a child of the auto industry in Windsor, Ontario, I grew up with a growing sense of uncertainty about the future. My father made tires in Detroit but we were not shielded from the "boom or bust" mentality of industrial dependency. My life options were very clear – get an education or go onto the assembly lines. I always remember the stories about the line workers at the Ford Motor Company who would dash out the plant gates on their breaks to down a row of draft beers and shot glasses of whisky ("boiler-makers") at the nearest tavern to ease their tedium and low self-esteem.

After "dropping-out" of school to work in a succession of dead-end and part-time jobs (textile plant, retail sales, pumping gas, theater usher) I "smartened up" and went back to school to get enough education to qualify as an elementary school teacher.

In my first job, teaching grade 5, I still recalled the words of the Master at Teachers' College responsible for School Management: "Remember, don't smile until Christmas or you will lose control of the class." This preoccupation with discipline and structure seemed to be most important in the eyes of the Principal and Inspector of Schools, whose satisfactory evaluations were needed to secure a permanent teaching position.

Because I had not yet achieved a Bachelor's degree, in the early 1960s I attended university courses at night and during the summer. I was fortunate to be enrolled at Assumption University whose applied sociology program, pioneered by Dr Rudolf Helling, encouraged me to involve myself in experiential learning, including "original research" in the field. One of my service learning assignments consisted of more than a year's volunteer work at St. Leonard's. This was Canada's first half-way house for ex-prisoners which was in the process of being founded by Fr. Neil Libby, an Anglican priest (much to the dismay of area residents).

My job as a volunteer was to be a "friend" to those who had recently been paroled from prison into St. Leonard's. I soon discovered that there were only two types of people in their world: the "squares" and the "rounders." Needless to say, I never did achieve the status of a "rounder."

I will always remember sitting around watching television one evening with Bob, a grade 7 dropout with the "gift of the gab." Bob pointed across the living room at Jake, a newcomer to the House. "See Jake," he said, "he ain't gonna make it." "How do you know?" I asked. "He's just too institu-tionalized" (his words) said Bob with conviction. Sure enough Jake went back to "the joint" about two weeks later after trying to rob a confectionery store. Bob maintained that prison was the only place where Jake had a sense of identity and felt secure. The outside world was a pretty frightening and confusing place for Jake.

It was then that I began to understand the nature of institutionalization. Both Jake's prison and my elementary school had something in common. They were both "top-down" custodial institutions with a strong commitment to external control and a culture which encouraged dependency. I also began to ponder the question of whose needs were really being served in such institutions.

My next career assignment was as a school–community worker in a public housing estate in the Borough of North York in Metropolitan Toronto. I went from a school authority with 60 teachers in six schools to work in one school with 60 teachers and more than 1,200 students from junior kindergarten to grade 6. These children and their parents inhabited a community of 5,000 with a fence around it to separate the housing project from the more advantaged homes in the surrounding residential area. This enclave of "institutionalized poverty" was commonly referred to by outsiders as "The Jungle." Children who strayed beyond the chain link fences surrounding the project were often told "Get back in The Jungle you monkeys." Is it any wonder that children, parents and ultimately the teachers and other professionals who served the community suffered from low self-esteem?

In 1971 I went to work in the City of Toronto as Vice-Chairman of a Task Force established to study problems of inner-city education and school–community relations. A group of poor mothers and community organizers were confronting the school authorities with the rallying cry "Our kids can't read!" It was soon apparent that the Task Force had been created to protect the bureaucrats from the fire of community indignation, particularly around the issue of streaming low-income children into special education "opportunity classes" for slow learners. As a result the Task Force took much of the heat, as it was "middled" between the community activists and the institutional administrators. Consequently, no one really trusted us and we were "shot at" from both sides.

The Task Force brought down its final report in 1972 and I was asked to implement the recommendations – many of which were seen as being threatening, if not subversive, by the administrative ranks. For the next eight years I struggled to initiate policies and programs in inner-city education, multicultural education, community school development, cooperative education, school-based day care, the education foundation, community resource learning, day use of vacant space, alternative schools, community education programs, school–community relations, employment programs for school-leavers and education in the workplace, to name but a few. As a "change-agent" I again found myself in hot water most of the time; but it was also a wonderful opportunity to study the politics of education first hand as an "intrapreneur."

During the decade of the 1980s, I became a superintendent for the York Board of Education responsible for community services as well as school supervision. I was able to transfer much of my learning experience from North York and Toronto while developing similar policies and programs. The Adult Day School and the Learning Enrichment Foundation were new initiatives, however, which built upon my experiences in adult education and community development. The "York Model" for community education and economic development has now been emulated both nationally and internationally. In 1987, I was named an expert consultant to the Organization for Economic Cooperation and Development (OECD) in Paris. In particular I have participated in two studies:

- *The Social and Economic Integration of Young People*, which was published as a report entitled *Towards an Enterprising Culture* (1989).
- *Business/Education Partnerships*, which resulted in *Partners in Education: The New Partnership Between Business and Schools*, a report to be issued in 1992.

My work with the OECD has given me an international network of contacts which has broadened my vision and provided a much more in-depth understanding of the role of schooling and employment in the cultures of the western world.

Allen Tough describes a "learning project" as: "a highly deliberate effort to gain and retain certain definite knowledge and skill, or to change in some other way" (Tough, 1978).

The writing of this book has been the outcome of many such projects. This personal learning odyssey has become a life-long quest to better appreciate and serve the needs of those discarded by the traditional education and economic institutions of the industrial age. It represents a "resource inventory" of experiences, case studies and alternative strategies to better prepare us to survive, and perhaps even prosper in the new millennium.

Dale E. Shuttleworth, Ph.D.
City of York, Ontario, Canada.

Acknowledgements

I'm pleased to dedicate this book to my father, Harry James Shuttleworth. Born in 1900, a product of the agrarian society, he had to leave school at the age of 14 when his two older brothers went off to Europe to fight in the "Great War." He was soon "doing a man's work" – able to plough a straight furrow behind a team of horses. After working as a carpenter's helper – building barns – and serving in the United States Marines, he joined the industrial age making tires for 39 years at US Rubber in Detroit. Upon retirement in 1965, he returned to his love of the soil as a gardener whose beautiful floral displays have continued to be a work of art to this day.

Therefore he has transcended both the agricultural and industrial eras to create beauty and achieve personal fulfilment in the post-industrial age. His more than 92 years of very productive life have been an inspiration to me. His continuing devotion to work, creativity and commitment to the well-being of his family have been qualities and values which I will always try to emulate.

I must also pay tribute to other mentors and role-models whom I have been privileged to know throughout my career. Both the late Rudolf Helling, former Chairman of Sociology at Assumption University of Windsor, and the late Fr. Neil Libby, founder of St. Leonard's House, in Windsor, helped me to appreciate the needs of the "discarded" and challenged me to pursue a life of service to the community; Wilson Head taught me about social welfare, poverty and human rights and first recognized that I might have something to contribute as a scholar and community educator; Alec Dickson has given me a better understanding of the real meaning of "community service learning"; Malcolm Roberton shared his insights into community economic development; Allen Tough introduced me to the power and potential of nonformal personal learning; Bill Quinn and John Phillips have been my models for the humane educational administrator who "really cares" about students, parents and teachers. I have been truly blessed by having known and learned from these outstanding individuals.

I also wish to especially thank the following persons: Joyce O'Connor, Erik Wallin, Dave Turner, Anne Jones, Colin Ball and Jarl Bengtsson, colleagues from the OECD, who shared their knowledge and experience; Leslie Starkman, who introduced me to Celestin Freinet; Kristina Tomory, Rita Zanter, and Sara Wolch, who offered suggestions and encouragement; along with my editors at Routledge – Mari Shullaw and Cyril Poster. Most important, I wish to express my profound appreciation to Ambalika Naresh, who prepared the manuscript, provided encouragement and always had faith in my ability "to get the job done." And finally my wife Marilyn and children Tara, Tracy and Todd, who "put up with me" during the fifteen months it has taken to complete the enterprise.

1 Education and employment security

REDEFINING EMPLOYMENT

As we open the 1990s with a global recession, western economies are facing the grim reality of seeing traditional sources of employment in manufacturing, construction or natural resources down-size their workforces, automate their operations, relocate to low-wage zones or simply go out of business. What social theorists have characterized as the "post-industrial age" (Toffler, 1980) began to be sharply felt in the 1981–82 recession when jobs lost were never replaced. The recession of the 1990s promises to have an even more profound effect on the nature of employment in western industrialized countries.

For example, fewer than 20 per cent of Canadians now earn their livelihood by actually producing goods such as automobiles, buildings, food products or fuel. By far the majority, more than 80 per cent, are employed by governments, commercial enterprises or not-for-profit organizations that provide wide-ranging services (Statistics Canada). Unfortunately, employment opportunities related to business and personal services may be low-paying and structurally unstable.

The Economic Council of Canada in its 1990 report *Good Jobs, Bad Jobs* divides the economy into the following sectors consisting of "goods and services":

- primary industries – agriculture, fishing, forestry and mining (including oil and gas);
- secondary industries – manufacturing and construction;
- tertiary industries – all kinds of services that are intangible, non-transferable and nonstorable involving direct contact between producer and consumer.

Technological innovations and industrial restructuring are beginning to blur the traditional separation between goods and services. Within the service sector there are now three subsectors:

- dynamic services in two divisions – distribution (e.g. transportation, communications, utilities and wholesale trade) and commercial (e.g. finance, insurance, real estate and business services);
- traditional services – retail trade, accommodation and food and personal services (e.g. hair-cutting, cleaning, repairing, amusement and recreation etc.);
- nonmarket services – education, health, social services and public administration.

However, rapid technological and organizational innovations are changing the economy. Interrelated computer and telecommunications technologies are "transforming both the nature of service activities and the contribution that they make to economic growth" (Economic Council of Canada, 1990). The new information-age technologies of robotics and automation continue to devastate our workforces as large multinational corporations use recessionary times to introduce new labor-saving devices which improve the bottom-line by sacrificing jobs. As a result traditional industrial heartlands are becoming known as the "rust-belt," often beset by an abundance of vacant industrial spaces and a redundant workforce. Because the new technologies are so sophisticated, they often require an advanced level of education and technical skill to operate. The dislocation of workers from relatively high-paying manufacturing jobs to low-wage service employment or lingering unemployment is a tragedy of profound importance to the future social and economic well-being of the western world.

YOUTH IN CRISIS

In the new technological age it is expected that many graduates of high schools and post-secondary institutions will be following careers for which they were not trained and in this process displace less educationally advantaged workers who could have been employed in the past (Donner, 1983). A US study indicates that by the end of this century the best bet for employment will be in low-skill jobs such as building maintenance, fast-food workers and kitchen helpers (Levine, 1983). Even these jobs may be in jeopardy, however. As Willard Daggett, Director of Occupational Education Instruction for the State of New York observed in a speech to Kansas legislative and educational leaders:

> In some communities you can go in, push one button to indicate you want a quarter pounder and another to indicate how you want it cooked . . .

You can also indicate what you want on your hamburger. You put in your money and 13 seconds later you get a cooked hamburger untouched by human hands. Nobody takes your order, and no one prepares your food . . . the fast food restaurant has gotten tired of trying to attract quality workers that can do the level of work they want for a price they are willing to pay.

(Daggett, 1989)

While we know that the employment potential increases with the amount of education or skills a person possesses, young people still are not staying in school. A 1989 study from the Organization for Economic Cooperation and Development produced a table related to enrolment rates for 15–19-year-olds (see Table 1.1).

In 1981–82 a large proportion of young people of the western world had to shoulder the major burden of a global recession whose recovery left them ill-prepared for future employment and economic security. The resulting cost to our industrialized societies of a generation of unemployed or under-employed school-leavers in social and economic terms is staggering. In North America, for every 1 per cent rise in unemployment, there is an exponential increase in mental health admissions, homicide, suicide and

Table 1.1 Enrolment rates for 15–19-year-olds, 1986/87, expressed as a percentage of the cohort

	Age				
	15	*16*	*17*	*18*	*19*
Canada	98	94	79	54	40
Denmark	97	90	75	68	52
France	95	88	80	60	43
Germany	100	100	100	84	57
Netherlands	99	93	78	60	43
New Zealand	92	69	39	23	20
Norway	100	87	76	62	30
Sweden	98	81	83	43	22
Switzerland	92	85	56	53	37
United Kingdom	99	69	49	33	11
United States	98	95	89	60	49

Source: OECD, 1989: 37

arrests. There is clinical evidence that the high school dropout rate and youth unemployment are closely tied to crimes of violence, vandalism, delinquency, suicide and heavy drug abuse. These effects can be translated into permanent losses in billions of dollars to society each year (Kirsh, 1983).

Since the Second World War, our young people have been told to "play the game – stay in school, study hard and you'll have a job for life." They could look forward to even more material rewards than their parents – bigger house, more cars etc. Today's youth realize, only too well, that this has become a hollow dream. They have had to learn to struggle, just to survive.

SCHOOLING AND THE INDUSTRIAL AGE

There continues to be ongoing debate among educators, politicians and the tax-paying public as to how well our educational systems are serving the needs of youth. The fact that the majority of western young people do not go on to higher education or often even finish secondary school would seem to be an indictment of our ability to respond to the social and economic needs of young people. Perhaps an historical analysis of our systems of public schooling is in order.

Public education in the agrarian age grew out of the expressed needs of local citizens for literacy and numeracy skills. Since the industrial revolution, however, the physical structure of the education service, organizational style, management and supervision, curriculum content, and ability to evaluate and renew itself have all been shaped by the industrial model.

In North America the early nineteenth-century rural schools were often crude one-room log structures. Furniture was rough and scanty, print materials almost nonexistent and most pupils used slates and slate pencils.

Schools in the towns and industrial centers were quite different, however. They were either multi-roomed structures employing several staff or large, open halls with rows of benches in the Lancastrian or Monitorial style. These nineteenth-century buildings were often influenced by the architecture of European private schools and churches (Phillips, 1957).

By the late nineteenth and early twentieth century, urban schools adopted the now familiar style of long corridors with a series of standard classrooms on either side. These three- to four-storied structures, in design, were remarkably similar to the burgeoning industrial-age factories of the day. In fact, some industrial-area schools (such as Brant Street Public School in Toronto) were actually built so they could be converted to factories should the need arise.

Even in the 1950s, when single-storey schools began to appear on large sites in suburban communities, they were once again quite similar to the industrial architecture of the time. Even the open-plan schools without walls were strongly influenced by designs first applied to business offices and industrial facilities.

The organizational style of urban school systems was also based on a centralized administration building serving schools as branch plants located in areas with a high density of children and adolescents. The central facility provided senior management and financial support, as well as supplies and equipment, much like the industrial model of the main plant with warehouse and distribution centers spread across the country.

Each school had a principal (head teacher), department heads at the secondary level, and regular teachers supervising students in classrooms. By comparison, the factory might have a general manager or superintendent, supervisors or department heads, foremen and workers. This supervisory model still prevails in the industrial and educational institutions of today.

Supervisory or management techniques have been "lifted" from industrial experience whether through labor/management relations or quality-control procedures. Such industrial terms as "collective agreements," "cost effectiveness" and "management by objectives" have been directly applied to educational policy and practice.

The supervisory emphasis in large secondary schools has most often dealt with concerns of control and the efficient and productive movement of bodies, as opposed to responsiveness to the needs of individual learners. For example, principals-in-training must master the intricacies of timetabling, which is often seen to be more important than their abilities as curriculum leaders. This efficiency of production ethic has strong origins in the assembly-line model as envisioned by Henry Ford.

The nature of the curriculum and program in our schools is most often mandated by central government and reinforced by the administrative office of the school authority. The content seems to be either a reflection of tradition or an outgrowth of real or imagined political pressure. Business and industrial interests, because of their disproportionate influence on the political process, are often more able to encourage or retard change, at both the central government and local levels. The fact that most politicians are traditionally drawn from business and professional ranks reinforces this phenomenon.

The educational philosopher, John Dewey (1915), has described the role of the schools as either preservers of the status quo or anticipators of the future. However, most of our schools have acted as a stabilizing influence, serving to socialize the young in the mores of society, conserve and pass on culture, and provide a basis of social coherence.

Schools also provide a custodial function in the care and protection of children and adolescents while their parents work. High schools, colleges and universities keep young adults occupied who cannot be absorbed into the labor market. To quote Norman Henchey of McGill University:

> Schools teach the industrial model of roles, norms, and expectations; and they exercise their investment, sorting, stabilizing, custodial, and residual functions through the operation of the hidden curriculum of rituals, instructional organization, discipline codes, schedules, accepted behaviour patterns, curriculum organization, evaluation procedures, and certification mechanisms.
>
> (Henchey, 1983)

Large organizations have been characterized by social scientists as devoting their collective strengths and energies to maintain themselves (Drucker, 1985). This "systems maintenance" behavior is to be found in government bureaucracies, large corporations, and educational authorities. This drive to control change may serve as a comfort to those who supervise our institutions but how accountable is it to the real social and economic demands of today and tomorrow? In the 1950s US President Dwight D. Eisenhower first warned of the dangers of the "military–industrial complex." In the intervening years we have seen his fears more than realized. It is my belief, however, that we have also suffered from dependence on an "education–industrial complex" which is now having an even more profound influence on our social and economic well-being.

LIVING WITH LESS

It has been said that "the technology we call 'school' will have as much place in the twenty-first century's learning system as the horse and buggy have in today's transportation system" (Perelman, 1986). While the post-industrial population has growing unmet needs for learning, our traditional educational institutions are still locked into the industrial age. Large manufacturing and resource industries are no longer the major sources of employment but our educational systems are still modeling themselves on these forces.

We know that the best hope for employment in the next century will be in small entrepreneurial enterprises stressing the provision of quality services, consumer accountability, compatibility with changing technologies, and an international trading perspective. Our large, bureaucratic, inbred, insular, inflexible educational institutions would seem to be the most inappropriate venues possible to prepare young people for the future. To quote Peters and Waterman (1982):

In excellent companies, small, in almost every case, is beautiful. The small facility turns out to be the most efficient; its turned on, motivated, highly productive workers in communication with their peers, out-produce the workers in the big facilities time and time again.

We can no longer afford the current educational/industrial model of "bigger is better" when the costs of creating such physical environments far outstrip our abilities to finance these facilities. Indeed, the ideal of "living better with less" seems the direction in which most governments are being forced because of declining revenues and mounting national debt.

AN ENTERPRISE CULTURE

Schooling has long been criticized for its role in creating a sense of dependency among students and teachers inhabiting those institutions. As manufacturing increasingly moves "off-shore" in search of cheaper labor pools and to escape unionization, our economies have been forced to adjust to a new age of service employment and global interdependency.

Our formal educational systems, however, have most often stressed an abstract, academic style of institutional learning which has resulted in an average school-leaving rate of 46 per cent (18 years and older) among eleven western nations (OECD, 1989). It is estimated that the majority of workers at all levels will require substantial retraining every five to eight years, regardless of whether they change careers or stay in existing jobs.

Because education and employment are both facing this "crisis in confidence" at the same time, it would seem that only a massive joint campaign which mobilizes the resources of the governmental, commercial and voluntary sectors to attack the problem at the local level will result in a new more enterprising culture. Such a culture should recycle existing resources, embrace appropriate technologies, and encourage innovative design, cooperation and sharing. Education for employability in the post-industrial era will need to incorporate these values in an experience-based service which is responsive to the needs of all learners and consumers. The chapter which follows will explore current theory and practice to prepare for employment in an age of small enterprise and global interdependency.

2   A new age of enterprise

THE CHANGING ECONOMIC ORDER

The word "enterprise" has to do with the skills of initiation, imagination, creativity, being able to organize, make decisions and take control in a wide variety of contexts (OECD, 1989). These are qualities which have always been of vital importance in building the economy. The pre-industrial agricultural age was built on a foundation of local enterprise in marketing commodities, goods and services. In the twentieth century, the economic focus shifted to manufacturing and resource industries to generate wealth and employment in our increasingly urbanized societies.

As we reach for the twenty-first century, employment in manufacturing and primary resource industries is declining at an alarming rate. The major sources of new jobs would appear to be in small local business and service enterprises in both the public and private sectors including voluntary not-for-profit ventures (Canadian Press, 1992).

To compete in the post-industrial age, it will be necessary to strengthen innovative and entrepreneurial skills to access world markets for goods and services and decrease economic dependencies. What existing models, past or present, will help us to cope in this new age of economic instability and globalization?

OUR ITALIAN HERITAGE

Italy has taught the world perhaps more than any other nation about urban life and urban form. In the pre-industrial age the famous trading centers of the Mediterranean – Venice, Genoa and Florence – formed separate city states from whence merchants ventured forth and artisans aspired to economic success, prosperity and security.

In Florence, the craft guilds became a power that dictated laws to the governments. The merchants' companies became bankers whose symbol, the gold florin first minted in 1252, was to remain for three centuries the most solid and precious currency in the West. These rich and powerful cities became the cradle of the Renaissance, producing many of the great architects, painters, sculptors, scientists and scholars who founded our modern Western civilization (Bargellini, 1980).

New industrial networks

Today this same north-central region of Italy is experiencing a new age of industrial renaissance that may serve as an inspiration for economic renewal in the western industrialized nations. To quote Fritz Schumacher, the renowned German economist, from his book *Small is Beautiful*:

> We need the freedom of lots and lots of small autonomous units, and, at the same time, the orderliness of large scale, possibly global unity and co-ordination . . . For every activity there is a certain appropriate scale, and the more active and intimate the activity, the smaller the number of people that can take part, the greater is the number of such relationship arrangements that need to be established.
>
> (Schumacher, 1974)

In the early 1970s, factories in the region between Florence and Venice began to close under the dual impact of exploding oil prices and double-digit inflation. As a result, cities, unions, and trade associations learned to work together to establish a large number of very small, flexible firms that depend upon motivated workers and multiple-use, computer-based machines. These small independent enterprises, averaging only six or seven employees, act like departments in a large company but are free to combine with other small firms to form networks capable of complex manufacturing for world markets. Subcontracting within networks allows product specifications to be upgraded and product lines changed according to market demand.

The majority of the new entrepreneurs and former factory workers practice a high degree of shop-floor democracy to allow for the ongoing redesign of products and processes. The diffusion of knowledge and skill, together with the relatively small amount of capital needed to get started, encourages experienced workers to continually move on to open their own shops.

This new network of interdependent firms concentrates on quality rather than quantity, recognizing that large-scale production will inevitably migrate to lower-wage areas. Their flexibility allows them to produce efficiently even in short production runs because of the involvement of all workers in solving production problems and the availability of program-mable, numerically controlled machines. Experimentation and training are encouraged to ensure that innovation and quality are maintained (Hatch, 1986).

The Modena model

These networks of socially innovative enterprises came about because of the active involvement of government, artisans' organizations, educational and financial institutions, labor unions, planners, and architects. For example, in 1956, the City of Modena in Italy's Emilia–Romagna region, established its first "artisans' village" in response to layoffs in major industries in the area. Unemployed workers were encouraged to set up their own shops by making venture capital loans readily available. As a result, 75 small firms occupied space on the ground level with apartments on the second floor. These workshop/homes on city-owned land were municipally financed and sold to the new entrepreneurs on long-term contracts.

Since 1973, Modena has used funding from the central government to establish 27 similar projects. Shops range from 2,500 to 10,000 square feet and share utility costs. Sports fields, coffee bars, and cafeterias are standard features in the larger apartments. The city's planning and architecture departments work closely with the local branch of the artisans' confederation and the labor unions in the design and allocation of the new artisans' villages. As a result, the small city of Modena has planned and built working neighborhoods for over 500 small firms and several larger ones employing nearly 7,000 workers.

Besides providing physical accommodation, technical training and marketing services are available to foster entrepreneurship. This is an alternative to the alienation and deskilling characteristic of modern manufacturing. By distributing the benefits of technological improvements, investment is encouraged in human capital and increased opportunities for initiative. The city as a whole is strengthened because participatory workplaces reintegrate life and work and sustain blue-collar employment. It is not surprising that the Modena model for flexible industrial networks has now been emulated in Sicily, Denmark, Sweden, Germany and the United States (Hatch, 1986).

THE JAPANESE PHENOMENON

During the 1960s millions of Japanese managers and workers took part in a massive training program in quality control. One outgrowth of this national effort was the beginning of employee participative problem-solving programs known as Quality Circles (QC). Quality Circles are credited as one reason for Japan's phenomenal economic success.

The focus of a Quality Circle is problem-solving. With management support and employee commitment, work-related problems are identified, analyzed and resolved. Problem-solving in QCs may be described as a seven-step process (Sanders and LaRoe, 1983):

1 A problem is identified.
2 Causes for the problem are determined.
3 The most important causes are identified and analyzed.
4 A solution is chosen.
5 A plan of action is developed.
6 A presentation is made to management to obtain support for recommendations.
7 If the plan is accepted by management, the circle monitors implementation and undertakes to see if the problem is resolved or alleviated.

The QC model has spread quickly throughout the western world as Japanese corporations have moved their manufacturing operations closer to the marketplace. North American and European companies have adopted this method to satisfy consumer demands for better product quality.

It is a mistake, however, to assume Japanese industry is made up of massive manufacturing/banking conglomerates or "keiretsu." Of Japan's 874,471 manufacturing plants, 75 per cent employ fewer than 10 workers, according to the Ministry of International Trade and Industry. Only 0.15 per cent of Japanese companies have more than 1,000 employees. Small- to medium-sized manufacturers employ nearly three times as many of the 13.5 million factory workers as large ones.

Subcontracting is obviously the key to Japan's corporate success. Small household industries are rewarded with steady business during good times plus access to research and development knowledge. During economic slowdowns, however, it is these same small firms that bear the brunt of the down-sizing and reduced revenues. It would appear that the prevalent image of the giant paternal corporation providing a "job for life" is a myth for most Japanese (Hirsch, 1990).

COOPERATIVE ALLIANCES

Pioneering executives in the United States, Europe, Japan and other countries are now redefining the role of individual enterprise in an age of high technology and global economy. A new blend of competition and cooperation combines the entrepreneurial freedom of markets with the social values of democracy. Experimental prototypes developed by leading-edge corporations, communities, and entire nations include: participative leadership, client-driven marketing, decentralized structures, "intrapreneurship," democratic corporate governance, strategic alliances, deregulation and privatization, business–government partnerships and other innovations.

New democratic forms of business are emerging which serve social interests rather than profit alone. By gaining the support of workers, customers, suppliers, distributors, investors and the public at large, a new collaborative model of governance has emerged which produces better products while contributing to the social well-being of the community. To quote William Andres, Chief Executive Officer of the Dayton Hudson Corporation in the United States: "We find no conflict in serving all our constituents because our interests are mutually intertwined. Profit is our reward for serving society . . . It is enlightened self-interest."

Another innovation has been research consortia where competing companies form collectives. In the United States, the Microelectronics and Computer Technology Corporation is a joint venture of 20 computer firms working together to advance the cause of research and development in computer science for their material benefit.

Many large corporations in the auto, steel, electronics and other industries are forming strategic alliances to combine the advantages of cooperation and competition. North American, European and Japanese corporations, who normally are fierce adversaries, are now cooperating by jointly making and selling products in each other's markets.

American cities and states have formed partnerships with local corporations, universities, labor unions and civic groups to encourage economic development. On an international level economic partnerships, such as the European Community and the Pacific Basin Alliance, are growing rapidly because they offer the powerful advantages of cooperation for competing corporations and governments. Even such traditional ideological enemies as the United States and the former Soviet Union signed 230 joint venture agreements between socialist state enterprises and capitalist corporations (Halal and Nikitin, 1990). It appears that the new age of global enterprise is being built on a foundation of joint venturing, international and sectoral cooperation to enhance social as well as economic well-being.

THE RISE OF THE THIRD SECTOR

A new economic vehicle for the nurturing of employment skills and economic development has been third-sector initiatives. The third sector refers to voluntary not-for-profit enterprises, which together with the governmental and commercial sectors, comprise the post-industrial economy. Third-sector enterprises incorporate most of the business principles commonly associated with the for-profit sector but in most instances must be even more cost-effective and well managed to survive. To quote Peter Drucker in his book *The New Realities*:

> The third sector has grown fast, especially in the last ten or fifteen years. Indeed during the eighties it has been the fastest-growing part of American society . . . A church-related health-chain, owning a dozen large hospitals and a dozen nursing homes, has increased its income by a third in the last ten years during which most American hospitals suffered sharp income drops . . . The Girl Scouts of the USA, the world's largest women's organization, has managed to maintain its membership at 3.5 million despite a drop of almost one-fifth in the number of girls of school age between 1978 and 1988 . . . The third-sector institutions, in sum, not only practice management, in some cases more seriously than American businesses, they are becoming management innovators and management pioneers.
>
> (Drucker, 1989)

The value of volunteer work performed in Canada is estimated to be $12 billion according to a report by the Secretary of State entitled, "Economic Dimensions of Volunteer Work in Canada." Over a 12-month period in 1986–87, an estimated 5.3 million Canadians performed an average of 191 hours each of volunteer time. Using an average service-sector wage, it was calculated that these 1.108 billion hours of time were worth between $12 and 13 billion in 1990 dollars. When converted to full-time positions, this total number of volunteer hours would amount to 617,000 jobs, equivalent to 6 per cent of all full-time employment in the Canadian labor force in 1987 (Ross, 1990). It has been said the voluntary not-for-profit sector now contributes more than twice as much to the Canadian Gross National Product as does the primary forestry industry (MacInnis, 1985). Rather ironic as Canadians have traditionally been viewed as "hewers of wood and drawers of water."

LEARNING TO COMPETE

To compete in the new economic age, western nations should help all their people strengthen their innovative and entrepreneurial skills. A process of economic renewal should begin in the local community focusing on large-scale unemployment and underemployment among youth and redundant workers. This period of economic uncertainty could be a crucial time to build an enterprise culture including commercial, governmental and third-sector interests. Such a process of enterprise learning should involve primary, secondary and adult education to engender the attitudes and skills of self-reliance, cooperative problem-solving, innovative action and entrepreneurial zeal so important for survival in the global marketplace. The next chapter represents a survey of some public education programs in the western world which have been designed to bridge the gap between school and employment.

3 Schooling for work

BRIDGING THE GAP

A variety of school-to-work transition programs have traditionally been offered by public educational authorities to assist young people in choosing a career or preparing for employment. In general, they fall into the following categories as described by Barnes and O'Connor (1987):

- *Experiential learning* is conducted wholly or in part through practical, community-based, on-site experience. Examples of such activities include cooperative education, internships, experience-based career education, work study, work experience, and job shadowing.
- *Cooperative education* is an experiential method of learning that is intended to integrate a student's in-school program of study with a community-based training station for learning. This provides students with an opportunity to apply classroom theory to a realistic hands-on experience by spending part of their time in school and part of their time at the training station. Students are not remunerated for their work although a small honorarium and/or travel expenses may be provided at the discretion of the employer. However, academic credits are usually awarded as a result of the experience.
- *Internships* generally offer after-school opportunities (e.g. 2:30 to 4:30 p.m.) to apply those skills acquired in school to the world of work. Academic credits are earned but a wage is not paid. The intention is to offer the student a chance to experience a career choice by giving a more realistic view of the inner workings of that career.
- *Career education* involves a collaboration between the business/labor/ industry community and the formal education system to meet the goal of education as a preparation for work through a variety of in-school curriculum and out-of-school vocational experience (Hoyt, 1986).
- *Work study* is a type of learning where periods of in-class instruction are augmented by learning at a place of employment for specified time

blocks. These programs do not link in-class and out-of-class activities, contact between school and employee is limited, and the work is completed for pay by low-income students.

- *Work experience* is an approach in which relatively short-term experiences, usually of one or two weeks, are arranged as part of a student's overall school program. This usually takes place in the graduating year.
- *Job shadowing* refers to students spending time observing or "shadowing" someone in a work situation. This usually involves professionals (doctors, lawyers) high-profile positions (politicians) and highly skilled people (artists) where students would not have the skills for "hands-on" experience.

COURSES OF STUDY

Several countries have now implemented courses of study, as part of the regular school curriculum, to better prepare young people for the post-industrial age. A sampling of such programs is as follows.

Ireland

In Ireland the Social Research Center of the National Institute for Higher Education in Limerick has developed *Enterprise: The Key to the Future* as a resource package for young people exploring their career options. The package includes a video and a student's manual which can be used with both senior- and junior-level students, pre-employment students and community and youth groups. Enterprise is seen as fundamental to all activities and students are shown how "to explore various avenues towards controlling their own lives and reaching their full potential" (O'Connor, 1987).

The aim of the material is to enable young people to develop the confidence to create opportunities for themselves by taking a more active part in planning their own lives and to develop their creativity, assertiveness, self-reliance, self-determination and willingness to take risks. The video focuses on living in a changing society and examines the changing nature of work and employment and investigates opportunities for enterprise within the person, the home, the school, at work and at leisure. The approach is action-learning whereby students are encouraged to undertake a wide range of exercises and activities and examine realistic case studies, to explore how enterprise and being enterprising can become an approach to life (OECD, 1989).

The package is being presently used in approximately 300 schools, some community groups and youth training programs throughout Ireland.

Funding for the project has been provided by the National Board for Science and Technology and the Seven-Up Irish Bottlers.

Canada

An entrepreneurial studies curriculum has been implemented in two Canadian provinces – Ontario and Alberta. The Ontario Ministry of Education, with assistance from the Canadian Foundation for Economic Education, has developed a new curriculum in the Business Studies – Senior Division, entitled *Entrepreneurship Studies.*

Students examine the nature of entrepreneurial activity and the role of the entrepreneur in our economy and society. They explore the motivation that lies behind entrepreneurial initiative and identify the characteristics and attributes that are important to successful entrepreneurship. There is an emphasis on the broad application of entrepreneurial skills and attitudes as they apply to a small business enterprise, a large business, government and community programs, as well as to their personal/family/school endeavors. Students are encouraged to understand the role of initiative and creativity in all their activities and to appreciate the need to prepare themselves for tasks that will extend their capabilities. Steps in the entrepreneurial process include the identification of an opportunity, formulation and testing of ideas, planning the implementation of an idea, and launching and managing the initiative. These attitudes and skills are then applied to a broad range of possibilities in the areas of community service, business enterprise or the achievement of personal goals and aspirations. Students may earn credits at the basic, general or advanced levels of difficulty (Ontario Ministry of Education, 1990).

In Alberta a course called *Career and Life Management* is mandatory for grade 11 students in senior high schools. The core of the course is organized into five main, interrelated themes: self-management, well-being, relationships, careers and the world of work, and independent living. Optional additional themes include entrepreneurship, and dealing with crises. This content is different from that of the Ontario course in that it blends and updates traditional forms of personal development and career education. The Ontario course has enterprise at its core while the Alberta course has enterprise as one among many elements such as communications, decision-making, taking initiative, stress management and problem-solving skills (Alberta Education, 1987).

United States

Enterprise-related initiatives in the United States are found in both rural and urban areas as courses of study or school-based projects. Perhaps the most influential voice in advocating an approach to education for enterprise in rural areas has been Jonathan Sher. In his book *Education in Rural America: A Reassessment of Conventional Wisdom* (1977), Sher developed the concept of *Rural Education for Active Learning (REAL)*. A major concern of vocational agriculture studies in schools and colleges in rural areas has always been economic decline, and the dislocation of the family farm by large-scale agribusiness, often resulting in a migration of youth from their home areas. Sher envisioned school-based enterprises, mounted by young people, as a means of creating jobs, strengthening ties between youth in rural areas and their communities, giving young people real-life responsibilities and offering entrepreneurial training. He felt that school-based enterprise should initially complement but eventually replace traditional vocational training as a community development process to improve both the economic and social well-being of the local community (Sher, 1977).

As an outgrowth of Sher's vision, Paul DeLargy, of the University of Georgia, established *REAL Enterprises* as a non-profit organization, located in Athens, Georgia, which works through state affiliates to assist school systems and community organizations interested in school-based enterprises. Such enterprises involve businesses created and operated by students in cooperation with local educational institutions that fill gaps in the local economy while providing entrepreneurial, vocational and academic training. Schools act as small business incubators, helping rural students to understand the local economy and to find ways of tapping the potential for self-employment and small-business development – not through simulations but rather by starting and managing *real* enterprises having long-term economic viability. Existing pilot school-based enterprises include a child development center, a feeder pig operation, a printing company, a retail store, a community theater, a sheep farm, a tourist railway, a community newspaper and a construction company.

It is hoped that these enterprises will help rural students escape the trap of being unable to stay in the local area after leaving school because of declining local employment and having nowhere to go to find good jobs because of high unemployment in the cities. They build upon the economic opportunities existing in their areas to help them, their families and other local people become primary beneficiaries of their own community's development. Students are motivated to stay and succeed in school by providing an experiential base for learning both academic subjects and business-related skills (DeLargy, 1987).

The Mid-continental Regional Education Laboratory (McREL) is one of nine regional educational laboratories funded by the Office of Educational

Research and Improvement of the US Department of Education and serves schools in Colorado, Kansas, Missouri, Nebraska, North Dakota, South Dakota and Wyoming. The *McREL Rural Institute* "helps school districts create educational policy that recognizes the problems and opportunities in a diverse rural sector and contributes to rural rejuvenation and human development" (McREL, 1990).

McREL has developed a *Blueprint for Entrepreneurship in Your School*, whereby communities (school board members, administrators, teachers, students, parents, business people etc.) begin by agreeing that student learning can be enhanced if students learn how to create jobs, as well as how to work for someone else.

School officials identify a teacher eager to expand the regular curricula. Students are either selected for their academic ranking or risk-taking abilities or they may choose the class as an elective. In some schools participation is limited to the junior and senior years while in others it is open t o all high school classes.

The project may fit into existing curricula (e.g. English, Social Studies, Business, Math, Economics etc.) or be offered as a free-standing course. Student-created businesses must serve real needs and are either profit-making or community-service not-for-profit ventures. Steps in the process are as follows:

1 A community survey is undertaken to identify unmet local needs that student enterprises can address. This may consist of a demographic or economic analysis or a survey instrument (questionnaire or interview schedule) which is student-developed and administered.

2 A business plan is formulated which includes the following sections: executive summary; description of the enterprise; the industry and the competition; a description of the product or service; the production process; a market assessment; plans for management and personnel; financial data and supporting documents. A community-based development advisory committee may be convened to enlist the support and expertise of local business leaders in implementing the enterprises.

Student-developed ventures have included a restaurant, school store, home repair service, firewood sales, small-business directory, Cable TV show, and a dinner theater (McREL, 1990).

In the state of Oklahoma, a national vocational/entrepreneurship demonstration project, the *Rural Entrepreneurship Program*, was launched in 1981. Classes in entrepreneurship use a curriculum package known as *PACE* (*Program for Acquiring Competence in Entrepreneurship*), developed by the National Center for Research in Vocational Education based at Ohio State University. Three "votech" (vocational–technical) schools participated in the Oklahoma project, which involves study courses and the development of "industrial incubators" at each of the three centers to initiate business ideas developed by students. The courses include *Introduction to Entrepreneurship*, a short course mandatory for all students, and *Creating a New Enterprise* for those students actually planning to start a business. Participating schools are linked by computer to the state's Rural Enterprise Development Center, which is a source of information on new ventures (OECD, 1989).

In urban areas, one of the most comprehensive initiatives is *Enterprise High*, an alternative program for potential school-leavers, located in Macomb County near Detroit, Michigan. Established in 1982 with 25 students in an abandoned elementary school, the program now operates in 10 centers involving more than 500 students each year and is being replicated in three other states.

Enterprise High lets students combine their academic learning with experience in running their own small businesses. Students master the basic academic and vocational skills which complement their business ventures. Producing and selling products or services enhances student self-esteem and cooperation while they learn about the economic system. It is the intent of the program "to give those at risk of a life of dependency the option of autonomous living" (Benedict, 1988).

The program at Enterprise High consists of four elements to encourage "autonomous functioning":

- *academic* – mastering basic skills of reading, writing, mathematics and communication;
- *adult role preparation* – developing roles as autonomous adults (e.g. money managers, consumers, tenants, home-owners, employees, taxpayers, heads-of-households, spouses, parents, voters etc);
- *social adjustment* – working effectively and cooperatively as members of a team;
- *self-adjustment* – building self-esteem.

All of these four elements are built into four "curricular interventions" which include: the enterprise itself; integrated academics; integrated adult role preparation and quality circles for both businesses and academic work. Students spend 50 per cent of each day on academics and 50 per cent on enterprise, beginning and ending with a quality circle meeting. Enterprises started by students have included woodworking, food services, commercial arts and crafts, data and word processing, the performing arts, auto-mechanics, general merchandising, computer repair, plastics and metal fabrication and graphic arts (OECD, 1989).

Another curriculum package has been developed by *ACCESS Inc.* (The

Association for Cross Cultural Education and Social Studies) for use in high schools – particularly among female students interested in entrepreneurship. The *Be Your Own Boss (BYOB)* program encourages students to examine personal interests, skills and values, increases awareness of barriers confronting women in the business world and helps students apply basic skills in decision-making, planning, communicating and organizing (ACCESS Inc., 1986).

United Kingdom

The most comprehensive program to prepare British students for adult and working life has been the *Technical and Vocational Education Initiative (TVEI)*. TVEI began in 1983 with a small number of pilot projects in selected schools as a program of the Manpower Services Commission and in 1987 was extended to all education authorities. TVEI equips young people of 14–18 for the demands of working life in a rapidly changing society (The Training Agency, 1989):

1 By relating the whole curriculum to the world of work.
2 By equipping all young people with the knowledge, competencies and qualifications for working in a highly technological society which is itself part of Europe and the world economy.
3 By providing young people themselves with direct experience of the economy and the world of work e.g. through work experience, work-shadowing; projects in the community.
4 By enabling young people to learn how to be effective people, solve problems, work in teams, be enterprising and creative through the way they are taught.
5 By making sure that young people have initial guidance and counseling, and opportunities for education and training, and progression throughout their lives.

In practice TVEI represents a new approach to the delivery of curriculum and program for many educational authorities. Schools and colleges often work together to provide a wider range of opportunities than would be available in a single institution. New and enhanced courses have been developed in most subject areas which were never before available. New teaching techniques and learning styles have been adopted which incorporate active learning.

Benefits to students have included the opportunity to (The Training Agency, 1990):

• take more responsibility for their own learning;

- acquire an appreciation of the potential and application of technology, and undertake studies with a significant technological content;
- have practical experience of enterprise through problem-solving activities;
- have planned work-related experience, together with much wider experience outside of the classroom generally;
- apply knowledge and skills to the solution of real life problems;
- have access to supported self-study and open-learning techniques;
- develop personal qualities such as self-confidence and resourcefulness and communication skills through a variety of activities inside and outside the classroom.

The Mini-Enterprise in Schools Project (MESP) and the Community Service Volunteers (CSV) have jointly published *Enterprise Education in the National Curriculum: Agenda for the 90s*. Both agencies have previously developed resources for teachers who have involved young people in enterprise initiatives. CSV has focused its work on the role of community enterprise in the curriculum while MESP has developed the mini-enterprise model. Both programs complement the ideals of TVEI.

As British schools move towards a national curriculum (as set out by the National Curriculum Council), the importance of "education for enterprise" has been emphasized in two ways:

1 The ability to tackle problems; take initiatives, persevere, be flexible and work in teams.
2 The opportunity to take part in small-scale business and community enterprise for economic and industrial understanding.

The joint publication, *Enterprise Education in the National Curriculum* (MESP and CSV, 1990), advocates Five Key Elements to form the core of an enterprising approach to education:

1 *Self-determined learning* – students take greater responsibility for their own learning.
2 *Enterprising skills development* – students are involved in applying the skills of enterprise such as: planning, problem-solving, decision-making, negotiating, communicating, risk-taking, creativity.
3 *Team work* – students work with others and cultivate the ability to recognize that the contribution of all team members is important to successful undertakings.
4 *Access to resources* – students use their initiative to draw on a range of human and physical resources within the school and the broader community to complete their task.
5 *Accountability* – students are challenged to work within the constraints

and realities of life outside the classroom. They have a responsibility to other team members and to community partners in the venture.

BUSINESS/EDUCATION PARTNERSHIPS

An issue of vital importance in the development of school-based curriculum and program is "relevancy." How are educators assured that the content of these initiatives is relevant to the ever-changing nature of the workplace? One approach has been to establish joint ventures with employers and employment-related organizations to assist in shaping program content to reflect "real world" conditions. There are a variety of terms used to describe these developmental initiatives the most common being business/education partnerships.

Public education has become increasingly subject to external influences, particularly to the interest and involvement of employers. There are several reasons for their change in emphasis (Stone, 1991):

* Concerns about the quality of teachers, particularly math and science;
* the social burden placed on schools by poverty, drug abuse, violence and youth unemployment;
* the dropout rate in general and the diminishing number of students pursuing education at the highest level;
* concerns about the current educational and skill levels of employees in the workplace in light of the challenges of the global economy.

In 1990 the Organization for Economic Cooperation and Development (OECD) in Paris began an analysis of business/education partnerships in the western world. They have concluded that partnerships beyond the school, should be a two-way process benefiting both business and education. The level of cooperation between partners, however, may vary widely. The first dimension identified was simple "links" involving no more than a joint activity which one or both participants pursued out of self-interest, with no shared goals. "Partnerships" involved a deal between the sides to do one thing in exchange for another. "Strategic Coalitions," however, involved genuinely common goals, and a range of committed partners, to improve the education system (OECD, 1992).

The nongovernmental sectors have traditionally contributed to curricular development by participating in a vast array of programs designed to assist young people to better prepare themselves to achieve and maintain employment. One model, that was originated more than 60 years ago in the United States but has been emulated around the world, is *Junior Achievement*. This is a non-profit organization dependent for its support on the interest of the business community. It offers the high school student the opportunity to discover, first hand, the value of individual initiative and effort. In a practical learning-by-doing situation, students organize and manage small-scale businesses with the aid of professional business people who are willing to share their knowledge of production, administration and marketing.

Each JA company, comprised of 12–15 students, establishes an administrative system, work and sales forces. They select a product or service to market and then raise capital through the public sale of stock in their companies. Production lines are set up for manufacturing and sales. Businesses keep complete corporate records, pay taxes, meet payrolls and encounter the realities of corporate decision-making.

At the end of the program year, a shareholders' report is issued, dividends paid (where applicable) and the JA companies are liquidated. Students gain a realistic understanding of the organization and operation of a business enterprise (Glendinning, 1987a and b).

Project Business is a program of Junior Achievement for grade 9 students to increase their awareness of the role business plays in their family lives. A resource consultant from the business community meets with the students on a weekly basis for approximately fourteen weeks. This flexible economic education program fits into a school curriculum supplementing an existing social studies or guidance course. Working with the teacher, the consultant shares with the students a practical first-hand approach to any one of the following topics – economics, the national economy, the marketing system, money and banking, financial statements, consumerism and choosing a career. Because the business consultant becomes a live "case study" in the classroom, students should develop an understanding of key business concepts while experiencing an enjoyable and interesting introduction to the world of business (Glendinning, 1987).

In Australia *Young Achievement Australia*, established in 1977, encourages secondary school students to set up and run their own out-of-school business ventures over a period of 28 weeks, usually during Year Eleven. In the Netherlands *Youth Enterprise* was established in 1980 to further the understanding of secondary school students as to how businesses operate through setting up their own business projects. Britain has had a program called *Young Enterprise* in place since 1963. Currently, about 1000 "YE" companies are formed by 15–19-year-old students each year, spread over a period of nine months, and taking up a total of approximately 55 hours per student (OECD, 1989).

Another major trend in North America has been *Industry–Education Councils (IEC)* whereby local business and industry join together with government and education providers to plan and implement curriculum and program initiatives. One such venture in Canada has been The

Hamilton–Wentworth Industry–Education Council. This Ontario based IEC is a non-profit corporation established to match community resources with student and teacher needs in an attempt to ease the transition of youth from school to work in Hamilton–Wentworth, a steel-making, heavy industrial area.

The IEC became fully operational in 1980, with representatives from business, government, labor, education and community organizations. The original seed funding came from the provincial government, but continued support has been provided by three boards of education, two post secondary institutions, the federal government, the commercial sector and community organizations.

One of the IEC's primary aims is to make students active in their career search, rather than reactive. IEC programs encourage students to actively pursue various methods of inquiry into potential careers, rather than passively waiting for an opportunity which may never arrive. In addition, the IEC has established and continues to develop programs aimed specifically at facilitating the transition from school to work. A third aim of the council is to increase understanding, cooperation and collaboration between schools and the community.

Education and employment needs and interests are communicated to the council by community resource volunteers and educators. Advisory committees are established to respond to these concerns. These committees review suggestions and develop guidelines for pilot projects. Before pilot projects can be implemented, final approval must be sought from the IEC's Board of Directors, which includes representation from all sectors.

The IEC has developed many programs aimed at bringing together representatives from business, industry, education, labor and government. They include the following activities: Career Resource Directory; Career Resource Center; Career Information Seminars; Student Marketing Conference; Career Awareness Seminars for Students and Educators; Job Search Handbook; Ontario Career Symposium; Operation Employability for Handicapped Adolescents; and Adopt-a-School – Partners in Education. By establishing and coordinating numerous innovative career education programs, the IEC hopes to successfully foster positive attitudes and promote learning activities for local youth that will be realistic in terms of career orientation (Industry–Education Council, 1987).

In the United States, the *Boston Compact* was established by business and education in 1982. The compact was a guarantee on the part of the business community to hire area youth and on the part of schools to improve attendance and skill competency. Trade unions and universities later joined the compact. The National Alliance of Business, after the success of the Boston Compact, extended the concept to 12 US cities according to local needs. From these experiences, the following criteria for successful partnerships were drafted (OECD, 1990):

- A common vision statement and dedicated leaderships from all sectors (business, education and city government) to remove impediments to changes in education and business employment practices.
- A sound definition of the goals and action plans of the partners both long- and short-term. The goals should be measurable.
- The proper means of managing change including a review forum to monitor progress, sufficient staff to organize and analyze, the use of key personnel to act as change managers and an institutionalization plan to integrate funding into regular institutional activities.

As part of the Government's *Action for Cities* initiative, the Training Agency in the UK has funded 30 compacts in England and Scotland. The first "British Compact" was established in East London. "School, colleges, training providers and young people, actively supported by employers, work to reach agreed standards and goals. In return employers undertake to provide further training and jobs for those who reach the required standards" (The Training Agency, 1990).

Adopt-a-School initiatives, whereby a local employer establishes a special relationship with a neighboring secondary school to enhance learning experiences and upgrade the overall quality of education, have also been popular in North America. Adopt-a-School programs may include involvement of the employer as follows (Industry–Education Council, 1987):

- Allow students to visit business sites.
- Conduct classes at the place of business in special skills areas.
- Donate surplus materials, furniture and equipment.
- Share the organization's expertise through seminars, demonstrations, mock job interviews, and career days at the adopted school.
- Offer student scholarships and awards for outstanding achievers in academics and athletics.
- Establish an extra-curricular club to motivate students in math, computers or electronics.
- Provide tutors in subjects like math and English.
- Sponsor teacher professional development and internship programs.
- Provide cooperative education / work experience placements or summer/part-time jobs.
- Display student achievement at the place of business.
- Provide funding for special programs.
- Serve on an advisory or curriculum committee.

- Establish a mentor program to match students on a one-to-one basis with industry volunteers.

In France, there is a widespread use of *jumelages* (twinnings of schools and companies) and *alternance* (alternating classroom and on-the-job training). The Lycée Fortuny maintains partnerships with well known fashionhouses and cosmetics companies. In addition to training periods and career lectures, these companies take students on *séquences éducatives* in various departments for credit as part of the schools curriculum (OECD, 1990).

In Sweden, business and labor play more than an advisory role in the curriculum as they provide places for students within their organizations. Several large Swedish corporations (e.g. SKF, Volvo) maintain on-site secondary schools providing standard education supplemented by technical courses. Teachers come from both the company, and the Education Department and three-quarters of the funding is provided by the company which may also hire many of the graduates (OECD, 1990).

British Petroleum has provided leadership in the UK through *Learning for a Changing World*, a project which aims to enhance the development of general competencies and skills in young people regardless of the career path they may choose. Other parts of their *Link Scheme* promote projects such as teacher secondments, BP employee attachments to schools and in-service training for teachers to assist schools in developing problem-solving skills across the curriculum. The latest innovations to promote technological and scientific literacy have included a *Problem-Solving Pack* for secondary schools and direct links of industry to the primary school level (OECD, 1990).

Germany's *dual system*, which combines formal apprenticeships with vocational education, has been very successful at producing high standards in the workplace with low rates of youth unemployment. *Apprenticeship*, the largest form of upper-secondary education, is jointly operated and financed by private industry and the government. It enrols more than 60 per cent of Germany's 16–18-year-olds. German apprentices spend one day in school and four days in the workplace. School subjects include German, social studies, and specialized math and science courses related to their prospective trades.

On the job, they receive minimal "learner's wages." They may take specialized classes in large companies, while in smaller firms they are usually assigned to a master craftsman for informal hands-on instruction. To ensure that high-quality standards of theoretical training are maintained, the schools use uniform curricula developed jointly with industry representatives. The government also maintains technical centers to supplement the training smaller employers can provide. After three years of training and after passing a written and practical exam, apprentices become journeymen with credentials that are recognized throughout the country. However, it should be noted "while the rest of the industrial world envies German workers' exacting standards and precision, many Germans fear that their workforce is so precise – and narrow – that it lacks the flexibility global competition demands" (Perry, 1988).

Magnet Schools have been popular in school districts in the United States where theme programs have been established with curricula built around a particular discipline, often with the support of local business. For example, the Chesterfield School system in Virginia has a partnership with a regional department store related to marketing involving teachers, administrators and students. Educators receive paid internships and orientation programs to increase awareness of industry requirements. Students have the opportunity to work as a sales associate with performance evaluations at the end of the period.

The *Philadelphia High School Academies* program began in 1970 combining academic and vocational education with on-the-job experience for low-income students. Executives from 40 companies including Continental Bank, Philadelphia Electric and Rohm and Haas meet with teachers to help plan courses suited to employee needs. In New York City, General Electric works with top students from the Manhattan Center for Science and Mathematics, a magnet program in Spanish Harlem, preparing mostly minority students for careers in engineering and science. The company provides mentors and special classes to help its "GE Scholars" get into prestigious universities (Perry, 1988).

Another magnet program, the *High School for Engineering Professions (HSEP)*, was established in 1975 in Houston, Texas. The Houston Independent School District received financial commitments from Houston business and industry totalling about $100,000 (e.g. Exxon, NASA, Hewlett-Packard, Rohn & Haas, Texaco, IBM etc.). An independent school-within-a-school, HSEP is hosted by the Booker T. Washington High School. The primary objective of HSEP is "the development of resourceful, self-activated, well-rounded graduates who are capable of analyzing new situations, making intelligent decisions, and communicating their ideas."

Highly gifted and talented college-bound students, who are interested in engineering or scientific disciplines, receive a strong program in communication skills and humanities within the total school population. HSEP maintains its own instructional coordinator and specially selected faculty to provide continuous progress and subject mastery in English, mathematics and science. Courses are based on specific proficiencies in each subject. Hands-on experience, particularly within science and engineering, is emphasized. Teachers fill two roles – as facilitators of subject matter and as advisers. Students are encouraged to become as independent and responsible as possible for their own learning. The result of the HSEP program, to date, has been 100 per cent acceptance of graduates into university, with 96 per cent studying engineering, science and mathematics. Seventy per cent of students are from minority backgrounds (Marshall, 1983).

THE FORGOTTEN ONES

Most in-school curricular initiatives and out-of-school learning experiences tend to be offered to senior-level students in their last two years of high school prior to graduation. Employers working with local schools, or receiving students in the workplace, are most often interested in involving those who have excelled academically and are seen as "good citizens" by their institutions. The fact that the school-leaving age in most western countries is 15 or 16 years would seem to separate out the low achievers and behavioral problems from the process. For example only 37 per cent of British youth, aged 16 to 18, were in full-time education in 1989.

The employment models being emulated are often large corporations whose organizational style and management methods are still very much part of the industrial age. Most secondary schools seem to reflect a sense of devotion to large scale corporate efficiency and insularity which may be completely out of step with a new era of innovative problem-solving, shared decision-making and enterprise creation in a global economy.

Curriculum development related to entrepreneurial skills and small-business venturing has been an important addition to the content of what is taught in secondary schools. Unfortunately, only senior students seem to be allowed to participate, and even they must be specially selected in some instances. The teachers who offer these courses may not be qualified in that they have never gone through an entrepreneurial experience. In fact, sociologists have long maintained that those who go into teaching do not tend to be "risk-takers" but are more often "security-seekers." There is also a continuing debate as to whether it is even possible to teach a person to be a successful entrepreneur. These qualities to be sharpened may be already inherent in the personality rather than acquired through some form of "entrepreneurial conversion." There is little doubt, however, that we can all benefit from "exposure to the life skills of the new age of small enterprise."

EFFECTIVENESS OF PARTNERSHIPS

Serious doubts are now being raised about the effectiveness of "business–education partnerships." To quote Donald M. Clark, President of the

National Association for Industry–Education Cooperation in the US:

> Business–education partnerships – a term invented in the '80s by policy issue types who haven't spent a day in the trenches with hands-on experience in collaboration – have been a flop in terms of any impact on education. . . . The state of practice of business–education partnerships is fragmented, unstructured, unco-ordinated, unconnected, duplicative and conducted on an ad hoc basis.
>
> (Clark, 1989)

Kenneth B. Hoyt, a nationally known US authority on career education, makes the distinction between cooperative and collaborative partnerships. He sees cooperation as a willingness to help the education system solve "its problems". Collaborative partnerships, on the other hand, are seen as (Hoyt, 1986):

1 Convincing the education system to share its "authority" for making decisions.
2 Convincing the business community that it should accept appropriate shares of "responsibility" and "accountability" for the success or failure of the total effort . . . . the challenge has been to convince the education system to let loose and the business–industry system to take hold. Of the two problems, the first has usually been tougher than the second.

Marsha Levine of the American Federation of Teachers, co-editor of *American Business and the Public School* has stated "Companies should ask: Does this change the way things are done, or add on to an existing structure that isn't working very well?" The Committee for Economic Development in its report *Children in Need* has focused on early prevention as opposed to trying to reorient youth later in life. They conclude that "to save the kids most in risk of failing, it is vital to reach them in their earliest years and even, in some cases, before they are born. Just one dollar spent on early prevention and intervention can save six dollars in costs of remedial education, welfare and crime down the road" (Perry, 1988).

While these school-to-work programs have attempted to prepare young people for future employment, they have too often been limited to senior-level students who are the "achievers" in the school system. These opportunities have traditionally not been available to younger potential school-leavers or unemployed adult learners. They have also tended to focus on traditional sources of employment in large-scale manufacturing, primary-resource industries or large institutional service structures while the challenge of preparing young people for employment in the small business, entrepreneurial sector has not been met.

The fact that school-to-work programs have always emphasized the adolescent years also has neglected the reality that nearly three-fourths of the people who will be at work in the first decade of the twenty-first century are already on the job. A report by the US Office of Technology Assessment (OTA) entitled *Worker Training* estimates that between 20 per cent and 30 per cent of US workers lack the basic skills they need to work effectively in their current jobs, participate fully in training programs and implement new technologies successfully. To compete in the global economy, OTA believes that US business must invest heavily in basic literacy and computer-related skills in the workplace. They found that two-thirds of corporate training dollars spent on formal programs go to college-educated men and women in professional, managerial, professional sales, technical and supervisory jobs while front-line workers receive little training (Stone, 1991).

It is becoming increasingly apparent that "schooling for work" programs, traditionally offered to senior secondary students, may be irrelevant unless the needs of early-leavers and non-achievers are addressed as part of a commitment to life-long learning and industry/education restructuring to meet the demands of the new economic age. The chapter which follows will review some exemplary programs initiated to serve early school-leavers or "dropouts" as they are commonly called.

4   The discarded generations

PATTERNS OF DROPPING-OUT

The definition of a dropout varies widely. Some jurisdictions may define the dropout as any student who fails to graduate from secondary school. Others refer to students who leave prior to graduation as "early school-leavers." In Britain the majority of young people graduate from secondary school by age 16 and choose to go out into the labor force rather than continue their schooling. In North America, where four years of secondary school is mandatory to reach graduation, more than 40 per cent have left school before their eighteenth birthday (OECD, 1989). The early school leaving rate in inner-city neighborhoods is often twice as high as the national average. Many students leave as soon as they can legally do so – at the age of 16 in most countries.

Danzberger, Lefkowitz and Hahn, in their 1987 book *Dropouts in America: Enough Is Known for Action*, made an extensive review of the literature and concluded that early school-leaving is a multifaceted problem. It starts early, has many causes, and grows incrementally worse with each successive year. It includes the social, emotional and environmental concerns of school children, as well as the policy and program procedures of the educational providers. The authors identified ten conditions as major risk factors indicating that a student might be in danger of dropping out:

1 Behind in grade level and older than classmates – approximately 40 per cent of all high school students were found to be at least one year behind their modal grade level.
2 Poor academic performance – dropouts are more likely than other students to have scored low on, failed, or not taken proficiency examinations.
3 Dislike school – over one-third of dropouts cited this reason, males more often than females.

4 Detention and suspension – dropouts are more frequently suspended and placed in detention.
5 Pregnancy – four out of five girls who become pregnant in high school drop out, while less than 10 per cent of those who do not become pregnant do so;
6 Welfare recipients and members of single-parent households – dropouts are three times more likely than high school graduates to come from families that receive welfare.
7 The attractiveness of work – many take entry-level jobs which have little hope of long-term employment security.
8 The attraction of military service – for many dropouts in later years of adolescence, the military is a "safety net of last resort."
9 Undiagnosed learning disabilities and emotional problems – estimates of the learning-disabled high school population range from 5 to 10 per cent while less than 3 per cent of this group are ever diagnosed;
10 Language difficulties – a facility in the national language is clearly a critical element in achieving success in school.

Another study undertaken by Barber and McClellan – *Looking at America's Dropouts: Who are they?* (1987) identified the following categories of school-leaving:

- The "classic dropout" exhibited poor attitudes towards school, most likely was falling behind in academic progress, had a lower grade-point average and was probably male.
- The "work-oriented dropout" was most often male and had slightly better than average grades and achieved credits.
- "Homemakers" were girls with grade-point averages above passing but who didn't see school as necessary to gain their goals of setting up households and raising a family.
- "The intellectual elite" saw school as irrelevant even though they were the oldest and closest to completing their academic requirements.
- "Family supporters" while aware of the need for education felt obliged to help their family economically.
- "Cultural isolates" because of language problems and social distance were behind their peers in credits completed.

SEEKING A REMEDY

What are the personal and human effects on these young people who have left school to join the ranks of the unemployed or marginally employed in entry-level jobs with little economic security? Dr. Saul Levine, Professor of Psychiatry at the University of Toronto, has identified eight emotional stages suffered by unemployed youth (Levine, 1980):

1 Boredom.
2 Apathy and withdrawal.
3 Negative sense of identity.
4 Low self-esteem.
5 Demoralization and alienation.
6 Guilt and shame.
7 Anxiety and fear.
8 Anger and depression.

As previously stated, the high school dropout rate and youth unemployment have been linked to criminal behavior, drug abuse and suicide which result in permanent losses of billions of dollars to the economy each year. Most of the programs which attempt to address this problem involve government agencies, the commercial sector or nonprofit voluntary organizations working with school authorities or operating community-based employment/training projects.

The Danzberger, Lefkowitz and Hahn study (1987) concludes that an effective dropout prevention program cannot be based on one single element, such as remedial instruction or the provision of social services. They believe it requires an integrated effort combining the following components:

• mentorships and intensive, sustained counseling for troubled youngsters;
• an array of social services, including healthcare, family planning education, and infant care facilities for adolescent mothers;
• concentrated remediation using individualized instruction and competency-based curricula;
• an effective school/business collaboration that provides ongoing access to the mainstream economy;
• improved incentives, including financial rewards, for completing high school;
• year-round schools and alternative schools;
• heightened accountability for dropout rates at all levels of the system of public education;
• involvement of parents and community organization in dropout prevention.

The following is a sampling of a variety of dropout prevention and community employment/training initiatives.

United States

In the United States, *Cities in Schools* is a nonprofit organization, based in Washington, DC, with more than 20 years' experience in working with high-risk youth. Cities in Schools rallies corporate support for the formation of a national partnership to aid dropouts. The first partnerships that grew from these efforts were called *street academies* and were funded exclusively by such corporations as Union Carbide, McGraw-Hill, American Airlines, IBM and First City National Bank.

The major element of their success was a small, caring staff that could respond creatively to both the social and the educational needs of students and their families. The street academies were the forerunners of a new generation of partnerships that offer alternative delivery of social services to alienated urban youths by bringing a community's human service agencies and its businesses into the high schools and junior high schools.

Prototypes of the Cities in Schools program now exist in fourteen US cities, with plans underway to add an additional nine cities. Some examples follow.

Oxford, Massachusetts

Here the school system joined with the Digital Equipment Corporation to develop a partnership called the *Cooperative Federation for Education Experiences (COFFEE)*. The core of this partnership is an alternative occupational training component which offers computer-related and other work-experience curricula. This program combines academic instruction with training for entry-level positions in high-technology fields.

Atlanta, Georgia

Rich's Department Store created *Rich's Academy*, in which 160 employees volunteered their time to be matched in one-to-one partnerships with students. The employees encourage, support and motivate the students. Rich's hires a number of academy students each summer and many have continued to work at the store following their graduation.

Silicon Valley, California

A not-for-profit organization called the *Stanford Mid-Peninsula Urban Coalition* joined with the Sequoia Union High School District in designing a program to reduce the high dropout rate of minorities, reduce youth and minority unemployment, and reduce the number of unfilled entry-level jobs in the region. Acting as a link between the schools and the Hewlett-Packard Company and other area businesses, the coalition created *Peninsula Academies* – a partnership to improve both educational and employment opportunities among minority youth.

Students in the Academies have improved academic performance, gained employment experience and improved their feelings of self-worth. Cities in Schools is demonstrating that the performance of even economically and educationally at-risk youth can be vastly improved by creating public/private partnerships to address their social and economic needs (Justiz and Kameen, 1987).

The federal government *Job Corps* program has been in operation for more than 25 years in the United States. Participants live away from home, to be free of distracting influences, and receive a mix of remedial education and skills training provided by federally contracted agencies. A longitudinal study has found that Job Corps participants earned an average of 15 per cent more per year than a similar group of nonparticipants. A higher percentage of participants also completed high school, entered the military and stayed off welfare programs. Throughout its existence, Job Corps has experimented with a variety of learning methods suitable for disadvantaged dropouts including its own approach to competency-based, individualized instruction.

Jobs for America and *70,001 LTD* are two nonprofit organizations which offer pre-employment counseling, job-readiness training and some remedial education to 16–21-year-olds. Private industry was encouraged to hire program participants who had been pre-screened by program staff. An evaluation of the programs found that 90 per cent of participants were school dropouts and two-thirds were racial minorities. The average reading level of the sample group was grade 6.

The evaluation study found that participants had significantly higher levels of employment and higher wage rates than comparison groups. These positive results generally declined after 14 months. The program did, however, succeed in placing disadvantaged youth into jobs quickly and in combining job placement with training in work maturity, pre-employment skills and limited remedial education. While not as successful as the Job Corps, with its intensive services and residential setting, Jobs for Youth and 70,001 LTD were comparatively low-cost, short interventions which led to short-term results.

Another program, *Project ReDirection*, had similar results. Disadvantaged teenage mothers received a variety of individualized services, including day care, work experience, skills training, basic education, personal counseling, agency referrals, and the guidance of an adult mentor.

At the end of one year, twice as many program participants had returned to school as had members of a control group. Subsequent evaluation, however, was far less positive (Hahn, 1987).

Overall, the *Dropouts in America* study (Danzberger, Lefkowitz and Hahn, 1987) made several observations:

- Isolated work experience programs have little value in increasing the employability of dropouts.
- Dropouts should learn, but the curriculum should relate to the "functional" skills needed in the workplace.
- Dropouts should acquire vocational skills but first they need to learn how to read.
- Dropouts should learn to read, but the learning environment should not resemble a traditional classroom;
- Dropouts should be taught by caring teachers, but the individuality of each student should be reflected in the teaching technology used.
- Dropouts should be prepared for the labor market through pre-employment/work maturity services – but not until they are ready to conduct a job search.
- Program services must be, to some degree, intensive.

United Kingdom

Some of the most comprehensive programs to assist school-leavers have been developed in the United Kingdom. *Community Industry* was established by the government Manpower Services Commission in 1972, modeled on an initiative developed by a national voluntary youth organization. It provided temporary employment for disadvantaged youth in 57 local areas. The manual and environmental projects, co-financed by central and local government, employed 10,000 young people per year.

In 1976 the *Work Experience Programme* provided private and public sector employers with funds to hire young unemployed people as trainees for 26 weeks of work experience. By 1978 this program was folded into the *Youth Opportunities Programme* which extended the range of employers to include voluntary youth and community organizations. Beginning with an initial objective of 100,000 work experience/training places the program provided funding for a variety of new initiatives including:

- community service agencies to gain personal experience in the fields of health, education, social welfare etc.;
- short-term environmental improvement sponsored by voluntary groups, government departments or joint venture schemes involving both sectors;

- training workshops in small-scale manufacturing to defray expenses but not to be competitive in the open market.

As a result community services agencies and training workshops were able to employ staff to supervise trainees who reflected a new body of expertise, concern and commitment.

One innovation which grew out of this program was a training workshop in Notting Hill, West London – an area with a large ethnic minority population. The *Notting Hill Information Technology Centre (ITEC)* was established in the belief that modern computer and information technology could form the basis of a training program for young unemployed people.

In 1983, the *Youth Training Scheme (YTS)*, replacing the Youth Opportunities Programme, guaranteed that all those 16-year-olds leaving school without employment were eligible for up to one year's training with a weekly allowance. The program consisted of both on-the-job and off-the-job training designed to achieve the following objectives:

1 To develop those basic educational skills in young people which will enable them to meet the demands for a more highly trained workforce.
2 To develop in young people an awareness of, and skills in, new technology.
3 To enable young people to experience and perform effectively in a "real job" situation.
4 To enable young people to develop the skills required for adult life.
5 To enable young people to acquire job-specific and broadly related skills in an area of work and the ability to transfer those skills to other situations.
6 To develop in young people the ability to adapt to new situations both in work and outside employment.
7 To enable young people to redeploy the skills they have acquired.

In 1986 YTS was extended to two years, providing 420,000 places for young unemployed people. As a result of the pioneering work of the Notting Hill ITEC, more than 175 ITECs were established nationally, through YTS and the Department of Trade and Industry, each training an average of 30 school-leavers.

The Youth Training Scheme, in addition to personal presentation, job-hunting and interview techniques now added personal effectiveness as one of its objectives. This involved the development of initiative, interpersonal skills, dealing with responsibility and self-reliance.

A concern for the needs of disadvantaged and ethnic-minority young people also spawned several other community-based employment/training initiatives with particular emphasis not just on a skilled workforce but one that is adaptable, versatile and entrepreneurial in nature.

Project Fullemploy was originally set up by a group of businessmen in the City of London who felt that:

> the resources and goodwill of the companies and finance houses of this business and financial capital ought to be brought to bear on the problem of youth unemployment and the problems of ethnic minorities, young members of which face particular difficulty in making the transition to the world of work.
>
> (OECD, 1986)

The program began adjacent to the main business area of the City, providing clerical and office skills training. Soon there were 12 training centers in operation – nine in London and three in other urban areas.

One spin-off from the original training was *New Ventures*, a course to help young people start their own businesses. The 20-week unit provided training in business planning, market exploration and development, as well as assistance in initiating small enterprises (OECD, 1986).

Project North East was established in 1980 by two young businessmen in Newcastle, a depressed area in the northeast of England, with a narrow industrial base consisting of a few big employers in steel, ship-building, coal-mining, heavy engineering and basic chemical processes. As a branch-factory economy, the northeast lacked an entrepreneurial tradition. Co-founders of the Project, David Grayson and David Irwin, began with less than £1,000 invested. A series of *Make Your Own Job* exhibitions and a *Business Bus* toured the region advertising how to find business ideas, develop business skills, secure premises and finance. *Commercial Break*, a competition launched on the local independent television station, resulted in 800 entries – the most promising of which received cash awards and business follow-up training.

As a result of the success of the exhibitions and competition, the Project next persuaded major companies such as Legal & Counsel, Marks & Spencer, and British Rail to back the establishment of Britain's first *Youth Enterprise Centre* in 1984. Financial assistance was also provided by the Department of the Environment, Newcastle City Council and the Manpower Services Commission to convert a derelict warehouse into a "one-stop-shop" providing young people with business advice, enterprise training, workspace, common services, access to finance and marketing support. In its first three years of operation the Center served more than 1,100 clients of whom 180 formed their own successful businesses employing nearly 250 people.

Other accomplishments of Project North East have included the following (Roberts, 1987):

- a second Youth Enterprise Center in Sunderland sponsored by local and national government and private sector companies;
- seminars and a training manual on setting up and operating youth enterprise centers;
- a *Northern Youth Venture Fund* sponsored by local government, major charities and private industry providing low interest loans to young businesses;
- *Business Information System On-line (BISON)*, a computerized view data service, sponsored by ESSO, which provides a range of information, quizzes, games and business tips for those interested in starting a small business;
- *Youth Business Kit*, developed as a training package to help young people and their advisers explore self-employment and enterprise creation;
- *Design Works*, a 72,000 square feet converted warehouse in Gateshead jointly sponsored by government and private industry, provides workspace, exhibition facilities, and training courses in design and marketing;
- *North Tyneside Brass Tacks*, with support from Levi Strauss, one of Britain's first Information Technology Centers (ITEC) training unemployed school-leavers for jobs in computing and electronics.

Instant Muscle

In 1981 four unemployed school-leavers in Wiltshire formed a cooperative to sell their labor doing odd jobs. Peter Raynes, father of one of the young people, suggested they should call themselves Instant Muscle. Leaflets were designed and delivered to homes in the area. The response was overwhelming and soon 30 young people were working in the group. Peter Raynes was asked to assist in setting up other cooperative groups and with the help of the Cooperative Development Agency a *Starter Pack* was created. Media coverage of the project resulted in assistance being offered by such companies as Rank Xerox, Rowntree and the Wiltshire County Council.

In 1983 Instant Muscle was incorporated as a registered national charity qualified to receive funding from the government's Community Program. Staff were hired to contact the 550 people who asked for help to set up Instant Muscle groups in their own neighborhoods. Unfortunately, however, few young people saw odd jobs as a career opportunity, and when older advisers were introduced to establish business principles they tended to assume ownership and young members became disillusioned and left. The areas hardest hit by unemployment also proved to have fewer odd jobs that people would pay to have done.

In 1984 the project underwent a major change in focus. Instant Muscle would concentrate on helping young people set up "real businesses", producing goods and services in areas of greatest need. The UK was divided into seven regions, each coordinated by an organizer with a number of business advisers both salaried and volunteer. Advisers help young people to identify their own skills and evaluate commercial possibilities. A business plan and cash-flow projection is then developed to be presented to the local authority, to banks or to governmental and charitable organizations providing sources of venture capital. As businesses are formed, the adviser assists in improving profitability and encourages growth. Enterprises tend to be smaller, three or four employees, involving youth from racial minorities with limited educational qualifications. In an average year, Instant Muscle assists 1,000 young people to become self-employed (Raynes, 1986).

Facilities for Access to Creative Enterprise (FACE)

Originally founded in 1982 to train unemployed youth in small "handskill" craft workshops, this project provides occupational and entrepreneurial skills as an alternative to traditional manufacturing jobs. Beginning with glass engraving and signwriting, FACE now offers training in over 200 handskill occupations including antique restoration, clothing manufacture, graphic design, masonry, sail-making, specialist joinery, weaving and wood turning. Funded through the Youth Training Scheme, FACE provides 800 training places in the west and northeast of England under the premise that even if the young people don't secure employment they at least will have the skills to create their own enterprises.

Based on its experience, FACE has developed, with the Royal Society of Arts, a Certificate in Small Business and Enterprise Skills. The aim of the certificate is "to develop the basic skills of enterprise across a range of occupational sectors, within small business and in general employment and which are applicable in a wide range of personal and social contexts outside work." Competencies include self-evaluation, decision-making, initiative-taking, resource and time management, opportunism and self-motivation, problem-solving, and learning-to-learn skills as well as communication and numeracy skills vital to personal effectiveness (OECD, 1989).

Standby

This is a scheme operated by a youth project in the depressed former naval dockyard area of Chatham in Kent. While still in receipt of unemployment benefits, young people can work on building and repair jobs. Instead of cash payments, they earn "credit" which can later be translated into a small sum of working capital to be used to create their own small enterprises after a minimum period of six months. National guidelines have been drafted to allow this initiative to be replicated in other parts of the UK (OECD, 1986 and 1989).

CREATE

In 1986 a new training agency, CREATE, was established in Cleveland, a county in the northeast of England, "to stimulate enterprise skills in the region." Tioxide UK, a large petrochemical company, approached the Manpower Services Commission (MSC) for funding to research and develop the concept of enterprise skills training in Cleveland. A committee was formed, chaired by the training manager of Tioxide, to include the Cleveland County Council, the Cleveland Cooperative Agency and the Cleveland Youth Business Center.

In 1987, MSC agreed to fund CREATE for a three-year period to assist students, trainees, public and private-sector workers and unemployed people to design and manage projects based upon their interests and aspirations. Initiatives range from "community service activities, to the formation of a 'quality circle,' to the research and development of a future business idea." Crossing traditional boundaries of education, training and employment, projects receive necessary working capital and the services of a skilled facilitator to identify, develop and transfer skills concerning the planning, operation and review of the enterprise (Turner, 1986).

In the first year of operation CREATE attracted nearly 200 participants from schools, the Youth Training Scheme and unemployed groups. The "bottom up" learner-centered approach to training has allowed each of the participants to progress at their own pace in a learning environment that is owned by the participant group. CREATE has been registered as an examination center for accreditation by the Royal Society of Arts. Overall, in its objectives of developing an enterprise culture to encourage economic regeneration, CREATE represents an innovative response to "the appalling deprivation, poverty and depression that mass unemployment brings" (Wilburn, 1988).

Denmark

In 1978 the Danish Minister for Education issued a report entitled *Experiments in Combined Educational and Production Programmes* in response to the plight of 70,000 unemployed school-leavers. The report found that half of these left school with no qualifications and very limited motivation to seek training opportunities. A lack of success in secondary school and a shortage of jobs for the unqualified combined to create an untrained pool of 16–24-year-olds entitled to neither training nor work experience.

As a result, a new alternative education program integrating teaching with manufacturing was envisioned. Local authorities and district councils were given the right to establish subsidized programs, approved by the Education Department, which became known as *production schools*. Building on the tradition of the "free or alternative school," the production school combines education and vocational training. It is physically arranged like a place of employment combining a number of manufacturing industries and job processes. Most of the teachers have vocational backgrounds as carpenters, joiners, bricklayers, farmers, blacksmiths, mechanics, engineers etc. The focus is workplace training with academics as needed. By experiencing life in a working environment, students learn to develop commitments which form the background for adult life. The trades teachers help to link the practical and the theoretical world to ensure that the relationship between working and learning is maintained. Young people know that their work is valued and what they produce is of good quality and can be sold.

Production schools began with a traditional craft curriculum in agriculture, horticulture, woodwork, metal work, textiles and catering. More recently the curriculum has been extended to include the new technologies of graphic design, environmental studies, commercial fishing, engineering and architecture. Manufacturing projects are chosen which are noncompetitive with local industry. Patents are taken out as necessary. Several schools may work together to fill large orders. Today there are about 40 different production lines in 70 schools with an approximate enrolment of 2,000. No two production schools are alike. Each reflects community needs combining cooperation and work so that young people may become active and productive members of society (Jensen, 1990).

Sweden

Several initiatives for the young unemployed have been funded, under the Swedish Labor Market Board provisions, to promote an understanding and practice of enterprise in a cooperative environment.

The Blade

This is a worker cooperative which has offered cooperative-oriented education and training since 1983 for young unemployed. A 63-week program of activities includes business organization and administration, finance, book-keeping, Swedish and history especially related to the labor and cooperative movements. Practical activities are in three stages:

1 On-the-job training (10 weeks).
2 Productive work within the cooperative (10 weeks).
3 Working in groups to plan the establishment of their own cooperatives (43 weeks).

The Varmlands Cooperatives

This is a foundation which endeavors to improve self-confidence. The knowledge and will to work independently is combined with the knowledge of cooperation in group relations. It is hoped that out of the project strong and knowledgeable individuals will become working members of strong and knowledgeable groups. The focus of the program has been the manufacture of a variety of craft products for sale.

The basic elements of the program have included the following principles (Wallin, 1988):

1 All participants must agree on the aims of the training to build self-confidence.
2 Decisions and their implementation are the responsibilities of participants;.
3 Great care is taken not to make the training setting "school-like".
4 Participants must take economic responsibility for their project.
5 They learn to make contact with state and local authorities to solve their own problems.
6 Participants are encouraged to try different ways of doing things and to recognize that making a mistake is important to the process of problem-solving and confidence-building.
7 All participants learn to teach others what they are good at.
8 Teacher-led classes in such subjects as book-keeping, theories of enterprise development, Swedish and mathematics are used to complement the practical training.

Norway

The Norwegian city of Drammen, once a great timber center, has developed a different approach to meeting the needs of school-leavers. In 1980 the local labor office, in consultation with the education committee, opened the *AI Work Center (Arbeidsinstitet)* in two buildings, one with offices and workshops and the other a large vacant fiberboard factory. Objectives of AI are as follows:

1 To assist young people who have difficulty in finding a job because of a lack of self-confidence and work discipline.
2 To provide practical training.
3 To find them jobs.

Courses are planned according to the expressed needs of local employers such as building construction and maintenance, warehousing, office work, and special "niche" areas in the local labor market (e.g. butchery). Instructors are recruited from the field of employment rather than education. Their relationship with the young people is that of supervisor–worker rather than teacher–pupil. Trainees stay in the program as long as they need to, up to a maximum of ten months, before finding a job. The AI Center has also been used for language and cultural training for immigrants and refugees.

The AI factory building has seen the conversion of a vast empty shell into workshops and classroom. Part of the building has been used as a test center for welders, while the recycling of automotive parts from old motor vehicles in a neighboring scrap yard has been a source of revenue. Other initiatives include winter storage of boats and a course in steel rod handling and bending. Most important, all renovations to the building have been undertaken by trainees and all training activities are in response to the employment needs of local industry (OECD, 1986).

France

In the Les Halles district of Paris, the traditional food market area, the *Center for Youth Employment Initiatives (CIEJ)* serves unemployed youth, aged 16–25, who are disadvantaged due to poor school performance, social or personal background. A reception and information center for young job-seekers offers group work leading to training, workshop or job placement.

The CIEJ operates its own workshops (*chantiers de relais*) where the young unemployed gain up to six months' work experience in productive enterprises such as printing, mail-order addressing and packaging, catering and building and maintenance work. Young people earn the minimum wage while learning the disciplines of work and receiving employment training and the information and skills needed to start their own small businesses. The training for future entrepreneurs has led to the creation of "intermediate businesses" to employ more young people and an investment fund to provide working capital and start-up money for new enterprises (OECD, 1986).

Australia

In 1978 the South Australian State Government, through its Office of Employment Training, established a new program entitled *Community Improvement Through Youth (CITY)*. Young unemployed people were provided with resources to develop personal skills by being involved in the design and management of community projects while continuing to receive unemployment benefits. The four broad aims of CITY were as follows:

1 To encourage young people to initiate and develop community projects.
2 To assist young people to develop confidence and self-esteem.
3 To assist young people to gain work experience and skills.
4 To develop support structures in the community and promote the skills of the young people to the community.

Projects initiated by young people through CITY varied widely, including:

- organizing recreation camps for handicapped children;
- running concerts and music workshops;
- undertaking research into issues affecting young people;
- producing arts displays and theater performances;
- organizing campaigns and fund-raising events.

In 1985 the program, in recognizing the existence of long-term structural unemployment, revised its objectives so that the relevance of CITY to education and training would be more explicit, as follows:

1 To enable participants to identify, utilize and further develop skills that are essential for a person to be enterprising and better cope with and/or combat uncertainty.
2 To enable participants to better understand how they can create social, political and economic opportunities and/or utilize limited and unexpected opportunities.
3 To develop support networks within the community to provide assistance to unemployed young people.
4 To develop linkages between involvement in CITY and future involvement in further education and training.

The CITY staff in recognizing the uncertainty of the labor market, the impact of rapid social change and insecure domestic and community life identified eleven "enterprise skills" for personal self-reliance:

- assessing strengths and weaknesses;
- developing communication and negotiation skills;
- planning time and energy;

- seeking information and advice;
- resolving conflict;
- problem-solving;
- dealing with people in power and authority;
- making decisions;
- carrying through agreed responsibilities;
- coping with stress and tension;
- evaluating one's own performance.

Since its inception in 1978, CITY (now known as the Youth Initiatives Unit) has assisted nearly 20,000 young people to identify, design and manage their own projects, utilizing grants and the services of a full-time facilitator. A small proportion of the projects have led to the establishment of permanent businesses, self-employment opportunities, self-help associations and youth organizations (Turner, 1985; OECD, 1989).

WHAT HAVE WE LEARNED?

The inability of young people to complete their formal education is viewed as a serious problem by most industrialized countries. A large proportion of secondary school students don't achieve a graduation diploma nor do they go on to a college, university or training institute. Their limited employment skills and diminished self-esteem make them ill-prepared to compete for jobs in the post-industrial economy.

The industrial and agricultural ages provided an alternative to schooling through on-the-job training and apprenticeships, which often no longer exist. The decline of manufacturing and primary-resource employment has left school-leavers scrambling for a decreasing number of service jobs without any hope for a future career. It has been very much a case of "teach the best and discard the rest."

It appears that the most innovative programs to serve the needs of school-leavers have been initiated by voluntary, not-for-profit organizations, government departments, commercial interests or some combination of these. Those programs which seem to have provided an alternative to the traditional pattern of economic sorting have had a number of common elements.

They have focused on some form of community-based hands-on training in which trainees gain practical entry-level skills which may be identified as a priority by local employers. The social and educational needs of the young people are often seen as complementary to the more concrete learning. In some instances, academic studies and life skills are integrated into the workplace training process. In other instances, trainees go back to educational institutions to receive these skills on a part-time basis. The inescapable conclusion, however, is that workplace-related training, not schooling, has become the learning alternative for these young people.

Another vital element which reappears constantly is the relative importance of gaining the enterprise skills of initiative, interpersonal relations, cooperative problem-solving, accepting responsibility and self-reliance. This is most often pursued through some form of small-business, entrepreneurial initiative whereby trainees prepare for employment in service-oriented or craft enterprises or actually create their own ventures. The process of venture-creation is not a pseudo-exercise but an actual hands-on experience of learning-by-doing. The cause-and-effect relationships of success and failure are learned within the context of a supportive environment with all the real-world dynamics.

The challenge remains how can some of the more successful elements of these training initiatives be integrated into public education? Conversely, should the needs of more concrete learners be addressed in the formal educational institutions we call "schools" at all? How are we adjusting our whole preparation system to service the post-industrial economy? What about the older redundant workers who are also discarded from the economic system? The next chapter will explore ways in which public education has tried to cope with the service economy in a social context.

5 Beyond the chain link fence

EDUCATION FOR COMMUNITY LIVING

Voluntary assistance has had a long tradition in the western world. Perhaps it has been exemplified best in agrarian societies, where people learned to pull together to survive climatic conditions or an inhospitable environment. The history of the early pioneers in North America and Australia produces many tales of neighbors helping neighbors in rural areas to clear the land, bring in the harvest, raise the buildings or rebuild after a fire. These elements of community service became part of the hands-on culture of the agricultural age which passed by example from parents to children.

Voluntary action in rural areas resulted in the creation of the first public schools in North America. In fact many of the social and health-related services grew out of the experience of volunteers responding to local needs as "good neighbors." This pioneering spirit of neighbors working together to share resources and solve mutual problems did not always survive rural–urban migration, however. The state gradually seized control of schools, hospitals and social welfare agencies in both cities and rural areas as they became more institutionalized and dependent on tax revenue.

The transformation of our economy from agricultural to industrial, our people from active-rural to passive-urban dwellers, has challenged the schools to introduce more concrete learning experiences into the curriculum. A traditional sense of community service, which seemed so natural in a rural society, did not always translate to life in our crowded, transient, industrial centers. As a result, a new emphasis on experiential education where students could study social and environmental processes through activities outside of the classroom was advocated.

One of the most profound influences on the growth and direction of public education in the twentieth century has been John Dewey. In his widely read text, *School and Society* (1915), Dewey condemned the institutional school of the nineteenth century for its sense of isolation from the social, economic and physical realities of life-experience:

> Personalities which become effective in action were bred and tested in the medium of action. Again, we cannot overlook the importance for educational purposes of the close and intimate acquaintance got with nature at first hand, with real things and materials, with the actual processes of their manipulation and the knowledge of their social necessities and uses . . . . From the standpoint of the child, the great waste in the school comes from his inability to utilize the experience he gets outside the school itself; while, on the other hand, he is unable to apply to daily life what he is learning at school. That is the isolation of the school – its isolation from life.

One educator who has been strongly influenced by John Dewey is Edward Olsen. In his 1945 publication, *School and Community*, he proposed five goals for "life-centered education":

1 The school should operate as an educational center for adults (as well as children and adolescents).
2 The school should utilize community resources to invigorate the conventional program.
3 The school should center its curriculum in a study of community structure, processes and problems.
4 The school should improve the community through participation in its activities.
5 The school should lead in coordinating the educative efforts of the community.

Olsen merges the life-experience philosophy of Dewey with his own model of the ideal school. His *Community School* model is not the inward-looking educational clinic which has become the tradition but rather a facility which "gets involved" with quality-of-life issues. The Olsen model of community education proposes an organization which would: focus on community needs; identify and mobilize resources in school and community to satisfy these needs; and serve as a learning center for people of all ages to acquire the necessary information and skills for community problem-solving.

What then is the curriculum of the "Community School"? Irwin and Russell in their book *The Community Is the Classroom* (1971) provide a rationale for a community-centered curriculum:

> The community is a laboratory for learning. In this laboratory children interact with their environment and their first and most enduring

learnings occur. The community-centered curriculum is an extension of the natural learning environment, with the classroom serving as a coordinating center for a variety of experiences whereby the child's in-school and out-of-school experiences are one and the same.

The content of the curriculum, centering around life in the community and community problems, encompasses a multidisciplinary approach and requires a wise utilization of resources.

The "community schools movement," whereby the school is seen as a natural extension of the community it serves, has been a strong influence on the development of public education in both North America and Britain; particularly at the elementary school level. An important component of the community school philosophy has always been a community-focused curriculum. If the school is to become a vital resource for community development, however, it seems essential that its personnel and facilities be actively involved in building and maintaining a network of voluntary and governmental services striving to improve the quality of life in the community.

THE HUMANE APPLICATION OF KNOWLEDGE

A US Tradition

The combining of classroom study with service/social action projects has had a long history in American education. In 1918 William Kilpatrick urged the adoption of the "project method" as a focus for educational reform. He believed that learning should take place in settings outside the school and involve efforts to meet community needs (Kilpatrick, 1918).

This concept was amplified by the *Progressive School Movement* during the 1930s which maintained that schools should "inculcate the values of social reform and teach the attitudes, knowledge and skills necessary to accomplish it." Such publications as *Dare the Schools Build a New Social Order?* and *Youth Serves the Community* promoted the ideals of using education for social transformation (Counts, 1932; Hanna, 1937).

During the 1950s the *Citizenship Education Project*, initiated by Columbia University's Teachers College stressed participation and direct community involvement through its *Brown Box* of teaching ideas containing hundreds of detailed guides to social investigation and social/ political action. In the 1970s such reports as the *National Committee on Secondary Education*, the *Panel on Youth of the President's Science Advisory Committee* and the *National Panel on High School and Adolescent Education* urged that:

young people be reintegrated into the community, encouraged to interact with a wider range of people, involved in real and meaningful tasks, and afforded more responsibility through a variety of direct experiences that included, but were not limited to service activities.

(Conrad & Hedin, 1991)

The most comprehensive approach to curriculum design was provided by Fred Newmann, who proposed community services as a stimulus for developing in students the attitudes, skills and knowledge required for influencing social policy (Newmann, 1975). Elliot Wigginton, of *Foxfire* fame, offered inspiration, theory and practice for teachers working with youth service programs. *A Place Called School* by John Goodlad and *Reconnecting Youth*, a 1985 report of the Education Commission of the States, both advocated community service to improve education. The William P. Grant Foundation report, *The Forgotten Half*, made a strong plea for non-college-bound youth performing community service as central to the fundamental education program of every public school (Conrad and Hedin, 1991).

A more recent proponent of community-service learning in the United States has been the *National Society for Internships and Experiential Education (NSIEE)*. In their 1990 publication *Combining Service and Learning – A Resource Book for Community and Public Service*, NSIEE observes that:

In the last half of the 1980s and the start of the 1990s, the surge of interest in involving young people and adults in community service experiences has been tremendous . . . . Hands-on experiences in the community are essential for educating the next generation about human needs and for building among young and old a commitment to social responsibility in their careers and in their lives as active citizens.

(Kendall, 1990)

Ernest L. Boyer, a former US Commissioner of Education, states that "the problems of our schools are inextricably tied to the feeling on the part of many of our youth that they are isolated, unconnected to the larger world outside their classroom." As President of the Carnegie Foundation, Boyer proposed that every American student complete a service requirement that would involve them in not less than 30 hours per year, or 120 hours over four years, to qualify for a "Carnegie service unit." Such voluntary service might be in the community or in the school – spending time with a lonely older person, helping a child learn to read, cleaning up litter on the street or working on a school-based service project. From a study of school service programs, Boyer (1990) identifies the following principles to be considered before embarking on a program:

1 A service program begins with clearly stated educational objectives – school at its best involves the humane application of knowledge to real-life experience.
2 A service program should be carefully introduced and creatively promoted – the planning, implementation and evaluation of service programs should be approached cautiously, with both teachers and students involved in the process.
3 Service activity should be directed not just to the community but also toward the school itself – most students see the school as belonging to adults and have little appreciation of what makes a school work.
4 A service program should be something more than preparation for a career – the values and skills gained from a service experience have universal application.
5 Students should not only go out to serve; they should also be asked to write about their experience and, if possible, to discuss with others the lessons they have learned – service is not just giving out, the joy, satisfaction, frustration and pain should be communicated and discussed with mentors and fellow students as an integral part of the total curriculum (Boyer 1990).

The UK experience

One of the strongest advocates for the integration of community service into the curriculum in the UK has been Alec Dickson. His experiences working with displaced persons after the Second World War and as a community development worker in Africa resulted in the founding of Voluntary Service Overseas in 1958. More than 1,000 university graduates were mobilized each year to provide service in developing countries. In 1962, as a result of these experiences, he established the Community Service Volunteers to encourage British primary and secondary school students to provide volunteer service in their own communities. These voluntary organizations were the forerunners of the Peace Corps and VISTA in the United States.

But there were obstacles to overcome. To quote Dickson in his book *A Chance to Serve*:

> The mechanisms of the Welfare State, the operations of the Affluent Society, convey the impression that the most basic requirements are really provided for . . . . Partly underlying this attitude is a change in the concept of the voluntary role in all aspects of western life. The volunteer is no longer a doer, but a committee member: the actual work is entrusted to professionals. The committees themselves reflect the

contemporary preoccupation with coordination rather than creativity, their temple a clearing house . . . . Endeavours that were reformist or even revolutionary in the 1860s have in all too many instances become set in hierarchic or institutional patterns, the fury of indignation that moved their founders now frozen into a formula.

The first obstacle encountered today by young volunteers is the resistance of professional social workers. Sincerely anxious to protect clients from exposure to the immature or unqualified and possibly mindful of their own struggle to achieve recognition, it is comprehensible that some of them feel as they do. No one today would argue that the concept of the Lady Bountiful going slumming was a substitute for the experienced social worker. But what is now implicit – that human relations are so intricate that without a university degree, a diploma in sociology, followed by casework and group dynamics, no one should be allowed to engage in this field – is tantamount to a keep-out warning to the volunteer.

(Dickson and Dickson, 1976)

Alec Dickson has been influential in having community service accepted as part of the curriculum in the UK. To quote Dickson's paper "Community Service and the Curriculum" (1980):

That service can be integrated into the curriculum is a relatively new idea. It is happening in many secondary schools in Britain . . . . Indeed, it has been quite a hard struggle to get it accepted in British schools. However, three official reports – "Community Service and the Curriculum" (Schools Council), "Community Service in Scottish Secondary Schools" (Scottish Education Department), and "Community Service in Education" (Department of Education and Science) – testify that this concept now has official approval . . . . Moreover, there is now an Association for Community Service in Education (ACSE), whose members are teachers actively interested in promoting this approach in their schools.

Dickson maintains that the great advantage of introducing community service into the curriculum is that all students can have the experience regardless of whether they aspire to go on to university or leave school early. "We say that young people can be educated to serve: better, that they can be educated by service. It is in helping that one learns to help." He believes that community service projects should be interdisciplinary, involve all staff and students in a school, and become more challenging as students mature.

LEARNING TO SERVE

What types of programs have been developed to encourage learning through service? Diane Hedin and Dan Conrad have identified six different stages in the integration of service learning into the regular academic structure of the school (as described in Conrad and Hedin, 1990, a publication of the National Society for Internships and Experiential Education). The following is a description of these stages together with selected case studies which illustrate the different approaches.

1. Club or co-curricular activity

Students perform community service through joining an after-school club or activity. They receive neither academic credit nor time off school, and participation is purely voluntary. Such clubs might be indigenous to a secondary school or operate as a local chapter of such national organizations as Future Homemakers of America, National Honor Society or Key Clubs. A faculty adviser may be provided and in some school systems the central administration may even offer assistance in establishing clubs and programs in individual high schools. Most often, however, students demonstrate leadership in organizing service activities.

Volunteers Unlimited is a co-curricular activity which I introduced in 1968 into three secondary schools in North York, a municipality within Metropolitan Toronto, Ontario, Canada. The project involved students volunteering in social service agencies on their own time and then meeting once a week with a staff adviser to discuss their placements and share ideas and perceptions. This program was similar in some respects to other extracurricular activities that students participate in. The project was open to senior secondary students who were willing to provide a maximum of three hours' service per week. Applications to participate in the program were made through the Guidance Department of the school.

The aims of the project were the following:

1 To provide a practical educational experience in the area of community service and human involvement.
2 To provide a source of additional auxiliary aid and volunteer service to the fields of health, education and social welfare.
3 To provide an introduction to the helping professions which might influence future career choice.
4 To promote a better overall understanding of community services and the part they play in urban development.
5 To promote greater liaison on a professional level between education, health and social welfare.

In setting up this service program, the following plan of action was followed:

1 A faculty adviser was appointed in each school to supervise the formation of a separate student organization responsible to the principal and affiliated with the Student Council.
2 Each student member was classified according to his or her individual interests (i.e. medical, social welfare, recreational, educational, etc.).
3 A list of institutions and agencies interested in making use of youth volunteers was compiled (i.e. hospitals, social welfare agencies, mental health agencies, recreational and educational bodies, institutions of rehabilitation and convalescence, residential treatment and cure centers, etc.).
4 Each agency accepting volunteers was responsible for orientation, instruction, placement and supervision.
5 Each agency operated its own autonomous program while maintaining liaison with the faculty adviser.
6 A fellowship of student volunteers was maintained within the school, providing an unstructured forum for the sharing of ideas, experiences and philosophies.
7 Operational costs were minimal and were underwritten through Student Council grants.

As with any new project a number of problems were experienced. Communication between the agencies and the schools was not clear at first, although the agencies were encouraged to communicate directly with staff advisers concerning personnel and placement. In one case the receiving agency was found to be too far away for volunteers to reach easily. In another there were not enough staff members to supervise the student volunteers. (Neither of these agencies became involved in the program.)

Both the staff advisers and the students in the program felt the experience was very positive. The students were highly motivated and sincerely interested in the problems of the people they were dealing with. In general they felt they were really doing something worthwhile. There appeared to be no conflict with academic performance and in some cases there was an improvement due to attitude change (Shuttleworth, 1968).

2. Volunteer clearinghouse

Some schools have created their own "volunteer bureau" to serve as a clearinghouse for school–community involvement and volunteer service. Students might choose from a wide range of activities, including voluntary clubs. No academic credit is granted and work must be done during unscheduled time during the day or after classes. Students may source service opportunities from a central resource list which might be developed during the summer as a student employment project. Typically, volunteers are required to sign a "contract" which demonstrates their personal commitment to the placement. The bureau is most often staffed by faculty and students who coordinate day-to-day operations, follow-up and review. In some instances, an outside voluntary service organization, such as the Junior League, Red Cross, Jaycees (Junior Chamber of Commerce) or a central volunteer agency, may provide leadership. *SerVermont* is a public service volunteer project for high school students established in 1986 in the US state of Vermont by Cynthia Parsons. Her "dreams" for the project were described in SerVermont's first brochure (Parsons, 1991):

- a dream that every student in Vermont's public schools will do some important community service;
- a dream that every community will be enriched by the voluntary service done by its student citizens;
- a dream that each nonprofit organization in Vermont will train and use students to enhance the quality of services it provides to clients;
- a dream that each government agency in Vermont will make a place for student volunteers, enabling them to learn by doing;
- a dream that school authorities will encourage and support community service for students as an essential part of free public school.

A primary object of the project was "to compile an inventory of the service opportunities available to students in each of the state's 59 school districts." Parsons envisioned a working notebook listing volunteer jobs for students with telephone numbers and contact names. The information could then be sent through the Vermont library system via computer and updated regularly by volunteer college students. A pilot project created an inventory of 100 community service agencies within commuting distance of one rural Vermont high school. The resulting information was accurate, readable and usable; but no one ever used it.

After two years of frustration, Parsons discovered the *Retired Senior Volunteer Program (RSVP)* a voluntary organization active in almost every county in Vermont. RSVP offered to provide any public school in the state with an adult volunteer to serve as a liaison between students who wish to volunteer their services and local agencies looking for volunteers. By the 1990–91 school year all but a handful of Vermont high schools had expanding programs of community service (Parsons, 1991).

3. Community service credit

Some schools offer community service as one of the semester (five-month term) credits, usually requiring 100 hours of volunteer service. This could be a course elective in place of such subjects as social studies or humanities, or in some instances a prescribed number of service hours is required to graduate. Service assignments may take place after school hours, for one full school day a week or as a block placement from one month to a whole semester in length. They are not however, performed as part of a regular school course but as an off-campus experience with minimal supervision by school personnel. The receiving agency is responsible for all training.

The *Community Involvement Program (CIP)* is one of the most in-depth credit programs in community service learning being operated in a number of Boards of Education in the Canadian province of Ontario. As described by Lesley Mang in her book *Community as Classroom* (1979), CIP goes much beyond being a volunteer service project. In many ways it encompasses the idea of career education, where students are given an opportunity to sample a "real-life" work situation that could lead to a future career in community service.

The program developed out of discussions surrounding a paper by David Brison of the Ontario Institute for Studies in Education. In his article, called "Restructuring the school system", he states: "schools have almost certainly failed to prepare students to cope with and resolve problems, some of which threaten our very existence or prevent us from living together in any reasonable harmony" (Brison, 1972).

The Community Involvement Program was organized as an alternative to present school programs. It was designed as an alternative within existing school buildings and with existing staff and budget allocations. However, its central purpose is:

> to develop a commitment to the solution of social problems and to teach the kinds of skills needed to build alternative solutions, where needed, to ones presently offered in our society . . . the role of education is not to teach a specific solution but in the broadest sense to impart skills and knowledge needed to derive solutions to problems and generate the appropriate motivation so that the individual will desire to find solutions to some of the pressing social problems facing society today.
>
> (Brison, 1973–74)

Within the frame of the above purpose the specific aims of the program are the following:

1 To develop an awareness and understanding of the social needs of the student's own community and the services organized to meet them.

Through study activities the student should attempt the analysis and solution to problems or needs the organized services do not always meet.

2   To develop appropriate inquiry and research skills.
3   To develop group work skills needed to help groups constructively to make decisions and solve problems.
4   To study interpersonal skills so that through the work experience, personal growth and maturity may result.
5   To develop a sense of confidence, poise, maturity and responsibility in students.
6   Within the area of values and moral reasoning, there are three main aims:
    (a) to help students clarify their own values;
    (b) to increase the importance students place on helping those in need and on solving social problems;
    (c) to advance the students' moral reasoning.
7   Within the area of practical politics the student should learn to develop a sense of applied civics in understanding how the political structure operates and can be influenced within social service agencies, with reference to the three levels of government and the agencies themselves.

The Community Involvement Program, which occupies 50 per cent of a student's time during the school year, is worth three or four credits. The program is comprised of three broad areas: the agency assignment, the in-school class sessions and the independent study project.

Each student spends ten hours a week working with a social service agency. Ideally the student has an opportunity to relate to different staff members and different clients. The assigned tasks become gradually more complex and require more responsibility and more initiative. The students have opportunities to observe agency procedures and to practice inter-personal and group process skills. They are able to observe "politics in action" within the agency and to see how government regulations affect the lives of people it serves. Students are able to practice data-gathering and interview skills to obtain social facts which can be shared with other class members.

In the classroom sessions students study the "theories" of interpersonal skills and group process skills and practice them in their work in the agency. They also have the opportunity to use reporting skills to give the class information about the social sector in which they are serving. From this data the class can, through discussion, get a picture of the social problems of the community, the agencies organized to deal with them and the need for further social reform.

The independent studies section offers the student the opportunity to do original research into an area of social concern. He or she may do a survey of use, opinion or need; undertake a case study of a client or a student (or a group of students). In this exercise the student learns and practices such skills as data-gathering, analysis, classification, hypothesizing, testing, concluding, recommending and writing a documented report. The students are encouraged to seek help from school resources as well as agency and community resources.

In planning the program the teacher or liaison person should first explore the community for agencies able to provide experiences in keeping with the aims of the program. In the initial contact with the agencies all areas of concern could be discussed: the concept of the program, the responsibilities of the school and of the agency, the kinds of tasks to be done, any reservations the agency might have about students doing some levels of staff work, provision of information about the agency for students and meeting with students and teacher to explain agency work.

As well, arrangements would be made to interview students who request a placement in the agency, so that students and agency can be matched as ideally as possible. An evaluation form should be designed for the use of the teachers to assess student work in the agency. A written commitment from agencies should be obtained as soon as possible before the next year's option sheets come out for students.

In presenting the course to possible students, certain points should be made. Students should know that there are a variety of agencies available, that the program is worthwhile for both boys and girls and that it is a valuable experience for students proceeding to university.

After students have been selected they should receive information about each agency provided by the agency and attend meetings where the agency personnel explain their programs. Then students decide which agencies interest them and attend individual interviews with the agency of their choice. Agencies list their choice of student in order of preference and then teachers match agency and student as well as possible. Agencies and students should be informed of results and students who have not been placed where they requested should be given the reasons why.

Once the students and agencies are matched, teachers should meet with agency personnel who will supervise students before the students begin working in the agency. Several weeks after the students begin work in the agencies a joint meeting should be held to review the placements: sometimes a transfer might be made, in the best interests of both students and agency.

The teacher of a CIP course plays several roles. He or she acts as a liaison person with the direct supervisor of the students in the agency. With the supervisor, he or she will work out the students' schedule and methods of evaluation. Teachers are also resource persons for their students in that they should be aware of the scope of resources available (e.g. library, other staff, agency personnel and community leaders). The teacher is a classroom teacher for the in-school portion of the course and a counselor for the students who will be moving into new and demanding situations. It is important that the teacher visit the agencies often, since classroom contact is so limited. As well, the teacher performs the duties of an administrator in arranging schedules and contacting resource people.

The agency's responsibilities include providing at least ten hours per week of involvement for the student. It should offer an orientation period during which the student becomes familiar with agency routines and meets agency personnel. There should be training provided for tasks in the agency. The program should be defined as far in advance as possible, with tasks assigned so the work can increase in challenge and interest as the work year progresses. The agency should also be responsible for evaluating student work in the agency (with student and teacher present during the discussion of the evaluation).

The student should be made aware of his or her responsibilities in being a part of the program. He should carefully study the material provided by the agencies, attend the agency meetings prepared to ask questions and handle the agency interview in a mature way. After he or she has begun working he should be in time for work, ask for clarification if he does not understand his instructions and inform the school and the agency if he will be absent. If the student encounters personnel problems at the agency he should discuss the problem with his supervisor; if the problem involves his supervisor, he should then discuss it with his teacher. When the student requires assistance from agency personnel for a school assignment, she should allow them ample time to give it consideration.

There are agencies in many service areas where students could be placed. For example, students in this program have worked in day care centers, children's mental health centers, homes for the aged and physically handicapped, hospitals, probation offices, municipal and provincial social service departments, classes for slow learners and English as a second language, information centers, and Parks and Recreation Departments.

Some tasks that students have done through their agencies are the following: teaching crafts to the elderly, to children and to the mentally handicapped; assisting in special reading programs, including writing stories for them; teaching practical skills to the mentally handicapped; accounting, budgeting (for welfare applicants); assisting with physio-therapy; homemaker work in the field; assisting with counseling groups and individuals; supervising play activity; coaching sports (Mang, 1979).

4. A laboratory for an existing course

Students in existing courses do community service as a "reality test" of course content. For example, to gain an insight into poverty, students might volunteer for approximately two hours per week in a social welfare agency. The classroom teacher assists in finding appropriate placements and provides ongoing supervision. Service experience becomes an incidental part of curriculum content but the overall course structure does not change.

Community Service in Action is a program within the Abraham Lincoln High School in Philadelphia. In 1988, Governor Robert Casey of Pennsylvania launched *PennSERVE: The Governor's Office of Citizen Service* in the belief that "The qualities of a productive worker are the same as those of a good citizen, and community service is an effective means of cutting dropout rates and aiding in the difficult transition from school to work by giving youth direct career and citizenship experience" (Briscoe, 1991).

Lincoln High School, serving a racially-diverse working-class area, received two PennSERVE mini-grants to support curricular projects in environmental studies and local history. The environmental project involved students collecting water, soil, air and radon samples for analysis. The nearby Pennyback Creek was monitored, and tons of trash and refuse were removed from the creek and a neighborhood park. Students in an oral history class presented their ideas to community groups, recruited an advisory board and published a 160-page book on the history of the local community.

The experience with the two seed grants and the introduction of community service into the curriculum has resulted in a whole new approach to funding innovative projects. Rather than just depending on traditional means of support from the school system, teachers are now learning to solicit resources from outside sources to enrich the learning opportunities of students. As a result, horticulture students now have summer jobs in the local park, a major nursery for the park system has been established on the school campus and students were hired to design and install a historically accurate garden at the local museum. Finally, the business community has donated over $2 million in environmental equipment to create the *Lincoln Environmental Laboratory* – the only such facility at a high school in the United States (Silcox, 1991).

5. Community service class

In this instance, a community experience forms the central focus of the course but is combined with classroom experience to provide information and skills to assist students in interpreting their experiences and to operate more effectively in their placements. A one-semester social studies class might meet two hours per day with a student spending four days (eight hours) in the field and one day (two hours) in class. The additional hours per day are achieved either by giving a double social studies credit or by making the course multidisciplinary, combining English, home economics, humanities and social studies.

Alec Dickson in his paper "A curricular approach to community service" (1973) provides this insight into a community service class in action in the UK:

> At Brierly Street School in Crewe, situated in the poorest area of a city famed only as a grimy railroad junction and as the place where Rolls-Royce manufactures its automobiles, the boys are as far removed from the social background, academic ability, and career prospects of Eton students as can be imagined. Indeed, recently, half the members of one class of 15-year-olds were known to the local probation officer. This was the class that the handicrafts teacher took to the hospital in Crewe and confronted with nine spina bifida children. The boys learned that neither surgery nor medication could do much to rectify the children's congenital spinal defects, one immediate consequence of which was their immobility. No child could move unaided, and a nurse had to lift each one for every human function. Could the boys help?
>
> Back at school, in their handicraft session, they wrestled with the technicalities of this problem, trying out this material, testing out that design. Eventually, in the last week of term, led by their school principal, they returned to the hospital ward and handed over nine low carts, boomerang-shaped in front to fit the children's splayed legs, and mounted on casters, so that each child, when seated in one, could propel himself in any direction with his fingertips.
>
> At the presentation ceremony, the hospital staff were astounded; the children, euphoric; the mothers, in tears of joy; and the 15-year-olds themselves, strangely silent. Why had this experience made such an impact on them, their own principal asked later. "Because it's the first bloody thing we've made in this school that we didn't have to take home afterwards" was one reply. "Because nobody said this was good for us. They said it was serious, dead serious" was another.

6. Community service as a school-wide focus or theme

The most comprehensive approach is where community service provides a focus for the total curriculum of the school. For example, a magnet school in human services might involve all students pursuing field placements in service agencies for career exploration and the development of social responsibility. In this model, community service is not just for the selected few motivated students but a key organizational principle for all students:

> Biology students might work in a food co-op, where they teach nutrition to low-income elderly people; home economics students run a day-care center several mornings a week for neighborhood preschoolers; and advanced math students offer their computer skills to small businesses to manage inventories and do financial projections.
>
> (Conrad and Hedin, 1990)

Service to the community program

The St. Paul Open School is an alternative public school from kindergarten to grade 12 established in 1971 in St. Paul, Minnesota. From its inception the Open School has promoted the use of the community service as a base for experiential learning. To quote Mike Scott, a teacher at the Open School:

> Students' experiences have ranged from building bridges and harvesting crops in Nicaragua to working in hospitals or performing service at food shelves and drop-in shelters. Students have worked at theaters, women's advocate shelters, day care centers and Meals-On-Wheels. They have tutored younger students at other schools and coached teams for young children in their neighborhoods. They have served on boards of directors for neighborhood community councils and as student resource persons on state and local committees.
>
> (Scott, 1991)

Students have worked on political campaigns, participated in advocacy programs, served as language interpreters for refugee families, assisted the elderly in seniors' high rises and worked in neighborhood justice centers. To graduate, students must demonstrate certain basic and applied skills and knowledge in six areas: career awareness; consumer awareness; information finding; community knowledge and service; personal and interpersonal skills; and communication and cultural awareness. Each student develops a packet of validations with teachers, employers, parents and others documenting that the student has demonstrated the required skills (Nathan, 1991).

SCHOOLING FOR THE REAL WORLD

The last half of the 1980s and the beginning of the 1990s has seen a strong upsurge in interest in involving young people in community service, particularly in the United States. In November 1990, President George Bush signed into law the *National and Community Service Act*. The Act provides funding for community service programs in schools and colleges and support for a full-time service corps that students can enter after high school. Why the renewed interest in service learning as an alternative education strategy?

Urban school-leavers have little to look forward to except employment in entry-level jobs at fast-food restaurants and all-night gas (petrol) bars. As heavy users of drugs and alcohol, they have the lowest voting rate of any age group and the teen pregnancy rate has become an epidemic. As academic standards in public schools continue to fall the plea for educational reform has become a desperate cry.

To quote Nathan and Kielsmeier in their article "The sleeping giant of school reform" (1991):

> We believe that these problems stem in part from the way adults treat young people. Unlike earlier generations, which viewed young people as active, productive, and needed members of the household and community, adults today tend to treat them as objects, as problems, or as the recipients (not the deliverers) of services. Young people are treated as objects when they are routinely classified as a separate group, isolated in age-based institutions . . . . They are treated as problems when they are feared, criticized, and made the focus of preventive and remedial programs. They are treated as recipients of services when they are viewed as creatures to be pitied, fixed and controlled.

Largely unsuccessful reform proposals and frightening new societal concerns have resulted in a political climate more open to school reform derived from the skills and experiences gained from service learning and social action. For example the *Governor's Youth Service Recognition Program* in Minnesota has produced the following criteria for successful programs (Kielsmeier and Cairn, 1988):

- significant, necessary and measurable service is accomplished;
- youths are directly involved in planning and implementation;
- clear institutional commitment to the service program is reflected in goals or mission statements;
- community support for and involvement in the program are strong;
- learner outcomes for the program are well-articulated;

- a well designed and articulated curriculum for service exists that includes preparation, supervision, and active reflection on the experience;
- regular and significant recognition of the youths and adults who participate takes place.

The influential Report of the William P. Grant Foundation Commission on Work, Family and Citizenship, entitled *The Forgotten Half: Non-College Youth in America* (1988) makes the following observation:

> The plight of the "forgotten half" never easy, has become alarming. This nation may face a future divided not along lines of race or geography, but rather of education. A highly competitive technological economy can offer prosperity to those with advanced skills, while the trend for those with less education is to scramble for unsteady, part-time, low-paying jobs.

The Report recommends unpaid community service as a complement to paid work and cooperative education in the belief that:

> young people need experience not only as workers but especially as citizens . . . . By engaging in activities that are important to adults, young people would not be seen, or see themselves, as dependents or as mere takers from parents, families and the community. Rather they would become contributors, problem-solvers and partners with adults in creating a better society for all, young and old alike.
>
> (W.P. Grant Foundation, 1988)

The greater part of the literature on service learning focuses on the older adolescent and young adult. If we are to realize the goal of a more caring, compassionate, service-oriented society it seems that we must begin much earlier to encourage "the humane application of knowledge." Barbara Lewis' 4th to 6th grade students in Salt Lake City, Utah, have been responsible for the clean-up of a hazardous waste site, the passage of two new environmental laws, the planting of hundreds of trees and the completion of a number of neighborhood improvement projects. All these accomplishments from students of a school with the lowest per-capita family income in Salt Lake City. To quote Lewis, "One thing they do have is courage. They don't give up easily. They believe that the future depends on them. They're not afraid to attack things that other people say can't be done" (Lewis, 1991).

The application of service learning to the education process would seem to be a viable alternative to the abstract, static information-assimilation method prevalent in most classrooms. The experiential hands-on nature of most service activities may be a way to reach young people who have not benefited from the traditional institutional model. How do we ensure that these non-classroom experiences engender the "intellectual rigor" so necessary for survival in the post-industrial age? The chapter which follows will explore a more developmental concrete approach to the needs of the disadvantaged learner.

6   Hands on the future

UNDERSTANDING THE CONCRETE LEARNER

There continues to be ongoing debate among educators, politicians and the tax-paying public as to how well our educational system is serving the needs of our youth. The fact that the majority of students do not go on to higher education, or often even finish secondary school, would seem to be an indictment of our ability to serve the needs of students who are not academic abstract achievers, but may possess above average concrete learning skills. To quote Canada's Report of the Special Senate Committee on Youth:

> While it is the responsibility of schools to prepare youth for the next stage in their life in the workforce, they must do it in a way which balances practical and more general preparation. Unfortunately, the effect of many curricula is to polarize students. Academic courses serve the "achievers" and the 33% most likely to continue their schooling in post-secondary institutions. Specific skills training meets the needs of those who have already decided that they wish to pursue a certain vocation. For those who are somewhere between the two, the scenario is not as promising. They see little relevance in the courses they are taking as they lead neither to a guaranteed job nor to higher education. These students become bored, discouraged, disillusioned and therefore leave school. This is the group of young people who need an additional effort on our part, both before they drop out and once they have done so.
>
> (Senate Committee on Youth, 1986)

These concerns are not new to education. In 1916, the educational philosopher, John Dewey, in his essay entitled "Vocational aspects of education" stated:

> An occupation is a continuous activity having a purpose. Education through occupations consequently combines within itself more of the

factors conducive to learning than any other method. It calls instincts and habits into play; it is a foe to passive receptivity . . . . Since the movement of activity must be progressive, leading from one stage to another, observation and ingenuity are required at each stage to overcome obstacles and to discover and readapt means of execution . . . . Such organization of knowledge is vital, because it has reference to needs; it is so expressed and readjusted in action that it never becomes stagnant. No classification, no selection and arrangement of facts, which is consciously worked out for purely abstract ends, can ever compare in solidity or effectiveness with that unit under the stress of an occupation; in comparison the former sort is formal, superficial and cold.

(Dewey, 1916)

In more recent times, research into student learning styles and brain behavior has shown that the human brain consists of two potentially independent mental systems. To quote Frederick Staley:

The left hemisphere, for most people, is the site of logical, analytical, linear and propositional thought. It has primary control not only of the right side of the body but of such functions as talking, reading, writing, mathematical calculation, immediate verbal recall, time sense, order and most activities involving linguistic and numerical processes.

The right hemisphere controls the left side of the body and perhaps more important it is the locus of intuitive, imaginative, metaphoric and holistic thinking. As such, it controls dreaming, fantasizing, special perception, body awareness and movements, tactile sensations, visual memory, and perhaps many of our emotions. The right hemisphere is virtually nonverbal . . . . Additional support for the importance of the right hemisphere in effective learning is found in many important theories and practices related to language development, learning to read and learning to understand and do mathematics and science.

(Staley, 1980)

Max Rennels asks:

With Western man's primary institutional emphasis upon left cerebral functions, are educators overlooking a significant number of students who have highly developed right hemispheres?

(Rennels, 1976)

Becky Crossett further develops this theme:

Teaching as viewed in many educational settings, is tightly sequenced and students progress through the grades in a linear direction. The main subjects students study are verbal and numerical: reading, writing and arithmetic. Time schedules are strictly followed; seats are set in rows; learning converges on answers; teachers give out grades – and everyone senses that "something" is amiss.

(Crossett, 1983)

Betty Edwards in her 1979 text *Drawing on the Right Side of the Brain*, which documents research in "split-brain" studies at the California Institute of Technology, reaches the following conclusions:

> The right brain – the dreamer, the artificer, the artist – is lost in our school system and goes largely untaught . . . . the emphasis of our culture is so strongly slanted toward rewarding left brain skills that we are surely losing a very large proportion of the potential ability of the other halves of our children's brains . . . . Perhaps now that neuroscientists have provided a conceptual base for right-brain training, we can begin to build a school system that will teach the whole brain.

(Edwards, 1979)

What do we know about serving the learning needs of children with a predominant right-brain learning style? Who are these concrete learners and what is their place in public schooling? How can we build an educational strategy to address these concerns? The section which follows will draw upon my personal career experience.

DEVELOPING AN INSIGHT

My first experiences serving the needs of the "concrete learner" were in the 1960s as a school–community worker in an elementary school (kindergarten – grade 6) located in a large public housing area in North York, Ontario. As part of my duties, I was expected to counsel children (mostly boys) who were having behavioral problems in their primary and junior classrooms. However, I soon found that traditional Rogerian counseling was useless because, frankly, these children lacked verbal skills besides initially being very distrustful of me. It was only when I formed social development groups, with the help of our school psychologist, that I started to make any impact on their lives.

Social development groups were a form of activity group therapy drawn from the work of S. R. Slavson (1961). Each group of six was made up of two aggressive, acting-out children, two who were passive and withdrawn and two who might be classed as social isolates in that they had real difficulty in forming relationships and tended to be victimized, particularly on the playground. The important aspects of our weekly two-hour group sessions were mostly nonverbal communication relying upon such activities as crafts, model building, puppetry, active games, short excursions in the neighborhood or field trips to parks and other places of interest, such as the museum or science center. Out of these experiences new skills and abilities emerged which were valued. Lasting positive relationships were formed which were transferred to the classroom and playground. In my first year, I made 32 court visits with these children. Two years after the project was in place, the incidence of court appearance was reduced to just two occasions during the year.

These remarkable results gave me a new sense of insight into needs of socially disadvantaged children. Nonverbal, tactile experience was the only way to really reach them and to form lasting relationships. Unfortunately, this type of behavior was generally not appreciated or understood in the classroom, where mostly abstract learning skills were rewarded. Consequently, I was able to identify at the grade 3 level, those children who would be future school-leavers, often before their sixteenth birthday. In fact, they were already mental dropouts at the age of eight. This seemed to be the time "when the lights went out." The original glow of interest and wonder in their eyes had flickered and died.

Other responsibilities in operating an evening drop-in center for street youth confirmed my theory that the only way to reach these people was through some form of physical, concrete experience such as informal games, music, dance, and craft activities. It was obvious that hands-on expression was the primary focus in their lives. Academics, at best, were an incidental influence. It was no wonder that the great majority of the 200 14–20-year-olds who frequented the drop-in had already left school.

During the 1970s in the City of Toronto, I experimented with a variety of educational/training programs in which school-leavers were formed into small enterprise groups to develop employment-related skills in such areas as paper-recycling, wood craft, furniture refinishing and food service and catering. Each cottage industry also had an incidental academic learning component, in that a teacher was assigned to the workplace to offer upgrading and lifeskills on a withdrawal basis.

During the 1980s, I established this education in the workplace concept as a major department of the York Board of Education's *Adult Day School*, combining skill-training and upgrading in basic literacy, numeracy and English as a second language within such small community-based business enterprises as renovation and construction, industrial maintenance, healthcare aides, day care assistants, industrial sewing, bus-driving, home repair, courier/light-delivery services, restaurant services, landscaping, office skills and furniture upholstery.

Another component of this employment preparation package has been training in how to be successful in a small business. As more than 70 per cent of Canadians work for firms with less than 100 employees, programs in entrepreneurial skills and worker ownership were added to the training package.

In September, 1986 *MacTECH*, a new alternative school program in integrated machine technologies, was established utilizing accommodation at George Harvey Collegiate Institute and Standard-Modern Technologies – Canada's last machine tool manufacturer. Students used individual learning modules to develop skills in machine tool operation, electronics, computer control and microtechnologies, as well as traditional academic skills. After achieving a secondary school diploma, they were able to go on to secure a Humber College certificate in machine technologies – all offered in the same facilities. The program stressed personal initiative, problem-solving, inventiveness and self-reliance to better prepare students for the workplace of the twenty-first century.

All of these experiences have confirmed my belief that there is a way to reach the majority of students who are not successful in school. We must begin much earlier to create an educational environment where concrete learning skills are encouraged and valued (Shuttleworth, 1989).

IN SEARCH OF A STRATEGY

How should our curriculum and program be reformed to recognize the needs of the concrete learner?

Britain

Here, where youth unemployment has reached 25 per cent, there has been a demand for major reforms in educational practice to recognize economic and social realities. The movement for a fundamental change in the culture of education has been strongly influenced by the Royal Society of Arts (RSA):

> We consider that there exists in its own right a culture which is concerned with doing, making and organizing. The culture emphasizes craftsmanship and the making of useful artifacts; the design, manufacture and marketing of goods and services; specialist occupations with an active mode of work; the creative arts; and the day-to-day management of affairs.
>
> We believe that education should spend more time in teaching people skills and preparing them for life outside of the education system; and that the country would benefit significantly in economic terms from this re-balancing towards education for capability.
>
> (RSA, 1986)

In 1983, a group of leading thinkers and academics within the RSA signed the *Education for Capability Manifesto* supporting the idea of getting education to be as much concerned about capability as about knowledge. To quote Anne Jones, one of the signatories:

> By capability was meant the application of knowledge,the ability to do and complete a task, to solve problems, to use initiative, be enterprising, be self-managing, creative and practical . . . . The effect of the Education for Capability movement has been to influence government policy and educational practice at all levels.

> (Jones, 1990)

One example of such influence, undoubtedly, has been *Science in Primary Schools*, a publication of the Department of Education and Science (1983) which identifies four aspects of science for primary schools:

- Living things and their interaction with the environment;
- Materials and their characteristics;
- Energy and its interaction with materials;
- Forces and their effects (DES, 1983).

The content criteria for these science courses are as follows (DES, 1983):

- The content should, wherever possible, be related to the experiences of the children.
- It should, in accordance with their stages of development, provide them with knowledge and understanding of scientific ideas to help them to understand their own physical and biological environments and to understand themselves.
- It should, where possible, lay the foundations for a progressively deepening knowledge and understanding of scientific concepts and facts that will be useful to them as future citizens.
- It should include examples of the application of science to real-life problems including those of technology.

Other links to the man-made world are to be found in primary craft, design and technology initiatives using materials, sources of energy and natural phenomena to solve problems. The skills to be used in these activities are as follows (Evans, 1983):

- investigation – problem identification and definition;
- invention – proposing solutions;
- implementation – construction of selected solutions;
- evaluation – in relation to the problem.

Technological concepts to be applied include (Evans, 1983):

- Control – over the man-made environment;
- Energy – sources, forms, transmission, conversion, costs, etc.;
- Materials – sources, costs, useful properties, limitations, manufacturing processes.

Another form of communication to solve problems is to be found in mathematics, where students are encouraged to use imagination, initiative and flexibility while working both independently and cooperatively. The introduction of microcomputers and microelectronics into primary schools provides other hands-on activities to reinforce interactive learning through practice and simulations in which observations are recorded, stored and retrieved. Computer languages such as Logo are used to introduce students to electronic control devices (DES, 1985).

Another outcome of the Education for Capability movement has been the *Technical and Vocational Education Initiative (TVEI)* launched by the government in 1983 to make education for secondary school students (aged 14–18) more relevant to the needs of employers (see Chapter 3). In 1987 TVEI became a national initiative designed to change the culture of the whole secondary educational system.

It seeks to equip young people for the demands of working life in a rapidly changing world economy by the following means:

1 To relate what is learned in school to the world of work;
2 To make sure that all young people are scientifically and techno-logically literate (including information technology skills) and able to speak more than one language;
3 To ensure that young people have the experience of work and do projects in "real settings" so that they understand the world of work better;
4 To help teaching and learning styles to change so that young people learn "how" as well as what, can manage their own learning, can work with and through other people, can use modern technology as a tool of learning;
5 To improve the system of guidance counselling and progression, to help young people set goals and targets for their learning, to provide a record of achievement which records "capability" as well as academic achievements, and to help young people see 16+ as a stepping stone to further learning, not the end of it all.

(Jones, 1990)

What types of initiatives have emerged from these policy and procedural guidelines?

Lewknor Primary School, Oxfordshire

Children at this school have the opportunity:

> to manage their own work, take responsibility for it and make decisions about it for themselves. This operates at three levels. First, they manage an individual programme of work in basic subjects in which they must decide what to do and when. Secondly, they are asked to plan one afternoon's activity a week entirely by themselves, determining what to do, with whom, where, how and for how long. They then have to do it and cope with whatever may arise to frustrate or inhibit their purpose, as well as the task itself. Finally, within study projects directed by the teachers as much of the planning as possible is handed over to the children and they are set leadership tasks in carrying out the planning decisions that have been made.
>
> (RSA, 1984).

St. Philip's CE Primary School, Salford

Here a junior class focused on the local textile industry. After visiting two companies, it was decided to set up a classroom production line to make drawstring bags under the name *B & B Textile Company.*

Children made decisions on initial planning and financing, allocated jobs and learned to work together as a team. Production was halted from time to time to allow for "fiber science" sessions to examine and test a variety of different textiles. For example, a fireman's uniform might be borrowed to consider its suitability for the job. Tests were conducted to discover fiber strength, flameproofing, waterproofing and windproofing.

Regular visits were organized to local industries (such as J. Milom and A & B Cutting Services) where the children watched bales of cloth being turned into garments. They examined machines and asked questions about their function. The local bank sent one of its staff to show the children how to set up and keep their accounts (Ward and Benfield, 1985).

Eden Valley Comprehensive School, Kent

All students complete a one year multidisciplinary course in the Faculty of Recreational and Creative Arts. The compulsory curriculum embraces seven disciplines – art, music, needlework, woodwork, metalwork, technical drawing and home economics. A problem-solving approach is taken where each pupil chooses a subject area and a project to tackle. A level 1 project is completed in all areas. Level 2 and 3 problems require greater thought, organization and skills, and frequently resources of more than one subject area:

> Pupils value the freedom of choice, find greater motivation through individual responsibility and sometimes surprise themselves by their reactions to subjects they had not expected to enjoy.
>
> (Royal Society of Arts, 1984)

Canada

A publication from the Ontario Ministry of Education, entitled *Issues and Directions*, describes each child "as an active participant in education who gains satisfaction from the dynamics of learning and as a self-motivated, self-directed problem-solver . . . . deriving a sense of self-worth and confidence from a variety of accomplishments" (Ontario Ministry of Education, 1980).

In 1988 the Ministry issued *Science is Happening Here. A Policy Statement for Science in the Primary and Junior Divisions*, which states that the "dynamics of learning include active involvement in playing, working, exploring, creating, taking risks, planning and initiating, asking questions, seeking solutions, and reflecting, both independently and with others" (Ministry of Education, 1988). The report envisions a learning environment where the learner is an active, enthusiastic and unique participant in the learning process. Children have opportunities for direct observation and hands-on experiences with a variety of materials. They interact with peers and adults in a safe environment. Both child-centered and teacher-centered learning experiences meet the changing needs, abilities and learning styles of children. They have the time and space to explore freely and to consolidate learning. The learning environment includes the outdoors and allows investigation of incidental events that may occur spontaneously. Learning resources include materials, people, places and the natural environment. Computers are used to: record, store, manage, analyze, share and retrieve data; report results; extend thinking and creativity; enhance communication and accommodate special learning needs (Ontario Ministry of Education, 1988).

A consultation paper entitled *Technological Education – The Way Ahead*, published by the Ministry of Education in 1990, examines technological education in a changing world:

> In the *Formative Years*, Grades 1 to 6, students should have the opportunity to manipulate materials and develop various models using mouldable materials . . . . The manipulation of materials such as large wooden blocks and boards in order to create a structure is a technological experience . . . . Students could be given the task of

designing and building a bridge made out of paper . . . . that could integrate mathematics, communications and science as well as technology into a social studies program.

This integrated approach will be fundamental to the experiences of students in Grades 7 to 9, the *Transition Years*. In a Grade 8 class that is discussing environmental concerns, for example, students could be asked to design and make can crushers that could be used at home to reduce the volume taken up by empty pop cans . . . . Mathematics (in the design stage), geography (in discussions about natural resources), history (in discussions about economics and previous manufacturing techniques), science (the processes involved in the production of steel and aluminium) could all form part of the project.

At the secondary level, technological education could be observed as a group of students and several teachers engaged in a series of diverse but connected activities over time . . . . A senior Construction Technology class might be involved with the design and construction of playground equipment for a day care center. A group of teachers could work together in the development and delivery of a program so that students could obtain credits in several subject areas. For example, the design of the project includes art, science and mathematics; the cost and purchase of materials could involve mathematics and business studies; the building and installation involves construction technology and a report on the project would involve language skills.

(Ontario Ministry of Education, 1990)

Samples of initiatives which have emerged from those policy guidelines are as follows.

Design Center

In 1989, the Board of Education for the City of York established the first Design Center in North America. To quote Geoff Day, Program Coordinator – Learning Resources:

Designing things brings together many of the things our students learn in their core subjects and puts them into a practical context. The techniques of designing develop a wide range of skills in our students. They learn co-operation, compromise, decision-making, planning, construction and evaluation.

(Day, 1989)

Students in kindergarten to grade 6 use a variety of materials such as wood, paper, wire mesh, glue and paint, to create solutions to problems. Tasks undertaken include designing a house for the disabled, learning about gears and levers or inventing better public transportation. Materials, products and curriculum resources were selected for the Center from around the world: Australia, Denmark, Japan, United Kingdom, United States, West Germany and Canada. For example the *Lego* company in Wrexham, England has developed comprehensive material from primary to secondary levels progressing from simple technological concepts such as structures and mechanisms to control technology incorporating computer interfacing (Day, 1989).

The York Board of Education's commitment to the development of technological studies has resulted in a number of innovations including: *The Teachers' Toolbox* – a resource guide focusing microcomputers in such curriculum units as Robotics, Flight, Communities and Icarus and Beyond; *Graphic Arts* – computer technology in high schools has been introduced to edit pictures in the same way that writers use word processors to edit text; *Satellites and Radio Signals* – the use of radio communications in the classroom to access live weather satellite images and radiofax weather charts; and *Information Retrieval and Presentation* – CD-ROM and laser disk formats are used to source information and enhance research skills and presentation techniques in libraries and classrooms.

To quote the publication *Technology in the City of York Schools* (Board of Education, City of York, 1990:

> Design and Technology will enable a student to develop approaches to problems with many solutions using the following basic technological ideas:
> - the effects of tools and machinery on materials, e.g wood, metal, plastic, paper, cardboard;
> - energy sources to create motion, e.g. electricity, clockwork, elastic, gravity;
> - connecting things together to form structures, e.g. frames, sheets, rigid materials, flexible materials;
> - transmitting movement via mechanisms, e.g. gears, pulleys, levers, cams;
> - making things work via systems control, e.g. manually, by switches, by computers;
> - how humans use products and how if affects the construction of the product, i.e. ergonomics;
> - understanding and using techniques to make things look better, e.g. aesthetics, appropriateness of balance, harmony, shape;
> - approaches to solving practical problems where no single answer exists, i.e. designing methods.

Construction Internship Program

This program at the Queen Elizabeth Collegiate and Vocational Institute (QECVI) in Frontenac County, Ontario is another example of "technology for the real world." Thirty-two grade 11 and 12 students from across the county enrolled in a one-semester pilot program offering four credits in construction, English and mathematics. The focus of the program was to build four portable classrooms to be delivered to school sites throughout the county. As described in the local newspaper:

> The essential philosophy behind the course is that students with an interest in the trades should get a real-life experience in seeing a project through to completion before they commit themselves to a career in the business. The students will all be given grades, but beyond the pieces of paper they will also have the completed portables as physical testimony to their abilities . . . . They'll be learning dry-walling, plumbing, electricity, decoration, environmental control, even horticulture. It gives students a broad base in many areas, so they can specify in the future.
>
> (O'Malley, 1990)

The students, assisted by teachers Lloyd Lockington and Don Voteary, worked together on four different design teams using resources of the school's new *Construction Technology Center* and local architect's offices. At a "Design Day" presentation on September 20, 1990, the concept drawings were displayed in a competition to see which plans would be built. The judges were so impressed with the designs that they recommended that all four projects be approved for construction along with a budget of $30,000 per structure to cover the costs of materials and labor.

The students had to tackle the bureaucracy to get construction permits, study and conform to municipal zoning-bylaws, building codes and fire regulations. A group of technical advisers from various architectural and construction firms also volunteered their time to the project.

Most important, math and English courses were taught as they apply to the construction of the portables. English included public speaking, the writing of technical reports, résumé and interview preparation. Mathematics included technical measurements, survey and statistical analysis, project financing and the preparation of cost projections. To quote Dick Melville, Principal of QECVI: "the program is a prime example of new ways of delivering curricula in schools, as well as a better way of teaching math and English for kids that need a different approach to things" (Rouse, 1990).

Gord Rogers, a member of the *Kingston Construction Association* board of directors, chaired an industry advisory committee for the internship programs: "One of the things we see as a problem in our industry in the future is qualified employees. So we want to work with students in this group to get them more prepared to get into the construction industry" (Rouse, 1990).

Michael Paquette, Project Manager at Mill & Ross Architects, volunteered to work with one of the design teams:

> They had some ideas. They knew what the problems were with portables that currently exist and they wanted to resolve that as part of their mandate. When I was in high school, we designed but we never actually built anything. This will give them 100 percent exposure to designing a project, building it and possibly even using it.
>
> (Rouse, 1990)

On January 27, 1991 the Frontence County Board of Education convened an Open House entitled "New Concepts on Portables – Designed and constructed by students from across the county." After a tour of the portables, the student design teams proudly presented the keys of the new buildings to each of the receiving schools. Seventeen-year-old Jonathan Bark captured the mood: "In 10 or 20 years I can drive by and say I built that thing myself, whereas when I sit down in a math or English class and write up an essay, really what do I have to show for it but a piece of paper?" (Rouse, 1990).

France

In France a source of inspiration in finding alternatives to traditional academic teacher-centered schooling has been found in the *Cooperative Learning* techniques of Celestin Freinet (1896–1966). As a casualty of World War I, Freinet returned to a public elementary school-teaching career at Bar-sur-Loup, a rural village in the south of France. Because of his war-damaged lungs, he was unable to operate in the traditional teacher-centered style – standing in front of the class all day, shouting orders and dictating lessons. He soon learned to rely on individualized and learner-centered activities such as child authorship, classroom presenting, school-to-school correspondence, project work and semi-autonomous learning based on self-correcting worksheets. Some parents enthusiastically supported these innovations while others were bitterly opposed. When he moved to a more middle-class school at Saint Paul, hostility mounted and he decided to leave public school-teaching. In 1935 he founded his own independent school at Le Pioulier, which is still functioning today.

While recognizing the need for classroom learning materials, Freinet rejected the rigidly-controlled texts and detailed syllabuses of the Ministry of Education:

> If the large mass of children rejected by the school system could speak, they would tell us how grammar and vocabulary textbooks have paralysed them, how the very thought of the intellectual and moral anguish they have caused makes them physically sick – a nausea bordering on neurosis. It goes a long way to explaining the almost total failure of such instruction.
>
> (Clandfield and Sivell, 1990)

Freinet decided to print his own child-authored materials. Beginning with a very simple printing press, he enlisted the children in selecting, editing, typesetting, printing and distributing the materials. The printing press became the foundation for cooperative and collaborative work within the classroom and a source of motivation for individual work as well. As Freinet said:

> Children setting type have the feeling that the text comes into existence in their own hands. They give the text permanent life and they make it theirs. With this technique, there is no interruption of the total process leading from getting an idea to expressing it, to producing the magazine, and finally to posting it to pen-friends in other schools. Each step is present; writing, group-editing, typesetting, illustration, preparing the paper, inking the type, printing, collating, and stapling . . . . Given the opportunity to create a permanent record of their memories, dreams, struggles and successes, children accept the challenge of overcoming similar obstacles. To reach their goal, they're capable of astonishing self-discipline.
>
> (Clandfield & Sivell, 1990)

The resulting child-authored texts, newsletters, flyers and school-magazines were soon being shared and exchanged with other schools. This mode of operation involved students in decision-making, peer counseling and labor-sharing – all essential aspects of cooperative learning. Other teachers and classes soon joined the network and by 1930 hundreds of printing-centered exchanges were in operation all over France.

Throughout his career, Freinet was intensely interested in technological innovation. He believed in "flexible techniques" where new inventions could be field-tested so the best of them might be incorporated into the classroom. For example, in classroom printing he experimented not only with metal type but also with stencils, dittos and lino-cuts. Dissatisfied with his first little printing press, he made his own design, which was produced by a local artisan. By 1937 Freinet presses were being distributed throughout France. He also pioneered the use of film, radio, one of the first teaching machines and later in his career, audio-tape. (It's unfortunate that Freinet did not live long enough to participate in the computer age.) He understood the power of well-chosen technology to individualize and enrich the users' learning by permitting a high degree of personal control over the content, order and rate of the experience (Clandfield and Sivell, 1990).

Another central focus of Freinet's belief was *work-based pedagogy* for young children:

> The worst punishment you can inflict on a child is enforced immobility. Children appreciate nothing so much as tasks that match their capabilities and that yield results they can see directly.
>
> Lighting or stoking the fire, cooking a meal, laying a table, bringing food to the table, riding a horse or a bicycle, these have always figured among the favourite occupations of children and they still do. It's only because such activities are thought to be dangerous expensive or obsessive for parents seeking a quiet life that they have been replaced by imitation versions in the form of toys: a dinner set for fun, toy soldiers or a set of miniature cars . . . . We have to direct the inexhaustible ingenuity of inventors and toymakers towards perfecting tools designed to meet the needs and capabilities of young children. Simple features that reduce the likelihood of beginners hitting themselves on the thumb, channels that reduce the risk of using a saw, but real saws, rasps, gouges, a transformer, a wirecutter, a lamp assembly and so on . . . .
>
> (Clandfield and Sivell, 1990)

But what about the unemployed school-leavers?

> Young people must be given the same opportunities that we provided to children in primary school. They must be offered genuine work, with a real purpose, that suits their personalities, that meets their needs, that stands a chance of restoring to them the self-confidence and dignity that they have lost.
>
> (Clandfield & Sivell, 1990)

To introduce his work-based education into the school/community culture Freinet advocated:

- reorganization, through work, of the life and education of children within the family;
- reorganization of work in the schools;
- reorganization of life and work at those times when children are not in the company of their parents or teachers.

To achieve these objectives, he saw administrators at all levels rethinking the construction, maintenance and development of school buildings to accommodate work-based education; teachers being retrained to adapt to the new working techniques and parents and commercial interests allowing young people to contribute meaningful, valued work to the community.

SCHOOLING FOR THE TWENTY-FIRST CENTURY

Abraham Maslow's *Hierarchy of Needs* envisions a pyramid (see the diagram) in which the physical needs (air, food, water, etc.) at the baseline must be met before a person will care much about safety and security (physical, emotional, etc.) which in turn must be satisfied before the person will be strongly moved by feelings of love and belonging which are dependent upon achieving a sense of esteem and respect for oneself and others (Conrad, 1991):

The Hierarchy
Self
Actualization
Esteem–Respect
(by self and others)
Love and
Belonging
Safety and Security
(physical, financial, emotional)
Physical
(air, food, water, sex, stimulation, etc.)

The preoccupation of public schooling with the three Rs (Reading, Riting and Rithmetic) may have neglected the basic tenets of developmental psychology as envisioned by Maslow. It may be that before a child is ready to tackle the three Rs the three Ss must be met. That is Sustenance, Shelter and Self-Esteem (or Social Well-being). Until these basic concrete needs are achieved the abstract agenda of the classroom is just not a priority. For example, the learner who comes to school hungry, and without adequate clothing and shelter invariably lacks self-esteem. Is it any wonder that children from impoverished neighborhoods often do poorly at school in academic work?

The developmental theories of John Dewey and Jean Piaget have been applied to childcare programs for preschool children which stress nutrition, social development and gross motor activity (e.g. creating structures with wooden blocks and learning about spatial relationships through water and sand play). Longitudinal studies into such programs as *Head Start* and the

Perry Preschool in the United States have demonstrated that these programs work. A fifteen-year study tracked 100 poor minority children in Ypsilanti, Michigan. All were considered to have low IQs. Half were randomly assigned to a preschool program; half were not. The preschool group had a third higher high school graduation rate, 40 per cent lower arrest rate, 50 per cent lower teen pregnancy rate, and were 50 per cent more likely to score at or above the national average on functional competence tests. They were twice as likely, after fifteen years, to hold jobs or be in college or vocational training as the children who didn't participate (Kearns and Doyle, 1988). Similarly, research by the US National Institute of Mental Health found that: "children who spent their early years in high-quality day care were well-adjusted and popular in elementary school and they performed above average in school work" (US National Institute of Mental Health, 1991).

Our understanding of the physiological needs of the concrete learner, gained through brain research, has indicated a need for more tactile, spatial stimulation which is not dependent on a person's verbal abilities. It seems logical that a developmental, activity-based school curriculum which rewards the concrete (craft, design and technology) as well as the abstract (reading, writing, mathematics) might be a better approach to building self-esteem in the learner. Of course in the case of the economically disadvantaged person nutritional, physical shelter (housing, clothing etc.) and socio-emotional needs would be prerequisites for learning. The person who lacks basic self-esteem would seem to be a poor candidate for academic achievement.

How can we identify, nurture and value these concrete capabilities within the school system? A few possible strategies might be as follows (Shuttleworth, 1989):

- A comprehensive high-quality early childhood development program (age 2–5) would be a foundation on which to build.
- Concrete materials such as wooden blocks, lumber, bricks, sticks, tubing, stones, plastic sheeting, etc. would be recognized as essential learning resources in the primary classroom (grades 1–3).
- Each room or space would have one or more work benches with simple tools with which children would be encouraged to create and invent technology.
- Visual arts activities would stress craft and design and use a wide variety of media including surplus materials from industry.
- Children as early as grade 1 would begin to learn how the provision of goods and services is essential to employment and economic well-being.

- Students would undertake community-service projects related to the needs of older adults and disabled people (e.g. intergenerational visiting, folding of dressings and bandages, art and craft activities to improve residential decor etc.
- Classroom enterprises might include envelope stuffing for voluntary organizations, fund-raising projects such as bake sales, flea markets, etc. in which children would actually participate in the making, collecting and selling of goods.
- Field trips would include visits to a variety of manufacturing and service industries.
- At the junior level (grades 4–6), concrete materials would also include lego and meccano sets, gears and pulleys, hydraulic and pneumatic kits, electronic assembly boards, patterns and cloth, sewing machines, modelling clay, microcomputer equipment etc.
- Students in the junior grades would be encouraged to develop their own classroom industries and business ventures including all the essentials of a business plan; proceeds from the sale of goods and services could finance field visits or be donated to the voluntary sector.
- Community service projects would stress problem-solving, program-planning and implementation, e.g. support to preschool and older adult programs, friendly visiting, environmental improvement, etc.
- An inventory of community needs and resources would be developed to establish priorities for service projects and small business ventures.
- At the intermediate and senior levels, students would be expected to develop and implement their own business ventures or service projects either as entrepreneurs or in worker cooperatives.
- Basic principles of market research, merchandising, inventory control, securing funding and venture capital etc. would be taught through practical experience.
- Students would design and create their own products or services utilizing a full range of manipulative and communication skills.
- Both intermediate and senior students would spend extended periods of time in manufacturing and service settings, not just in cooperative education, but as part of specific work projects to gain on-the-job training and through mentorships with tradespeople.
- Existing vocational shops would increasingly be devoted to enterprise development and the production of marketable goods and services which would not compete with existing private sector interests.
- Students at all levels would be encouraged to develop artistic abilities and craft skills to produce marketable products.

The twenty-first-century workforce may turn out to have much in common with the pioneers of the nineteenth century as the manufacturing industry, dominated by robotics and cheap third-world labor, will no longer be a major source of employment. While the information age may produce some new jobs for the accomplished abstract achiever, what about the needs of the concrete learner? Many service-sector jobs do require concrete skills, but are our young people prepared to assume these positions? How can we be assured that we will be able to harness and develop their creative skills and inventive abilities? How will we ensure the right of the individual to secure employment and to maintain an adequate standard of living?

It is my belief that public education must undergo a radical transformation if it is to be relevant or even exist in the next century. The strategy outlined above does not mean to imply that we abandon abstract learning, but rather that we recognize the importance of concrete expression in human development. Indeed, it may well be that those who gain confidence as concrete achievers may ultimately be much better abstract learners.

We do know, however, that the nature of the social and economic order is changing and we are no longer dependent on large institutional structures to deliver a service. Future employment opportunities will also be quite different – more decentralized, more related to personal and business services. We must rediscover the age of concrete learning to produce hands-on skills, inventiveness and entrepreneurial zeal – qualities which were so important in the pre-industrial age.

To ensure that everyone has an opportunity to be employed in meaningful and remunerative activity and we survive as an economic entity, it is my belief that a new *unity of purpose* must be forged, involving the three productive sectors of commerce, government and voluntarism. This alliance can identify needs and resources at the local level to provide education, training and employment opportunities for everyone. Public education can be a pro-active partner in implementing this process of social and economic renewal. The chapter which follows will explore the nature of economic development at the local level and as a strategy to create employment opportunities and promote economic well-being.

7 Building from the bottom up

CHASING SMOKESTACKS

Since the 1970s more than three million manufacturing jobs have been lost in the United States while the real income of American workers is falling. (A similar pattern might be found in other western industrialized nations.) The vision of a post-industrial, manufacturing-free economy has never materialized, as the best service jobs – in engineering, advertising, banking and information systems – are very much tied to the fate of the manufacturing sector.

Of the 355,000 small and medium-sized manufacturing firms in the US, close to half have less than 250 employees, accounting for nearly two-thirds of the blue-collar labor force. These small companies supply most of the parts and components used to produce the finished goods for both the domestic and export markets. As large firms downsize or relocate to third-world countries, the competitiveness of American industry is increasingly dependent upon small firms to meet the cost, quality and delivery schedules of major industrial customers (Hatch, 1990).

How have local areas undertaken to preserve or expand their industrial/employment base? In North America, during the 1950s to the 1970s, the predominant strategy to attract new manufacturing jobs was known as "smokestack chasing." Municipalities would compete with one another to lure manufacturing branch plants using such incentives as cheap non-union labor, cut-rate land prices and tax holidays. This was particularly true in the United States, where southern states regularly "raided" the traditional manufacturing heartlands of the northeast and midwest to attract new industries. These areas soon retaliated with their own recruitment/retention strategies – tax credits, training programs, low-interest loans and government subsidies.

By the late 1970s and early 1980s, however, it had become apparent that simply shifting manufacturing jobs from relatively skilled, higher-income areas in the north to unskilled, lower-income southern communities was no longer enough to keep a competitive edge in a global economy. Doug Ross and Robert E. Friedman, of the Center for Economic Development, describe this smokestack chasing as the "First Wave" of economic development:

> Evidence was growing that First Wave policies were losing their effectiveness. The South's success at closing its income gap with the rest of the country crested in 1976, after which the gap started growing again. Textile plants lured from New England to the Carolinas a decade earlier collapsed or fled off-shore to cheaper venues in record numbers. Manufacturing states like Michigan, Pennsylvania and Ohio found that, after the 1980–82 recession, smokestack chasing no longer provided a means to generate enough new jobs or overcome problems in their traditional industries – automobiles, steel, machine tools – that were losing both US market share and jobs . . . . Whereas in 1960 only 20% of US produced goods faced foreign competition, by 1980 more than 70% were fighting off international competitors . . . . Companies looking for cheap unskilled labor and low-cost locations were no longer confined to the U.S . . . . Mexico was cheaper, and Sri Lanka cheaper yet.
>
> (Ross and Friedman, 1990)

Another First Wave concern was the increasingly sophisticated technology available in some developed-world European and Asian countries (e.g. Germany and Japan). Robotics and other computer-based information technologies were resulting in better organized production processes producing higher-quality goods. Other factors affecting competitiveness, other than labor costs, were capital availability for modernization, new product development and market intelligence. Finally, existing firm expansions and start-up businesses were creating 80–90 per cent of new jobs in most states while recruited companies made up the remainder. The era of smokestack chasing was rapidly drawing to a close.

PRIMING THE PUMP

By the beginning of the 1980s a "Second Wave" of economic policy began to emerge. State governments and local municipalities realized that to attract new sources of employment, and retain existing jobs, a new support infrastructure should be created. To be competitive in the world economy, it seemed essential that a local area demonstrate the availability of a skilled workforce, risk capital, up-to-date technology, and modern telecommunications. A new role for state government, then, was to ensure these resources were available to maximize competitive capacities.

Public programs were launched to create new financial markets, modernize manufacturing, enhance technology transfer from university to business, sharpen worker skills, provide entrepreneurs with management information and encourage export expansion. For example during the 1980s more than 100 public investment funds, 25 public venture capital funds, and 200 projects to stimule technological innovation projects were established. Forty-seven states undertook specific educational reforms to improve quality and productivity. More than two-thirds of state budgets were directed to strengthening local businesses rather than attracting new ones.

Achievements of public sector "pump-priming" have been significant. Home-grown enterprise and increased public investment have improved the competitive capacities of states faced with ongoing industrial restructuring. In spite of these positive gains, however, serious limitations soon became apparent:

- *Limited scale* – while relatively small sources of venture capital (e.g. $5–10 million) became available, this was a "drop in the bucket" compared to the hundreds of millions of dollars needed each year to fuel the state economy. Workforce training, similarly, was limited to short-term projects without adequate needs assessment or continuity.
- *Fragmented service* – a proliferation of narrow-based training and development projects without integration or coordination may give the impression of a flurry of activity without tangible results. For example:

  > One program helps train workers but is out of touch with the latest technology applications. Another helps identify practical ways to apply new technologies, but disclaims any knowledge or responsibility for capital availability to finance new equipment.
  >
  > (Ross & Friedman, 1990)

- *Lack of accountability* – there was generally a lack of accountability concerning the performance of individual programs as well as overall collective performance of the initiatives. As public monopolies these economic developments often lack feedback between program customers and their managers. As political entities the programs may not be subject to independent scrutiny particularly if this could in any way affect the political fortunes of existing leaders.
- *A missing link* – these strategies may not address the gap between economic and social concerns. The assumption that an improved economy will automatically resolve social inequities is not borne out by experience. The separation of social issues from the economic agenda may serve to exacerbate the problem.

What the First and Second Waves had in common was that they used public funding as a solution to the issues of either building capacity or recruiting new industries. This "direct service" approach using public resources, however, suffered from a potential lack of dependable financial support through legislative appropriations and a growing civil service bureaucracy to complicate the programs. As public monopolies, these programs were constantly struggling for survival within shifting political priorities and fiscal restraint. Thus, they had difficulty being responsive to consumer needs for integrated services and social development.

RIDING THE THIRD WAVE

Recognizing the limitations of the other two approaches, Ross and Friedman describe a "Third Wave" of initiatives which incorporate a decentralized model that is not dependent upon government as the sole service provider. They use government finances and authority to mobilize other public and private resources to meet local development needs. The basic principles of Third Wave initiatives are as follows:

- *Demand driven* – government resources are utilized only when the benefits are valued by the end-users. Groups of employers define their common competitive needs such as improved worker training, process modernization or market identification. Only when the employers have defined their needs and committed their own energy and resources will government agree to invest.
- *Leveraged resources* – because government resources are almost always inadequate to meet development demands, other institutions must also invest their resources. Leverage and engagement techniques are used to attract private nonprofit and for-profit, as well as non-agency public resources. For example, a consortium of businesses, universities and private foundations joining with government provides a resource partnership to better supply the goods or services in demand.
- *Encouraged competition* – Third Wave governance encourages competition among resource suppliers. To ensure that world-class resources are available and integrated to meet customer needs, several private and public providers may compete to supply the necessary goods and services. Therefore, the actual buying power for a needed service is "consumer-driven," keeping quality up and prices down.
- *Automatic feedback* – feedback is built in to ensure automatic accountability and avoid political manipulations of the process. By defining the need and sharing in the investment, the customer becomes accountable for outcomes. Public purposes can therefore be met along

with the demands of intended beneficiaries and a decent return on investment in the marketplace.

In summary, Third Wave programs get some needed resource or service to the community by strengthening the operation of existing marketplaces, or by stimulating new ones. To quote Ross and Friedman (1990):

> Third Wave initiatives seek to achieve public economic needs by empowering the consumer beneficiaries, cultivating competitive public and private suppliers and designing new measurement, information and reward systems . . . . Public incentives may be required at the outset to induce people and institutions to think and act with each other in new ways. Those the community believes should have services, but who lack the resources to purchase them, may require subsidies to purchase services. Nonetheless, the goal is a functioning marketplace, independent of the day-to-day management by a government bureaucracy, that can provide area businesses and citizens with crucial world-class goods and services. The same holds true whether the resource in demand is education, capital, technology transfer capacity, or growth management information.

The rise of Third Wave initiatives does not signal the end of public economic development agencies, however. In Third Wave terms they compete with other organizations, both public and private, in service delivery. In certain circumstances they may serve as the direct supplier of last resort (e.g. inner-city or remote rural areas) if a public/private strategy is not feasible. "Government's critical role remains as the guarantor that essential services are available and consistent with core values of fairness, full participation and equity."

The following are examples of Third Wave initiatives in action.

United States

Pennsylvania's *Ben Franklin Partnership Program* links private-sector firms with the research capacities of educational institutions to "spin off" advanced technology applications to existing industries and new products and firms on the leading edge of innovation. The Program requires that each one dollar of private support be matched by one dollar of public support. For example, a university and a private sector partner involved in a project must reach agreement and put their commitment in writing before public funds are released (Plosila, 1990).

In Columbus, Ohio, the *Edison Welding Institute (EWI)* is a Third Wave organization for technology development. EWI, one of Ohio's nine Thomas

Edison Technology Centers, brokers and utilizes the resources of government, industry and higher education through shared ownership. EWI works closely with the Welding Engineering Department of Ohio State University to exploit the best basic research interest and expertise among faculty. The University, as part owner of EWI, provides rent-free use of one of its buildings and occupies two seats on the Board of Trustees.

EWI is operated by 228 industrial members who elect both its Board of Trustees and an Industrial Advisory Board. The Institute is organized into three units:

- *Research* may involve the University and one or more members, as well as EWI staff, in a single firm or group project. Members can determine how their dues are divided between core efforts, special services and research projects they wish to sponsor.
- *Education* and training through EWI builds on the results of research efforts. Activities include opportunities for member firms to consult EWI's 50-person staff, participate in workshops, seminars and conferences. Videotapes, instructional aids (such as operator and maintenance manuals) and customized training programs are also available for large and small firm members.
- *Applications* work can include providing problem-solving services, drawing upon EWI's research expertise, to assist member firms. This active hands-on service complements the knowledge base in improving manufacturing competitiveness.

To date EWI has received more than $30 million of financial support from state, industry and university sources (Plosila, 1990).

Italy

In the Emilia–Romagna region *Flexible Manufacturing Networks*, as previously described in Chapter 2, represents one of the most successful Third Wave initiatives. They have learned to engage entire manufacturing sectors in the process of modernization by building a capacity for continuous renewal through industrial networks. Through the identifying of profitable business opportunities for local firms, entrepreneurial energy is aroused and channeled into a taste for advanced technologies to improve manufacturing methods. Networks organize around common needs and opportunities. Dozens or even hundreds of firms share the cost of market forecasting, quality certification or financial management. Out of this process small companies may cooperate to exploit "niche" markets.

In building networks, public sector agencies and trade associations have been catalysts in forming "client groups." To quote Richard Hatch (1990):

Flexible manufacturing networks are the leading model of effective co-operation. In networks, groups of independent companies can work together to share overhead, access expensive technologies and blend complementary capabilities to bring innovative products to new markets. With activity ranging in complexity from the regular exchange of strategic information to joint ventures for product development and commercialization, flexible networks represent a general solution to the problems faced by smaller manufacturing firms as they attempt to regain competitive edge.

Denmark

In Denmark a *National Network Program* was launched in 1989 to prepare its industrial base of very small firms for the impending European Common Market of 1992. The program was organized in three steps:

1 *Broker training* – key industry consultants from both public and private sectors were trained as "network brokers." Brokers learned how to organize competing firms, spot mutual business opportunities, assess modernization needs and coordinate group services.
2 *Challenge Grants* – a multi-phase program of challenge grants was initiated by the Ministry of Industry. Up to US$7,500 was offered to groups of firms to conduct network feasibility studies. Later phases provided larger grants for long-term projects such as production coordination, export marketing and new product development.
3 *Business outreach* – the Agency for Commerce and Industry coordinated an information campaign which included direct mailings to all manufacturers, full-page newspaper ads, and regional conferences co-hosted with trade associations.

On July 31, 1990 the Danish government announced that more than 2,000 firms were now participating in the network program. The strategic alliances formed had resulted in an array of new products and services for export. The network program "had taken on a life of its own and became self-propelling" (Ross and Friedman, 1990).

Lessons learned

Experience to date with Third Wave initiatives has demonstrated several important lessons for local economic development. Governments can no longer act as mass suppliers of goods and services. Public agencies have discovered the need to operate more as facilitators, brokers and seed capitalists. Traditional "command-style bureaucracies" do not perform well in an entrepreneurial role. Just as private-sector organizations have had to restructure to meet the demands of the global marketplace, public organizations are now "under the gun" to embrace the future.

SMALL BUSINESS INCUBATORS

Another local economic development strategy which has gained widespread acceptance in both North America and Europe has been "small business incubators." Business incubators aid the early growth of an enterprise by providing rental space, management and financial assistance, and business services. By the spring of 1984 there were 12 business incubators operating in the state of Pennsylvania, of which four were privately sponsored while the others were sponsored by public organizations and/or government agencies. In a study of the 126 firms located in these incubators the following information was reported:

- the median size of the firms was 4.5 employees;
- slightly more than 60 per cent of the entrepreneurs were in the 23–40 age range;
- over 70 per cent of the entrepreneurs held a college degree;
- capital for the new ventures came from personal resources (51 per cent), banks and other lending institutions (26 per cent), business associates, family and friends (14 per cent), venture- and seed-capital groups (5 per cent) and government assistance (4 per cent);
- the median incubation period was 29 months, with most firms staying in the general area when they leave;
- over the two-year period an average increase of seven jobs per firm was expected;
- the most useful services provided by the incubators to entrepreneurs were – risk management and insurance, building security, mail service, government grants and loans, receptionist, inventory, copier, advertising and marketing, health and benefit packages and telephone equipment;
- most incubators were the result of converting a vacant, idle building into a productive center of business activity.

Overall, it was found that incubators were a valuable addition to community revitalization as well as job generators for the local economy (Allen, Ginsberg and Meiburger, 1984).

For example, *The Venture Center* was the first industrial incubator of its kind to be established by the town of Pasadena in the Canadian province of Newfoundland and Labrador. It serves a region with a population of 60,000 whose employment has been traditionally devoted to the forestry, pulp and paper, gypsum and cement industries, as well as farming and fishing. Plant closures and diminishing markets for primary resources have resulted in a chronic state of double-digit unemployment in the region.

The Center consists of 40,000 square feet divided into twelve business areas, six in each wing. Units are available in areas of 2,000–2,500 and 4,000 square feet, each with preconstructed workshop and office configurations. Space is provided over a period of years at a very low rental rate, common services such as secretarial, telephone answering, photocopying, telex and computer services are shared. "It is expected that with lower rental rates and support and common user services, the business will develop to the stage where it can leave the center and move into a multi-user industrial building or a building of its own" (Town of Pasadena, 1990).

Significant differences, however, exist between European and North American experience with incubators. In Europe such terms as "nursery units," "seedbed centers," "workspace and workshop developments" are used instead of "incubator." A high proportion of European centers have a craft orientation, are part of a formal training program or are run by a local agency whose primary function is small-business development.

Incubators in Europe, located primarily in Britain and the Netherlands, are quite small – well below 5,000 square feet. The tenants tend to be "microbusinesses" with two employees or fewer, occupying 400–700 square feet. For example, the British Steel Corporation built a number of incubators after the 1976–82 lay-offs of 200,000 engineers, craftspeople and artisans. These "enterprise centers" typically have a series of small tenant units serviced by a common pool of machine tools plus in-house technical and marketing advice. As a result, many of the existing incubators are metalcraft-oriented.

Another large group of British incubators have a broad community development focus. Operated by Local Enterprise Agencies (LEAs), they seek to help new and existing small firms gain access to technical and professional assistance. Another significant set of British and Dutch incubators are oriented towards vocational training and human resources development. Small units are made available to persons completing training courses, including youth, in the hope that their proximity to entrepreneurs will serve as a source of mentoring for future enterprises (Mt. Auburn Associates, 1986).

Business incubators continue to proliferate in North America. In Canada the number increased from four in 1981 to 28 by 1990. In the US, they mushroomed during the same period by nearly 400 per cent to 350. Incubators have a good track record of nurturing new-born companies. In a recent survey of 120 US and Canadian incubators, the National Business Incubation Association found that 22 per cent of tenants leave the centers each year, creating free-standing businesses and new jobs for their communities. The incubators studied graduated 270 businesses in 1989 alone, representing 1,850 new jobs (Zeidenberg, 1990).

THIRD-SECTOR ENTERPRISE

As cited in Chapter 2, Peter Drucker, one of the world's most respected authorities on business management, has become a strong advocate for the virtues of the "third sector" as an engine of the post-industrial economy. He describes North America's third sector as nonbusiness, nongovernmental, nonprofit "human-change agencies." Within this sector he includes the majority of America's hospitals, schools, colleges and universities, philanthropic organizations, healthcare associations, community service groups, churches and cultural enterprises. They are operated through fees and services governed by a volunteer board or, if tax-supported, run by administrators chosen by a locally elected board. Quoting Drucker (1989):

> The third sector is actually the country's largest employer, though neither its workforce nor the output it produces show up in the statistics. One out of every two adult Americans – a total of 90 million people – are estimated to work as volunteers in the third sector, most of them in addition to holding a paid job. These volunteers put in the equivalent of 7.5 million full time work years. If they were paid, their wages would amount to $150 billion a year; but of course they are not paid. The third sector largely explains why taxes in the United States are lower than in Europe. Spending on public and community purposes is actually quite a bit higher in the United States, but a substantial portion, as much as 15 per cent of the GNP, does not flow through tax channels. It goes directly, as fees, as insurance premiums, as charitable contributions, and as unpaid work, to non-governmental third sector institutions.

What makes these "human-change institutions" unique is that their functions are being discharged in and by the local community and, in the great majority of cases, by autonomous, self-governing, local organizations. Even more important is the role of these institutions in creating for its volunteers a sphere of meaningful citizenship. Because the size and complexity of government make direct participation all but impossible, third-sector institutions offer their volunteers the opportunity to exercise influence, discharge responsibility and make decisions.

This chapter has dealt with a variety of bottom-up economic development strategies designed to address local problems created by post-industrial dislocation. In preparing for a new age when employment is no longer dependent upon large manufacturing and primary resource industries, we need to continue to "spin off" employment alternatives, which maximize available resources within the community to create new models of social and economic well-being. The chapter which follows will explore how specific communities have discovered new vehicles for local economic development which combine the strengths of the governmental, commercial and voluntary sectors.

8 Grass-roots renewal

COMMUNITY ECONOMIC DEVELOPMENT

Community Economic Development might be defined as a plan of action to build new resources which will strengthen the local community internally as well as its relations with the larger world. The tool of this strategy may be a Community Development Corporation (CDC) which is organized and controlled by local residents to develop the economy of their own community. This "third sector" not-for-profit enterprise (as opposed to the governmental and private profit-oriented sectors) has the following objectives (Center for Community Economic Development, 1975):

- to identify and develop local skills and talents;
- to own and control land and other resources;
- to start new businesses and industries to increase job opportunities;
- to sponsor new community facilities and services;
- to improve the physical environment.

Community Development Corporations were first established in the United States in the late 1960s, with support from the federal government's "War on Poverty" programs, to improve disadvantaged urban and rural communities. By 1975 dozens of communities in at least 30 states had organized CDCs. These have ranged from such urban examples as the Bedford-Stuyvesant Restoration Corporation in New York City (with assets of 30 million dollars) to the Job Start Corporation in rural Kentucky. An evaluation of CDCs indicated that "they had demonstrated, as contrasted with conventional business, a remarkable level of performance in venture development and profitability in employment-related matters and in helping raise the level of confidence and opportunity in their communities" (Stein, 1973).

The following case studies are a sampling of economic development initiatives which are community-based and address local social and economic needs. They are derived from *New Age Business* by Greg MacLeod and my own experiences as Coordinator of Alternative and Community Programs for the Toronto Board of Education and Secretary-Treasurer of the Learnxs Foundation Inc.

New Dawn Enterprises

Cape Breton forms the northern part of the Canadian maritime province of Nova Scotia. Its population of about 175,000 is concentrated in various municipalities around Sydney harbor. Descendants of Highland Scots make up about 70 per cent of the population, with Acadian French and Micmac Indians inhabiting small villages within a region about 100 miles long and fifty miles wide. In the rural areas fisheries and forestry have traditionally been the major sources of employment, while coal-mining and steel production have been predominant in the more populated centers including the city of Sydney.

In 1900 Cape Breton was being touted as the "Pittsburgh of Canada" because of its access to raw materials to fuel a burgeoning steel industry. By the latter half of the twentieth century, Cape Breton had an unacceptably high rate of unemployment (26 per cent in 1985), as local coal-mining and steel production became increasingly uncompetitive in the world marketplace.

In 1966 the federal government had responded to Cape Breton's difficulties by establishing the Cape Breton Development Corporation to provide alternative sources of employment as the remaining coal mines were phased out. In 1967 the Hawker-Siddley Corporation declared that its Cape Breton steel works was no longer profitable and would be shut down. The provincial government responded by taking over the steel plant to continue operation at a reduced rate.

The Cape Breton Association for Co-op Development was established in 1973 to purchase an old downtown store to establish a handicraft school as a focus for craft-related employment. The building was improved with various federal "make work" grants to create commercial space at the ground level and eight bachelor apartments on the second floor. Using the original building for collateral, other properties were soon purchased and improved to provide much needed housing.

After consulting with community development corporations in the United States and with assistance promised from the federal Department of Health and Welfare, the Association devised a pilot project called *New Dawn*. In 1976, New Dawn was established under the Companies Act of Nova Scotia as a not-for-profit corporation concentrating on housing and general construction. From the beginning directors of the corporation were recruited who combined both technical competence and social conscience. They have included lawyers, engineers, business executives, tradespeople, housewives and pensioners. The *College of Cape Breton*, especially through its Bras d'Or Institute, has provided technicians, tradesmen, engineers, scientists and other academics with a wide range of specialized skills.

The New Dawn Board of Directors divided the corporation into three divisions: business, social and cultural. The social division was to assume an educational role as well as to initiate special projects of a social service nature. The Cape Breton Association for Co-op Development and the craft school became subsidiaries of the cultural division. An umbrella-like structure provided administrative services and management to a wide range of projects and enterprises.

By 1979 New Dawn owned over $1 million in real estate, including a senior citizens' home, group home for former mental patients, two dental centers, and a seniors' resource center. About 30 people were employed in the social division and New Dawn had sponsored a number of traditional folk concerts and other services. It had developed a clear policy of taking on any kind of project that was useful to the community provided that it was economically viable.

The first full-time manager was a successful real estate agent who guided the corporation in the fields of property acquisition and management which facilitated the generation of many labor-intensive, short-term projects. However, Board members were concerned that projects were being implemented without adequate assessment as to their profitability. The conflict between staff and Board resulted in all new projects being curtailed during a period of reassessment and consolidation. A new manager was eventually hired and told to "make things happen" under Board control.

Between 1980 and 1983 assets grew from $1,000,000 to $3,000,000 through construction projects under the federal Central Mortgage and Housing Corporation's nonprofit housing program. A consulting company, used auto-parts enterprise, Telidon (computer information) experiment and a land-clearing project were initiated. Conflict between Board and management arose again over project approvals and financial reporting. Again the Board ordered a period of reassessment and consolidation. A local chartered accounting firm was contracted to establish the required financial procedures. By 1991 New Dawn's operations consisted of: a real estate company with assets of $10,000,000; a volunteer resource center which recruits, trains and places volunteers; a small jobs construction company; a company providing homecare services to the elderly and a seasonally operated tour company (Macsween, 1991).

From these experiences New Dawn realized that an increase in size and scope requires a greater level of sophistication in Board approvals and financial control. Because the Board, not the staff, is legally responsible for everything that goes on in the corporation, the careful recruitment of staff and the active participation of Board members are as essential to a not-for-profit corporation as any other commercial enterprise. New Dawn has demonstrated, however, that the social and cultural needs of a community can be strongly addressed within a process of local economic development and job creation. To quote an evaluation conducted in 1979:

"It would be impossible to have contact with the enterprise for any length of time without being impressed by the quality, the dedication, and the energy of both employees and volunteers working with New Dawn" (Leroy, 1979).

In a recent article, Rankin Macsween, Executive Director of New Dawn Enterprises Ltd., observed (1991):

For all the ups and downs, New Dawn finds itself less and less required to justify its own existence. To its credit it will likely be more at home in the 21st Century than it has been in the 20th. Having started in the Seventies, and learned to survive in the Eighties, New Dawn looks forward to 'mastering its destiny' in the Nineties.

Mondragon

The Basque region on the north coast of Spain has a history which predates recorded time. Its many small ports shelter one of the largest fishing fleets in the world. The native language has no relationship to other languages in modern Europe, giving the region its own distinctive culture and traditions. Today the mountainous countryside has about 2.5 million inhabitants – 50 per cent of whom have migrated from other parts of Spain.

During the Spanish Civil War (1936–39) the Basque region supported the Republican side hoping to gain autonomy. The right-wing royalists, the Nationalists, were led by General Franco who launched a rebellion on July 18, 1936. Because the Basque and Catalonia regions had been declared autonomous republics, they bore the brunt of a bloody and cruel war which killed thousands of people before it ended in 1939 with Franco-led fascists in power.

Jose Maria Arizmendiarrieta was studying to be a priest when he was drafted into the Basque army. As a journalist he was assigned to the Department of Publications where he could observe the futility of pitting the Republican's passion, idealism and culture against the fascists' methodology, hierarchy, professionalism and economic power. After the fall of Bilboa he was assigned to Franco's army but continued his theological studies. In 1941 he was ordained and sent to the town of Mondragon as an assistant Pastor.

Mondragon was a wounded and divided town of 10,000 with a long tradition of metal craft. Don Jose Maria believed that Christianity implied socioeconomic justice and the full development of every human being's potential. To quote Jesus Larranaga, Don Jose Maria's biographer (1981):

> He did not limit himself to the mental framework of Heaven, Hell, Sin & Grace. Rather, he felt salvation was achieved in people's concrete lives. Salvation is achieved through community action and involves the development of the capacity to think, to invent, and to serve.

Don Jose Maria saw his priesthood as service consecrated to the community. To transform society he recognized that people needed technological and professional skills. In 1943 he established a new technical school where practical skills were taught along with the concepts of duty to the rest of society. From this small technical school some students went on to study engineering through the University of Zaragoza. The first nine graduates approached Don Jose Maria to establish their own company. The Franco government however was suspicious of Basque economic development and refused an application for incorporation.

In 1955, the group borrowed $5,000 from friends and purchased an electric stove manufacturing company in Vitoria, a city of 100,000 about 50 km from Mondragon. Five of them assumed the main responsibility for the business, which they called *Ulgor*, from the first initial of each of their names.

They redesigned the stove and were soon employing ten workers in the shop. In 1956 they decided to move the business to Mondragon because they felt that their economic model needed an environment where people were more inventive, self-supporting and used to solving local problems. The stove business prospered and in April 1959 the group decided to incorporate as a cooperative.

By the summer of 1959 the Mondragon founders were operating a foundry and producing stoves but they realized that further expansion would require a new financial structure to achieve the following objectives:

- capitalization of new cooperative enterprises;
- coordination of, and technical assistance to, new enterprises;
- management of a social security program.

In July, 1959 they incorporated their own credit union, *Caja Laboral Popular*, whose membership included producer co-ops as well as the bank's employees. The bank expanded quickly, opening branches in small towns and villages. As Don Jose Maria stated, "Savings are necessary to renew equipment and to create new enterprises."

Their motto was "Libreta o Maleta" ("Savings book or suitcase"). By investing in their own community, young Basques would no longer be forced to emigrate to find work.

By 1963 Ulgor had become quite large and it was decided to divide the corporation into several independent cooperatives. The foundry became *Ederlan*. Mechanical production adopted the name *Copreci*. The electronic division was incorporated as *Fagor Electronic*. While each co-op was legally independent, a unified complex was created with control vested in the bank.

Members of the cooperative bank or credit union purchased long-term debentures at low interest rates. Social security, as well as pension funds, were invested through the credit union. Cooperatives also invested in each other through the bank. Thus the credit union became the financial and ideological vehicle for the Mondragon movement.

In 1965 a new cooperative named *Ularco* was created to encourage collaboration between the cooperatives. Ularco's special functions were as follows:

- encourage the standardization of working conditions – wages, benefits, hours etc.;
- promote the movement of capital among the cooperative enterprises;
- promote benefit sharing;
- acquire new product licenses from such countries as the US, Germany, France and Italy;
- accept "turn-key" contracts for building new factories, especially in developing countries.

Each of Ularco's member co-ops was required to invest 20 per cent of its capital in another co-op with money to be available, as needed, as a loan on a demand basis. Co-ops were also encouraged to trade among themselves and to combine their purchasing power to reduce costs. Voluntary transfer of workers among co-ops was also encouraged. Finally, a General Assembly of Ularco was established, made up of a representative delegation from each associated enterprise including the local board of directors, the management committee and the accounts committee. The Board of Directors of Ularco consisted of one representative from each co-op board as well as the general manager of each member co-op.

The credit union has remained the financial and ideological vehicle for the Mondragon movement. It is divided into two branches, economic and entrepreneurial. The Economic Division promotes savings that can be channeled into the development of cooperatives. The Entrepreneurial

Division is responsible for ensuring that money deposited really benefits the community which provided the money. It offers its services to member co-ops by uniting the scientific treatment of problems and the professionalism of management with a capacity for risk-taking. The Entrepreneurial Division helps member groups take intelligent and informed risks in a world market which knows no nationality.

The success of Mondragon has been attributed to several factors (Caja Laboral Popular, 1969):

- the Basque industrial tradition;
- the economic growth which existed in the 60s;
- a favorable social climate;
- the financial support provided through the credit union;
- control of labor costs through social agreement;
- the support provided by the superstructure.

However, ultimately the Mondragon movement owes its success to the small band of dedicated people following the teachings of Don Jose Maria:

> Cooperativism is an association for social and economic purposes in a democratic structure; but at the same time, and always, it is an economic enterprise . . . subject to the same laws which rule all economic enterprises, whether capitalist or socialist. To be cooperative is not the opposite of capitalist – rather it is to assimilate the techniques of capital accumulation, such as developing capital and making use of technology and flexible forms of organization, but all the while giving priority to human values.
>
> (Larranaga, 1981)

Mondragon has been able to keep high-caliber leaders even though their pay scale is inferior to competing industries. Most managers are native to the Basque region and are committed to the social and economic improvement of their community. The *Ikerlan* research center, part of the support system, has kept Mondragon enterprises in the forefront of technological innovation – exciting places to work. Highly professional personnel guide the fortunes of the credit union and assist enterprises with their financial planning. Finally, no adversarial relationship exists between workers and managers, who all share responsibility for the success of the Mondragon experiment (MacLeod, 1986).

Youth Ventures

Metropolitan Toronto, in the Canadian province of Ontario, has been another focus for community economic development. In 1974 the Toronto

Board of Education's Research Department in their study *Patterns of Dropping Out* estimated that the dropout rate in Toronto secondary schools was 24 per cent or almost 8,000 students per year. Two of the largest groups within this population were the "Work Oriented" and "Family Supporters." Their main reasons for leaving school were to assume employment either as a demonstration of their need to feel more mature or to help support their families in times of crisis.

Each year about 600 14- and 15-year-olds were seeking employment through the Leaving School Early program. A survey of these students indicated that most did not like school and failed to see any value in formal education. Their reasons for wishing to leave school were related to financial need and/or problems of a family or personal nature.

The Research Department concluded that the dropout problem in Toronto was of "staggering" proportions. In fact, only 40 per cent of the students entering grade 9 would graduate from grade 12 and only 20 per cent from grade 13 (Young and Reich, 1974).

The severity of this problem to society became even more acute when the employment situation in Metropolitan Toronto was examined. A report from the Social Planning Council of Metropolitan Toronto observed that in the Metro Toronto Census Area during the first quarter of 1978 there were 14.5 unemployed persons for every available job. The rate of overall youth unemployment (age 15–24) in the Toronto area stood at 15 per cent, while a special survey of youth unemployment in the Regent Park Public Housing Project, in July 1977, revealed the rate for that area to be 51 per cent. Therefore, at a time when thousands of young people were choosing to leave school to seek a place in the world of work, there were very few employment opportunities available, even of a short-term or marginal nature. The result was an increased sense of failure and disillusionment among unemployed youth, contributing to serious social problems.

The profound impact of this movement was also felt in the schools where as many as 400 teachers could be displaced. When this situation was coupled with the beginning of a natural decline in the number of students entering secondary schools the problem was of crisis proportions as it affected teacher employment as well as the use of educational resources.

Traditional attempts to quell the dropout rate involved the provision of school programs based on the premise that an academic–vocational preparation system is the only valid approach. However, youth tend to be better informed about social and economic realities. Job experience may be more important to future employment stability than academic credentials. It seemed that a noninstitutional educational alternative which focused on work and used academic skills to support needs emerging through experience on the job might be appropriate. In 1978, the Job Creation

Working Group of the Community Policy Group on Unemployment of the Toronto Board of Education released a report recommending that the Board "undertake life-skills teaching programs in the workplace."

The Toronto Board of Education approached the *Learnxs Foundation Inc.* to assume sponsorship of a feasibility study on the employment of Leaving School Early students (14- and 15-year-olds) which had been funded by the federal government's Local Employment Assistance Program (LEAP). In July 1978 Learnxs received funding from LEAP to establish the *Student Employment Experience Center (SEEC) Project* to employ school leavers in a variety of small enterprises.

The Learnxs Foundation Inc., a nonprofit charitable organization, cooperates with the Toronto Board of Education in developing innovative and experimental programs. The SEEC Project provided full-time employment at the adult minimum wage for 14- and 15-year-old "hard-to serve" youth who had left school under the Leaving School Early policy of the Ontario Ministry of Education, as well as part-time employment for older students who were considered to be potential dropouts. At least eighteen student workers would be employed as well as five management personnel with industry and small business experience.

The Toronto Board of Education contributed surplus space, equipment and materials which resulted in the creation of the following "cottage industries":

- *Mario's Place*, a restaurant and cafeteria which used a vacant kitchen facility at Eastdale Collegiate to provide a food service for students, staff and area residents.
- *Mario's Community Kitchen*, a catering operation, served day care centers, meals-on-wheels, meetings, conferences and special events.
- *The Creative Wood Shop* (also at Eastdale) produced a line of novelty items made from pine (e.g. wall racks, bread boxes) which was distributed across Canada.
- *The Strip Joint* in the basement of Contact Alternative School refinished surplus wooden classroom furniture to be sold as antiques and memorabilia. Individual pieces of furniture were also received from the public to be refinished on a contract basis.
- *The Paper Chase* salvaged waste paper from the Education Center (administrative offices for the Toronto Board of Education and the Metropolitan Toronto School Board) for resale to a paper broker. The recovery system developed there was soon extended to other office buildings.

Each of these enterprises had been designed to operate as a small business on a cost-recovery basis. Therefore, revenue from sales was used to defray expenses so as to eventually make the Project self-sufficient and provide capital for further expansion of the concept.

It should be stressed that this was not work experience, where students take time out from their school-based academic pursuits to gain some experience in the workplace. It was a community-based job creation program for dropouts with an informal academic component built in to support the learning needs of the workers. The program focused on groups of youth organized into "working parties or work projects" (10–15 members) using a small-business or cooperative enterprise model. Each party had a manager with small-business experience and an "academic skills coach" provided by the Toronto Board of Education from the ranks of surplus teachers. The academic skills coach, as a working member of the enterprise, would also be responsible for developing remedial programs and other educational activities according to the learning needs of the workers.

This approach was similar to the "community development corporation" or cooperative enterprise model used in rural areas. However, instead of using natural resources to create employment, the work projects were developed on the basis of cost-recoverable service needs and the recycling of waste materials.

As a result of the SEEC pilot project, I met with Malcolm Roberton of the Bread and Roses Credit Union to explore possible models to employ youth through community economic development. It was decided to establish a planning group to form a community development corporation devoted to youth employment. Members of the group included individuals from the Toronto Board of Education, the Social Planning Council of Metropolitan Toronto, the Toronto-Dominion Bank, the Bread and Roses Credit Union, CEMP Investments, the University of Toronto and York Community Services.

In March 1979, Leon Muszynski, of the Metro Social Planning Council, submitted a report to the planning group entitled *Jobs Needed, Community Economic Development, A Job Creation and Social Development Strategy for Metropolitan Toronto*. This report became part of a working draft entitled: *Youth Ventures, A Community Economic Development Plan for Youth Employment in Toronto*.

The working draft called for:

- a survey of needs and resources in the local area;
- the creation of a community development corporation;
- the development of an ongoing evaluation system re cost-effectiveness and social benefit;
- the establishment of three or four urban cottage industries;

- the development of an academic skills support system to be integrated into each industry;
- the identification of sources of venture capital.

In April 1979 the working draft was endorsed by Toronto City Council.

That May the *Youth Ventures – Feasibility Study (1979–80)* incorporating the working draft was presented to LEAP jointly by the Social Planning Council and the Learnxs Foundation Inc. The sum of $87,000 was approved to launch a professional research and development study.

Four main objectives were established for the research work: the analysis of the feasibility of five potential enterprises and the development of business plans for those recommended for implementation; the development of a working profile of the target group (disadvantaged youth in the 16- to 24-year-old range); a review of experience in Canada and the US with various corporate models, particularly the Community Development Corporation (CDC), as the basis for developing the most appropriate legal form for Youth Ventures; and, the design of a management structure suitable for the achievement of the balanced social and economic goals of the organization.

Five potential enterprises were investigated:

- the operation of a visitors' guide service in Toronto;
- an office paper recycling system;
- The use of hydroponic gardening techniques in urban farming and/or the manufacture of hydroponic units;
- The production and sale of food products;
- The establishment of a light manufacturing facility.

In June 1980, *Youth Ventures Submission for Funding (1980–83)* was submitted to LEAP. Funding was granted in the amount of $249,711 to establish a paper and wood recycling business.

In October 1980, Letters Patent were issued for *Youth Ventures Developments of Metropolitan Toronto* as a nonprofit corporation with the following objects:

- to create employment opportunities for disadvantaged youth in Toronto by the creation and development of business enterprises;
- to create opportunities for imparting managerial and other work-related skills to disadvantaged youth whenever possible;
- to advance the cause of third-sector business development in Toronto and elsewhere.

In December, 1980 *Youth Ventures Recycling Incorporated* was established as a share capital corporation owned by Youth Ventures Developments of

Metropolitan Toronto. Youth Ventures Developments received second-year funding of $112,194 from LEAP and a teacher was seconded from the York Board of Education and assigned as *Academic and Life Skills (ALS) Coach* at Youth Ventures Recycling Incorporated. In February, 1982, York Wood Works was funded in the amount of $92,438 as a one-year Canada Community Development Project sponsored by Youth Ventures Developments of Metropolitan Toronto, to recycle, as firewood, waste industrial pallets and packaging. Youth Ventures received third-year funding of $158,325 from LEAP in September, 1982 to sustain the paper recycling enterprise.

As a third sector enterprise, Youth Ventures' target for employment was youth aged 16–24 who had poor employment prospects because of limited education and work experience. Fourteen staff were employed by Youth Ventures Recycling – eleven from the target group. One target employee served as Manager of Supply Development assisted by another target employee as Supply Development Officer and driver.

Youth Ventures Recycling recovered newspapers from Toronto households and fine papers from offices and businesses. The collection operation used three trucks driven by target employees and warehouse staff were rotated when needed as drivers' helpers. The processing operation, which involved sorting, staging, baling, stockpiling of bales and shipping, employed an Operations Manager and seven target employees – a foreman, a leadhand, two balers and three sorters / general warehousers. Entry-level employees had the opportunity to advance through the ranks and eventually assume managerial positions.

One of the most important innovations to emerge from the Youth Ventures experience has been the role of the ALS Coach. The following is an excerpt from an article entitled "What's a nice teacher like you doing in a place like this?" which I wrote in 1983 concerning the impact of this position on the Youth Ventures enterprise:

It should have been a day to be proud. Goodness knows, there hadn't been many in Donny's eighteen years. His family had wandered throughout Northern Ontario, from mining town to lumber camp, until his father just disappeared one day. Before Donny's ninth birthday, his mother took her four children to live in Toronto, where she suffered a nervous breakdown and had to be hospitalized. A series of foster homes and a stint in training school led to his current address in a group home in the east end of the city. No, it hadn't been easy.

He'd never spent that much time in school or been able to find a real job. One day he heard they were hiring in a waste paper recycling plant that was part of a program created to employ disadvantaged youth. He didn't think he'd have a chance but he sure could use the money. To his surprise, he got the job, learned to sort paper, drive a fork-lift, and operate the baler. He never missed work and felt a sense of accomplishment for the first time in his life.

The previous Friday, after Donny had been six months on the job, the General Manager called him into her office to offer him the position of Warehouse Supervisor. Although he'd always got along well with his workmates and had even trained new employees, he wasn't sure he could make the grade as a supervisor. But his probation officer encouraged him to give it a try, so he accepted.

The week had gone well. The General Manager was pleased when she handed him the pay cheques to distribute to the workers in the plant. Fifteen minutes later, though, he was still pacing back and forth in front of the office. When asked if something was wrong, Donny hung his head in shame and stammered. "I'm— I'm sorry M'am, I can't tell who they belong to." Only then did the General Manager realize that Donny was one of the five million Canadians estimated to be functionally illiterate, in that their reading problems put them at a distinct disadvantage in our modern society.

The answer does not seem to be to get people like Donny back into formal schooling. Too often, they view their original contacts with educational institutions as a negative, degrading experience. In fact, the most effective vehicle for adult basic education may well be an informal, responsive environment respecting the needs and interests of the learner as a person.

Successful literacy programs in developing countries have often integrated social and economic objectives – for example, in one area the establishment of a fisherman's cooperative with an adult basic education component proved to be an effective way to improve the quality of life because it met both literacy and employment needs.

A little over a year ago, an experimental project was undertaken to explore the feasibility of this integrated approach in Metropolitan Toronto. To help alleviate the more than 15 per cent level of unemployment among 15- to 24-year-olds, Youth Ventures Developments of Metro Toronto was established as a not-for-profit corporation devoted to community economic development. In June of 1981, Youth Ventures in turn approached the York Board of Education to request the services of a teacher to work with fifteen disadvantaged young employees in their waste paper recycling enterprise, Youth Ventures Recycling Incorporated. The teacher assigned to the project, who was given the title Academic and Life Skills (ALS) Coach, was to be responsible for individualized instruction in academic subjects, remedial upgrading, technical skills, vocational information, and counseling and life skills as required. He started that October and was to spend up to 30 hours a week at the plant.

This was not to be a traditional teaching assignment, however. To quote from the report of the ALS Coach after his first three months on the job:

Implementation of the teacher's role was achieved with careful consideration. Suspicious of the formal educational experience, the young people at Youth Ventures took an explorative "wait and see" attitude towards the academic support person and life skills coach. I saw clearly that if the business was to become a non-traditional learning environment, the "teacher" must necessarily become thoroughly involved with the day to day operations. Accordingly, I began work alongside the young people, sorting, baling, and loading in the warehouse and working outside on the trucks. In doing so, I learned from the "inside" just what the work demanded, how the company operated, and I established positive relationships with everybody. Through these involvements and a positive projection of my personality, much interest was generated in the possibilities of my functioning also as a "teacher."

I began to teach by finding out the educational standards of each individual, and by explaining that my presence at Youth Ventures meant that cooperative educational credit could be gained "on the job." The response was gratifying, in that the demands for "classes" became so high as to challenge my time in accommodating them. Happily, this situation has continued and my role as teacher has expanded into all aspects of the business and further into the lives of the young people.

The educational and skill-related benefits of the program are many. The following work-related topics were treated formally in small groups and individually on the job: (a) training in safety, sorting, baling, fork-lift, and maintenance; (b) kinesiology – human movements related to work operation; (c) work habits and attitudes; (d) design and technical drawings; (e) communication and social skills; (f) training for supervision.

Academically, I have tested all language skills and numeracy levels, and prescribed and implemented remediation where necessary. I have advised regarding procedures and options for upgrading related to night school, community colleges, correspondence school, individual study, return to school, and cooperative education as well as on continuing education courses and resources.

In life-skills classes we have dealt with health, communication, interpersonal skills, social attitudes and values, personal financial management, and driver education for classes G.M. and D. licenses.

In my developing role as counselor, I have dealt with the following areas: legal, interpersonal work-related, personal, health, financial, career, and educational.

But did the assignment of the ALS Coach compromise business objectives at Youth Ventures? This is what the General Manager had to say to the York Board of Education:

> From a social standpoint the concept of education in the workplace excited me; however, I was admittedly sceptical of the concept from a business point of view. Some of my business concerns were: the economic impact on a new business, the possible adverse effects on productivity, the potential increase in absenteeism, turnover and effects on employee morale, and the possibility of a clash in objectives between the ALS Coach and Management.

Despite these initial concerns, dramatic gains were noted in the business operation after the ALS Coach had been with Youth Ventures for three months:

- Productivity – increased productivity of 47 per cent.
- Employee turnover – prior to the arrival of the ALS Coach the rate was 97 per cent. During the first three months turnover decreased to 35 per cent.
- Absenteeism and lateness – the incidence of absenteeism and lateness declined from 140 hours in September to 45 hours in December.
- Literacy and numeracy skills – many employees had experienced difficulty doing fundamental calculations and reading staff memos and bulletins. The ALS Coach was instrumental in improving this situation.

To quote the General Manager:

> The ALS Coach has managed to prove to the individual employee-students that learning can be enjoyable, a point that failed to get across under the traditional educational system. As for Donny, needless to say he no longer has this problem . . . . I believe that education in the workplace has not only had a positive impact on the Company, but has also filled an educational void for our staff specifically, and potentially for young people in general.
>
> (Shuttleworth 1983)

During the 1981–82 recession Youth Ventures Recycling struggled to survive in a climate of reduced business activity and a depressed price for waste paper in the market place. Because of its unique "niche" position as a small enterprise, providing social as well as economic benefit, Ontario Paper (the primary purchaser of Youth Ventures product) continued to honor its commitments and even awarded extra baling contracts to bridge the difficult times. At the time of writing, Youth Ventures Recycling Inc. is a successful worker-owned cooperative.

EDUCATION AND ECONOMIC DEVELOPMENT

The case studies described above explore three quite different economic environments.

The New Dawn experience emerged from a semi-rural economy based primarily on the exploitation of natural resources to create employment through heavy industrial development. When the industrial infrastructure became outmoded and the natural resources were no longer competitive in the world marketplace, the region was faced with chronic structural unemployment – a fate which has also been visited upon numerous other communities in the Atlantic/Appalachian belt of North America. New Dawn has attempted to renew the economic base by recycling local skills to focus on more service-oriented needs of the community, particularly housing.

The Mondragon movement, on the other hand, grew out of the needs of a people to assert their own cultural and economic independence. Through the efforts of a charismatic leader, a new cooperative enterprise strategy emerged from the ashes of a civil war. Enhanced technological training, the pooling of financial resources, and a commitment to innovation have resulted in a new manufacturing infrastructure which remains competitive in the European marketplace while providing both social and economic benefit to the region.

Youth Ventures responds to the employment and training needs of early school-leavers who are at risk in a densely populated urban area. As educational non-achievers they are faced with the prospects of marginal service-sector employment, at best. A community economic development strategy, which focuses on this particular age group, demonstrated an alternative approach to better serve a sector of society which has been traditionally discarded in the industrial age.

What the three enterprises have in common, though, is their relationship to public education. New Dawn has been assisted in its development through its association with staff and resources from the College of Cape Breton. Mondragon has been the outgrowth of the original technical school founded by Don Jose Maria. Youth Ventures was a response to the employment and training needs of school-leavers and pioneered the role of Academic and Life Skills Coach in the workplace.

It seems that there is need for a different approach in which public education better relates its services to the realities of economic development. The next chapter will focus on the "education foundation," a purpose-built organization which helps public schooling to address both the social and economic needs of the community.

9 The education foundation

THE LEARNXS MODEL

One of the fastest growing trends in public education in North America today has been the education foundation. Since the late 1970s more than 350 school districts in the US have established nonprofit, charitable foundations to increase public involvement in schools, to support innovative projects, and most important, to raise money and stabilize school finances. Although innovations in Canadian education often reflect programs previously developed in the US or Britain, Canadians have, in fact, led the way in the establishment of the education foundation.

During the 1970s, while working as an administrator for the Toronto Board of Education, I established the Learnxs Foundation Inc., which has become a model for similar ventures in such municipalities as the City of North York, the City of York, the Borough of East York and the Regions of York and Ottawa–Carleton, in Ontario, as well as numerous other cities and regions across Canada.

In 1973, the Ontario government imposed ceilings on educational spending by school boards in the province, and it became apparent that public education was entering a new era of austerity. Budget priorities were changing, and the potential impact of declining enrolment on future revenues was being recognized. There was a need to explore alternative sources of support for innovative and experimental programs, since these were often the first to feel the impact of cutbacks in educational spending.

The effects of cutbacks were being felt by the Toronto Board of Education particularly with reference to the development of alternative and community programs. As Coordinator of Alternative and Community Programs, I proposed that a nonprofit charitable, community organization, to be known as the Learnxs Foundation be established. Learnxs is an acronym for the Learning Exchange System, a community education project which I developed in 1973. On June 26, 1973 the Board's School

Program Committee approved the following report:

1. Introduction

As budgets become strained and pupil enrolments decrease, a direction for the future is emerging. Boards of Education, in order to maintain the numbers of students, must become responsive to the needs of their potential and actual clientele. Inflation has accentuated the effects felt under the constraints of the present policy of educational spending. The Toronto Board of Education has a tremendous amount of experience in alternative modes of learning, responsive to community needs. This may be one area in which additional students may be brought back into the school system. One of the major problems in this area is the lack of short-term funding.

2. Rationale

There is a need to create a stable source of short-term funding to support innovative program and practice at the local school level. Such a fund would make research and development seed money available to initiate projects designed to alleviate specific problems as identified through schools and/or communities within the Toronto Board of Education. Since the present educational budget seems hard-pressed to provide basic services, it is proposed that the community be encouraged to become involved in education through a foundation to be established for the above purposes.

The funds required for this type of project could be solicited from industry, philanthropic groups, service clubs, and private individuals. By setting up a foundation, funds can be solicited, direction given, and projects implemented. The foundation would also act as a buffer zone between donor and recipient. Co-funding and multi-donor funding of single projects can also be considered under the umbrella of a foundation. Since foundations can be set up to conform to the regulations of the Income Tax Act (sections regarding charities), monies donated to a foundation could be used more efficiently taking advantage of the provisions for deduction of donations. There is also the possibility of cost-sharing arrangements with various levels of government to increase the purchase power of the foundation's dollar (e.g. Canada Assistance Plan). This flexibility in itself is a unique aspect of this type of short-term funding.

3. Objectives

To establish a foundation to be called the Learnxs Foundation, which will solicit funds from private and public sources, for the purpose of providing short-term funding for innovative programs within the Toronto system. The fund will encourage each program to build in a research aspect to document the developmental process by providing additional funds specifically for research.

Fund-raising will be carried out in two phases. The first phase will be the soliciting and administering of funds from established funding sources. This phase will enable the Foundation to establish credibility and gain acceptance as a funding source. The second phase will be the accumulation of sufficient capital to begin making grants from earned interest. This phase will require a wider base of grants, e.g. bequests, grants from community groups, etc. For this phase to be successful, the Foundation must have established credibility, and a proven administrative record. Once this is accomplished, the Foundation will have both a stable source of continuing funds, and the flexibility of interim grants.

4. Advantages

(a) Money channeled for innovative programs would no longer reduce funds available for on-going programs.
(b) Funded research components could be built in to each project so that projects could seek long-term funding as documented, evaluated, on-going projects.
(c) The Foundation could assist schools and community groups in the development of program plans.
(d) The Foundation could begin to develop skills among people in the schools and community familiar with alternative funding possibilities.
(e) The Foundation could maintain an up-to-date data bank of funding sources and maintain regular contact with them.
(f) The Foundation could coordinate funding appeals.

5. Possible projects

Although the initiative for projects will come through school and/or its community, it is possible to cite several possible categories of projects which may arise:

(a) *City-wide projects*
- e.g. Learnxs project (community resource learning);
- Students in business project;
- multi-cultural programs, cultural immersion for teachers;
- volunteer training;

(b) *School-based projects*
  • e.g. school-based day care establishment costs;

(c) *Innovative projects*
  • e.g. Science School and Art School.

6. *Proposed Method*

(a) The establishment of an incorporated charitable foundation, to be called The Learnxs Foundation, through the cooperation of the Toronto Board of Education's legal department.
(b) The formation of an interim nine-member board of directors composed of 3 representatives of the Board of Education staff (appointed by the Director), 3 Trustees (appointed by the Chairman of the Board) and 3 representatives of the community (appointed by the Social Planning Council), augmented by a non-voting advisory board.
(c) The preparation of a brief and prospectus to be distributed to various foundations and private sources of funding. This is to be an appeal for support and tentative funding, dependent on requests for support from school and/or community groups.
(d) Distribution of a brief, prospectus and explanatory material to all schools through normal channels. Schools will then be invited to prepare submissions to the foundation for help in possible funding.
(e) Submissions will be rated as to priority by the board of directors, budgets established, research components added, if necessary, and the completed document re-submitted to funding sources, which have indicated willingness to cooperate for funding.
(f) The Foundation will administer funds for projects, contract, if necessary, for research and documentation and gather interim reports.
(g) The Foundation will prepare semi-annual reports for distribution to schools and interested parties so that the progress of each project will be visible.

Recommendations

1 That the Toronto Board of Education assist in the establishment of the Learnxs Foundation as an incorporated charitable foundation as outlined in the proposal.
2 That staff time be allocated so that staff members be able to sit on the board of directors.
3 That one staff member be seconded from the Toronto staff on a part-

time basis for a period of one year to assist in the establishment of the Foundation.

4   That the solicitor of the Toronto Board of Education be allowed to assist in the legal work involved in this project.

5   That the Toronto Board of Education endorse publicly the concept of the Learnxs Foundation.

6   That the staff and community groups be encouraged to begin work on programs that might fall within the purview of the Foundation, and submit them to the interim board of directors.

7   That the staff of the Foundation be requested to prepare quarterly reports during the first year for the information of the Board, the officials, and other interested parties.

8   That the Toronto Board of Education absorb the costs involved in printing and distributing the brief and prospectus and the quarterly reports for the first year of operation.

(Toronto Board of Education, 1973)

Assistance in the incorporation and charitable registration of the foundation was provided by the Board's legal department. The Learnxs Foundation Inc. received its charter and charitable registration in April, 1974.

The Board of Directors of the Foundation reflected a cross-section of influential people. While each person sat on the Board as a private citizen, his or her other affiliations and interests could obviously prove beneficial in the future work of the Foundation. The mix among directors was also designed to ensure that the Foundation would not become just an extension of the administration or trustees of the Toronto Board of Education but would function as an "arms-length" organization oriented to community education. During the period from 1973 to 1980 I served as Secretary-Treasurer of the Board of Directors and administrated the activities of the Foundation.

In the intervening years, the Learnxs Foundation has worked cooperatively with the Toronto Board of Education to found a successful publishing house (Learnxs Press) and sponsor research and development projects in inner-city education (SCORE), arts enrichment (ARTS-JUNCTION), community education and development, and youth employment. For example, the Student Employment Experience Center (SEEC) project operated a restaurant and catering business, woodcraft manufacturing, furniture refinishing and a paper recycling enterprise to employ 14- and 15-year-old school dropouts. An important component of this program was education; a teacher was assigned to the workplace to teach basic literacy and life skills (Shuttleworth, 1986).

THE LEARNING ENRICHMENT FOUNDATION

The City of York, a municipality of 134,000 within Metropolitan Toronto, has the lowest levels of income and highest rates of unemployment and functional illiteracy in the region. Forty-two per cent of its residents speak a language other than English in the home and the largest proportion of newcomers in recent years has been from the West Indies, Asia and Latin America. More than 50 per cent of its students do not complete high school. York also has a chronic shortage of day care accommodation, as well as the second largest proportion of senior citizens in Metro Toronto. Although York is located several kilometres from the central business district, it has become the "inner city" of Metropolitan Toronto in the past decade (Statistics Canada, 1986).

A focus for community economic development in the City of York has been the Learning Enrichment Foundation (LEF). While still employed by the Toronto Board of Education, I assisted in the establishment of LEF by the York Board of Education as a not-for-profit community development corporation devoted to the promotion of multicultural arts enrichment. The provision of childcare services and employment/training schemes, particularly for youth, were later added. LEF's 11-member Board of Directors currently includes representatives from York municipal government, and the York Board of Education, but the majority of members are from business and industry and citizens from the community at large who bring particular skills and perspectives to the work of the Foundation. In 1980 when I became the Assistant Superintendent – Community Services for the York Board, I was elected Secretary of the Board of Directors of the Foundation.

Since 1981, LEF has grown from an annual revenue of $20,000 to a projected budget of $10 million in 1992 with more than 600 employees. Financial support has been received from four levels of government, corporations, foundations, community organizations and individual donations. The sale of goods and services has also contributed significantly to revenue. In addition, "in kind" support is received from the public and private sectors (e.g. donated space, materials and equipment). As a not-for-profit business, LEF operates with an administrative overhead of less than 5 per cent.

In August 1984, as a representative of the Learning Enrichment Foundation, and the Board of Education, I was approached by the federal Department of Employment and Immigration to convene a "local committee of adjustment" under provisions of their Industrial Adjustment Service program. The main objective of the Committee would be "to identify local needs and resources in order to develop a strategy to improve the economic well-being of the City of York" (Shuttleworth, 1988).

During that fall the Foundation approached the major governmental, labor and business interests in the City to become financial sponsors in the project. In December 1984, a Memorandum of Agreement was signed by the following partners to create the York Community Economic Development Committee: the City of York, the Board of Education for the City of York, the York Association of Industry, the United Steelworkers of America (District 6, Subdistrict 23), the Learning Enrichment Foundation, the Ontario Ministry of Labor and Employment and Immigration, Canada. This was the first such committee to be formed in a large metropolitan area in Canada.

The work of the Committee was divided into two main sections – research and development. The Research Work Group, chaired by a senior municipal politician, conducted a survey of existing industries as well as those who had left the City in the previous two-year period. Key factors drawn from the surveys were as follows:

- Almost 50 per cent of firms surveyed felt they could benefit from further training or retraining of staff.
- Most industries established in York because of its central accessible location, reasonable rents, available space, good labor pool and potential for marketing products.
- Negative aspects of location included small size of accommodation; inadequate space for delivery and parking; city building and zoning restrictions; and close proximity to residential properties.
- Commercial growth has been encouraged to the perceived detriment of industrial development.
- Most respondents were able to "access" city services; however, some experienced difficulty in obtaining information and building permits.
- Most industries left York because of a need for more and better space, high operating costs including taxes and rents, inadequate municipal services, residential versus industrial conflicts, inadequate public transportation and traffic problems;
- *Suggested areas for improvement* included: more space for expansion; better public transit; a streamlining of procedures to obtain Planning and Building Department approvals; resolution of industrial/residential land-use problems; improved access to local employment and training services; better communication between municipal, small-business and industrial interests; and more access to financial and other forms of support.

The Development Work Group, which I chaired, was established to assist new industries wishing to locate in York, as well as to support existing companies and agencies with their employment, development and training needs. Achievements of the group were as follows:

- Twelve potential new employers were identified as a result of liaison with real estate agents and personal contacts of Committee members.
- The Learning Enrichment Foundation was supported in developing the *Entrepreneurial Training Center* (16,800 sq. ft.) which accommodated 70 persons learning to establish small businesses as well as permitting the implementation of training and employment programs for more than 300.
- LEF also sponsored the *York Business Opportunities Center (YBOC)* a 28,000 sq. ft. facility to provide incubator space for at least 40 new businesses, creating 160 new jobs (in 1991 YBOC expanded to 74,000 sq. ft.).
- A letter of introduction offering assistance with marketing, venture capital, industrial space, training, zoning and building permits was sent to 378 employers in York.
- Training programs were undertaken in the following occupations: machine technology, restaurant and catering services; upholstered furniture; industrial sewing; renovation and construction; industrial maintenance; home helpers; healthcare; courier/light delivery; clerical/retail services; bus-drivers; and childcare assistants. Academic upgrading was provided by the Adult Day School.
- LEF operated two recruitment and placement agencies – A+ Employment Services and the Job Opportunities for Youth (JOY) Employment Center.
- Sources of venture capital were identified through banks, credit unions, government grants, the federal Entrepreneurial Investment Program, and the provincial Small Business Development Corporation program.
- Training programs were established for entrepreneurs and worker-owned cooperatives in cooperation with the Board of Education for the City of York.
- Positive relationships with municipal, provincial and government departments were generally maintained; however, definite problems were experienced with the City Planning and Building Departments and the Canadian Job Strategies program of the federal government.
- The York Community Economic Development Committee has become a model for more than 20 similar projects in Canada, the United States and Britain.

In April 1986, the Committee submitted its final report and recommendations to the sponsoring bodies. Since that time, a number of new ventures have been established as a direct outcome of the development work of the Committee:

- *MICROTRON Center* – a training facility for microcomputer skills, word and numerical processing, computer-assisted design, graphics and styling, and electronic assembly and repair. The project was jointly sponsored by the York Board of Education, Commodore Business Machines, Comspec Communications and LEF. The facility is available to serve the training needs of business, government, voluntary organizations and the community at large as well as the Board of Education.
- *MICROTRON Bus* – a refurbished school bus accommodates eight work stations from the MICROTRON Center. It visits small business and industry, and service organizations on a scheduled basis to provide training in word and numerical processing for their employees and clients. This project is jointly sponsored by the York Board of Education, the Learning Enrichment Foundation, Commodore Business Machines, Comspec Communications, Corel Systems, the York Business Opportunities Center and the York Lions Club.
- *MacTECH* – a training program for unemployed workers in integrated machine technologies (i.e. computer, electronics, machine operation) was established at George Harvey Collegiate Institute and Standard-Modern Technologies. It was jointly sponsored by the York Board of Education, West Metro Skills, Standard-Modern Technologies, Weston Machine and Tool and Magna International. This program provides a new source of training personnel in response to the direct needs of high-technology employers.
- *LWL-TV* – a distance education project of LEF, the York Board of Education and Graham Cable to develop a cable television version of the *Learning Without Limits* magazine which is published by the Board. The six hours of programming per week includes literacy and numeracy skills, English as a Second Language and preparation for citizenship, technical and business education and leisure-learn activities. The project reaches 90,000 cable subscribers and includes an advertising opportunity for local business and industry.
- *Small Business Owner Development Program* – this outreach program of the York Business Opportunities Center provides business consultation and a support network for 90 small businesses in the local area.
- *Industrial Advisory Committees* – the employer groups in York with the greatest potential for growth have been machine technology, industrial sewing, upholstered furniture, renovation and construction and childcare services. Advisory Committees were established in these fields to allow local employers to "drive" training and recruitment programs.

York was the first municipality in a large metropolitan region to be selected by Employment and Immigration, Canada, to host a local committee of adjustment. By bringing together the key economic participants in the governmental, commercial and voluntary sector, a new "unity of purpose" has been achieved. The York model has demonstrated the potential of community economic development as an important strategy to address local social, industrial and employment needs (York Community Economic Development Committee, 1986).

THE ADULT DAY SCHOOL

A key player in the education foundation process of community economic development has been the York Board of Education's *Adult Day School (ADS)*. I established ADS in 1983 as a secondary school devoted to educational upgrading, language skills and preparation for employment, or post-secondary education. ADS has grown from an initial enrolment of 265 in 1983 to more than 2,000 full-time students in 1990. Two departments of ADS – Education for the Workplace and Alternative Studies – have been particularly responsive to the needs of the employment community.

The *Education for the Workplace Department* has 23 teachers who provide basic education, and English-as-a-Second Language diploma credits on a withdrawal basis, to entry-level employment and training programs as well as cooperative education in a variety of business, industrial and service settings. Training programs (with LEF and other partners) include renovation and construction, industrial sewing, childcare assistants, machine technologies, healthcare aides, registered nursing assistant, electronic assembly and repair and small-business development. All programs are industry-driven, responding to the training and recruitment needs of employers in the City of York. Training partners in this community economic development process have included Humber College, the Learning Enrichment Foundation and employers who sit on Industrial Advisory Committees.

Alternative Studies comprises 27 teachers who provide individualized programs for those unable to participate in regular ADS classes because of physical, emotional, employment or cultural barriers. In addition, teacher-tutors visit a variety of employment settings to provide educational upgrading and language skills on the job. This service has been very popular with companies who employ an immigrant or functionally illiterate workforce (Shuttleworth, 1988).

An outgrowth of both education for the workplace and alternative studies has been *Adopt-an-Industry*. This demonstration project, which I established in the Fall of 1988, is designed as a joint venture between the employment community and the Adult Day School to increase the potential for education in the workplace. Each of a selected group of industries receives the services of an ADS teacher on a secondment basis. The teacher is assigned to the company's Personnel, or other appropriate Department, to perform the following duties:

- assess staff development needs;
- develop a training design;
- undertake training programs directly or through external resources utilizing continuing education provisions;
- provide direct service in the areas of educational upgrading and ESL training as appropriate;
- conduct an ongoing evaluation of the overall program in response to employer and employee needs.

As a member of the management team, the teacher reports directly to a company supervisor while maintaining liaison with the ADS Project Leader and other Adopt-an-Industry personnel. Initial response to the concept among employers has been enthusiastic. During the economic downturn of 1981–82 many larger companies lost their training officers, while small and medium-sized firms could never afford such a luxury. The benefits to the Adult Day School have included the professional development of participating staff, as well as a new source of students to serve. Therefore, it is hoped that both the economic and human development needs of both partners will be met (Shuttleworth, 1990).

BUILDING ECONOMIC PARTNERSHIPS

In a period of austerity and fiscal restraint an education foundation can be an important source of support for demonstration projects such as the Adult Day School. Through the pooling of public and private resources, it may ensure creative activity and program excellence when public organizations are struggling to maintain themselves.

A private foundation attached to a public body can also provide the means whereby committed persons from the public body and the community at large participate in joint problem-solving and collective action. However, the majority of directors of a foundation should be citizens of the community who are not affiliated with the Board of Education (or municipal government). This ensures a sense of objectivity and avoids the danger of the organization becoming politicized.

The education foundation can provide a vehicle to tap sources of funding in support of innovative practice which are not readily available to public education. It also provides an opportunity to involve the community as joint partners in the educational enterprise. With diminishing financial resources and a concern about credibility in a changing society, public education certainly needs the help.

Experiences in both Toronto and York, moreover, suggest that an education foundation, as a catalyst for economic renewal, should feature the following characteristics:

- Small business/entrepreneurial focus, both in job creation projects and in support for private sector businesses.
- Future oriented – emphasis on waste recovery, support services, and energy-efficient enterprises which do not compete with existing private-sector businesses and offer potential for long-term employment.
- Literacy component – each enterprise employs a teacher to do basic education, English as a Second Language, and life skills, or serves as a cooperative education placement.
- Cost-effectiveness through sound business principles and financial management.
- Worker participation in management of the companies through advisory committees.
- On-the-job training.
- Community development, by allowing local citizens to become active in needs assessment and resource identification.

The Organization for Economic Cooperation and Development in Paris has selected the Learning Enrichment Foundation (and the York Board of Education) as a case study of exemplary practice. Their report *Partners in Education: The New Partnership Between Business and Schools* (1991) makes the following observation:

In fact the foundation has been remarkably successful in maintaining links between its various interests, and in particular between its interest in community development and workforce preparation. Each of its activities seems to reinforce another. For example, the day care centers simultaneously teach a vocational skill to trainees, allow parents to study other courses while their children are being looked after and are themselves helped by other training schemes such as carpentry (which makes their furniture) and catering (which makes their lunch). Similarly, the co-existence of an office skills training course and a small-business incubator on the same site allows fledgling companies to use secretarial services provided by trainees.

This is a highly sophisticated coalition which manages to reconcile the various interests of a number of actors at community, enterprise and individual level. In some cases this involves building on shared goals:

the pool of goodwill towards the day care centers, for example is an important source of motivation. In other cases, goals can be very individualized and specific. When one of the city's hospitals seconded a teacher under the "adopt-an-industry" scheme, it aimed specifically to find a way of bringing the literacy skills of its auxiliary staff up to scratch to enable them to recognize and safely handle dangerous substances. A unifying theme is the foundation's commitment to ensure that adult education and training is made directly relevant to workplace requirements.

(OECD, 1991)

This and preceding chapters have dealt with the ability of schools and educational authorities to innovate and respond to community needs, particularly in relation to employment preparation and economic development. The next chapter will explore obstacles existing in the "traditional school culture" of the industrial era which resist change, and consumer responsiveness in the new economic age.

10 Challenging the gate-keeper syndrome

YABUTS AND WHYNOTS

As previously mentioned, in Chapter 1, John Dewey described the role of schooling as "either preservers of the status quo or anticipators of the future." The teacher, parent, student or administrator who advocates a new or different way of responding to a need or resolving a problem may soon find themselves in the land of the "yabuts" or the "whynots." The simple statement "I've got an idea!" may evoke two types of response:

- "yabut" you can't do that because – it's against the rules – it hasn't been tried before – who's going to pay for it? etc.
- as opposed to – that sounds interesting "whynot" give it a try, or how can I help?

The need to exercise control and encourage dependency has been a fundamental behavioral style for many industrial-age administrators and teachers. The introduction of an innovation in some organizations can be a bit like introducing a foreign substance into the body – the immune system white cells quickly attack in an attempt to neutralize or repel the intruder. Is the traditional yabut role of "administrator as gate-keeper" in conflict with the task of preparing young people and redundant workers for a whynot age of entrepreneurship, self-reliance and interdependency? Post-industrial enterprises have had to learn to encourage collaborative decision-making and bottom-up innovation. Can public schooling really afford to continue to dwell in the land of the yabuts while the new economic age surges forward into the world of the whynots? How do we ensure that tomorrow's administrators and teachers will be facilitators of learning in a global economy, not industrial-age gate-keepers?

EXPLORING THE CULT OF DEPENDENCY

As previously described, in Chapter 9, the Learning Exchange System (Learnxs) project spawned the Learnxs Foundation in the City of Toronto. Learnxs also represents a case study in challenging industrial-age dependency applied to schooling and other educative services as described in an article I wrote which was originally published in 1981:

> A considerable body of research is now available on patterns of non-formal learning. Tough (1977) has documented studies from Canada, Ghana, Jamaica, New Zealand and the United States about the individual learner's efforts to acquire certain definite knowledge or skills. These learning projects involve a series of learning sessions or episodes adding up to at least seven hours. Persons from all walks of life, and ranging in age from 10-year-old children to retired adults, were interviewed about their learning habits. It was found that of all learning projects, only 20 per cent were planned by a professional whereas 80 per cent were planned by the learner or some other "amateur" (Tough, 1977).
>
> (Shuttleworth, 1981)

In recognition of this fact, the Learning Exchange System, or Learnxs, was created in Toronto in 1973 as a three-year demonstration project concerned with the use of nonformal community-based learning resources for individual and group learning. Its services were made available to all levels of public education, as well as to educational support services, public libraries, and social and recreational agencies. The focus of the project was the creation and distribution of a directory of community resources known as the *Learnxs Directory*. Other activities included an information-sharing and retrieval system and an alternative secondary school known as *Subway Academy*. The project was supported through the establishment of a private nonprofit charitable organization known as the *Learnxs Foundation* which received financial assistance from community sources and goods and services from public education.

The sections which follow are derived from my thesis for the doctor of philosophy degree at the University of Toronto, which was entitled "The Learning Exchange System (Learnxs): analysis of a demonstration project in community education."

COMMUNITY-RESOURCE LEARNING

Community-resource learning may be defined as: the use of human, physical and organizational resources to support self-directed, as well as teacher- and agency-led, learning for individuals of all ages.

A review of literature and practice in the twentieth century indicates that the concept of using community resources as a classroom for life experience was originally espoused by Dewey (1915) and was later amplified by Olsen (1945), Irwin and Russell (1971), Tough (1971), and Illich (1970).

This concept may also be found as a focal point in several reports which were commissioned by the government of Ontario and which have been instrumental in shaping the direction of education in the province. The concept, therefore, has become a basic tenet for a more flexible and individualized education in elementary schools, for a series of alternative approaches in secondary schools, and for recognition of the nonformal, lifelong learning needs of the adult.

Although out-of-school learning may seem a very straightforward and rational approach, the educational tradition has been one of institutionalized learning, using a common set of curriculum guidelines and preprogrammed materials. To see the teacher as a facilitator of learning using out-of-school resources requires a major shift in emphasis from what has been known.

The predominant mode of out-of-school learning in public education in the postwar period has been the "field trip," where a class of twenty to forty students, supervised by their classroom teacher, participate in an excursion outside the school. Popular destinations have been farms and woodlands for "nature study" or museums, art galleries, and government buildings for "cultural enrichment." Primary school children might also study a theme known as "community helpers," which could include visits to the local police station or firehall. Programs in compensatory education at inner-city schools have encouraged field trips to places of cultural interest to improve the educational achievement of "deprived" students.

A continuing concern about this approach to education has been the limited number of places of interest to visit, resulting in a great deal of repetition and of ultimate boredom on the part of students ("Oh no, not another trip to City Hall!"). A second concern has been a lack of adequate preparation prior to the trip and of follow-up afterward. And a third has been the increasing emphasis on the safety requirements and operating procedures that govern the transportation and supervision of individuals and groups. That teachers can be held at least morally responsible for any accident has discouraged many of them from treating the field trip as a valid approach to learning.

At the secondary-school level, a time-tabling system of relatively short class periods makes it most difficult to arrange a block of time for a field trip. As a result, the onus is often placed on individuals or small groups to make the visit in their own time.

Practice and research in adult education continually stress the importance of self-determination and a more informal, participatory style of learning. The predominant approach, however, remains the group lecture method -- in both credit and non-credit programs. Since many adults are part-time students, difficulties in time allocation and scheduling are used as a justification to preserve the status quo.

The late sixties and early seventies saw the release of several very influential reports in Ontario, which spawned a new sense of openness, flexibility, and emphasis on the rights of the individual learner. Elementary education began to experiment with the open-plan school, a more flexible use of resources, and individualized programming, all basic principles of the Hall-Dennis Report (Ontario Ministry of Education, 1968). The H.S.–1 curriculum (Ontario Ministry of Education, 1972–73) in the secondary schools allowed each student to pursue a program of individual credits drawn from a wide range of options. The Commission on Post Secondary Education (Ontario Ministry of Colleges and Universities, 1972) coined the term "open sector education" to promote the needs of the lifelong learner. A basic premise of all these reports was the accessibility of the learner to a wide range of opportunities and resources.

Alternatives in Education projects, such as SEED (Yip, 1971), SEE (Etobicoke Board of Education, 1971), AISP (North York Board of Education, 1971), ALPHA (Toronto Board of Education, 1971), and CONTACT (Toronto Board of Education, 1972), seized upon these fundamentals and extended them even further as models of program flexibility, humanistic idealism, and shared decision-making. All of these projects stressed the importance of life experience as a focal point of curriculum development. All saw people, places and things in the community as vital to the realization of this objective.

When a school, organization, or project attempts to actualize this aim and build these resources into their learning program, an immediate problem becomes apparent. In a city, where there are thousands of potential supports to the individual and group learner, each resource must be identified, confirmed, categorized, and recorded. A means of access to these records should then be made available to the learner or resource leader. Without such a cooperative banking of information, individuals and groups may waste considerable time seeking out contacts. A readily accessible resource bank of people, places, and things could be supportive of the needs of many different learners.

The question, however, remains: how to create such a resource bank, ensure that it will be continually updated, and make it available to such individuals and groups?

LEARNING EXCHANGE SYSTEM

Learnxs was conceived as a demonstration project to support the needs of individuals and groups who wished to utilize community resources in their learning. While not the first of its kind in North America, it was the first time such a project had been attempted in Metropolitan Toronto.

In 1970, I was Vice-Chairman of a *Special Task Force* established by the Toronto Board of Education to study and report on matters concerning inner-city problems, educational programs and community relationships in Toronto schools. When the Special Task Force released its Final Report (Toronto Board of Education, 1972) it called for the establishment of ad hoc "work groups" to bring together capable individuals from the school system and the community to work on problems of mutual concern. Characteristics of such a group were to be: "their clearly defined goals, flexibility, integration of skills, strong sense of commitment, collaboration and their facility to disband as soon as the task was completed." I was responsible for the implementation of the recommendations of the Task Force in the City of Toronto.

One of these work groups, known as the *Cooperative Education Work Group*, had a membership of persons from business and industry, labor, government, and community organizations as well as persons from the Toronto Board of Education. A draft proposal entitled *Learning Exchange System, the Learnxs Project* was presented to this Work Group. The proposal recommended the establishment of three task groups as follows:

Learning Resources Exchange – to identify and compile a directory of community learning resources;
Information-Sharing and Retrieval System – to investigate a variety of media and technological applications with the purpose of establishing a retrieval system for the Learning Resources Exchange;
Subway Academy – to establish an alternative public secondary school (under the Board's alternatives in education policy) that would stress the utilization of community resources, independent study, and shared decision-making.

In February, 1973, the Cooperative Education Work Group approved the Learnxs proposal. The Learning Resources Exchange and the Information-Sharing and Retrieval System were to be further refined for submission to alternate sources of support. The Subway Academy plan was to be presented to the Toronto Board for consideration as a new alternative public secondary school.

THE LEARNXS DIRECTORY

In the spring of 1973, Learnxs received a grant from the Ministry of Education to employ four students under a program known as *Students Participating in Community Education (SPICE)*. Their task during July and August was "to compile a list of all the resources, human and physical, in the Eastend of Toronto (Yonge Street to the eastern boundary)."

That fall a group of volunteers organized the data into the first Learnxs Directory. A new proposal entitled *Resource Bank for Community Learning* was prepared by the Learnxs Foundation for submission to the Local Initiatives Program of the federal government. This was the first of a series of short-term grants received by the Learnxs Project from the federal and provincial governments and the J. P. Bickell Foundation. These grants allowed the Learnxs Directory to be further refined and extended to include the entire City of Toronto. Throughout 1974 and 1975, the Directory was distributed to schools, colleges, universities, libraries, social agencies, and citizen groups. During this period, the Toronto Board of Education continued to support the Project by providing facilities and services.

In the spring of 1975, the third edition of the Learnxs Directory was completed. It consisted of 213 pages, including six introductory pages describing its philosophy and use, and it contained 313 fully described contacts (people, places and organizations who agreed to be listed) plus over 200 partially described resources. A table of contents was placed at the beginning of the book and an eleven-page index at the back. This index listed the name of every resource in the Directory, as well as subject references, which greatly facilitated information retrieval.

The Directory was divided into thirteen, large, colour-coded sections – for example, Media and Health. Within these broad sections were fifty-nine subsections dealing with specific aspects of the topics. Each large section had its own table of contents listing all subsections contained within.

The page format allowed for a clear identification of the name, address, telephone number, contact person and description for each entry. As well, cross-references were included in some entries to guide users to additional information in other portions of the Directory.

SURVEY OF DIRECTORY USE

Part of the Learnxs process has always involved some form of evaluation of the use of the Learnxs Directory among the agents who receive it. The term "agent" refers to the person who orders the Directory and/or the person who is responsible for its use in the setting. As part of my thesis, I undertook a survey of these agents concerning the use of the third edition of the Directory. This survey involved the use of the Directory in elementary schools, junior high schools, secondary schools, alternative schools, post-secondary institutions, educational support services, public libraries and community services.

The agents saw the Directory as being of practical value to the learning needs of individuals and groups. However, its use by individuals was generally reserved for the older age levels; its use by the younger ages was restricted to group programs planned by professional staff.

These results are of interest in that Ontario Ministry of Education policy guidelines (*The Formative Years*, 1975) had stressed a more individualized approach to learning at the elementary level, while the predominant approach for older students and adults had been the group lecture method. On the one hand, it would seem from these results that younger students are not being adequately prepared for greater independence in learning. It would also seem that older students are assumed to have a sense of independence in learning which was not gained from earlier schooling experience and which is not being practiced in their later education.

The use of the Learnxs Directory by professionals in their program planning for group activities is certainly a valid one. However, if the intrinsic value of the directory as a vehicle to encourage independent learning is not being communicated by the professional, then a major objective of the Directory is not being met.

The survey indicated that the predominant source of information about the existence of the Directory within a setting was either through the "person in charge" or as a referral from a professional. Again, it would appear that the emphasis has been on ensuring that the user will be dependent on the professional rather than encouraged to learn and to seek information independently.

Although agents were asked to place the Directory in the most accessible locations within the settings, this was seldom done. Such omission also supports the premise that some agents or "persons in charge" viewed the Directory either as their own personal planning aid or as a specialized resource to be used selectively under their influence and control. Again, this role of the agent as "information-broker" would tend to create and reinforce learning dependencies rather than serving to encourage the growth of the independent learner.

It would appear that the Directory was proportionately more often used by students at the junior high or early adolescent age level. This could be a particularly crucial time to introduce and reinforce its use, as these students have a relatively high level of communication skills and their potential for mobility in out-of-school learning is enhanced. This would also seem to be an important period to develop independent study skills and an appreciation for lifelong learning.

Among professional and support staff, the Directory was seen as being used most often by school-related persons (e.g. teachers, librarians and consultants) as a program planning aid for group learning. The fact that other types of personnel were not involved would support the view that the Directory was seen as being of use only in relatively traditional settings. Schools used it for program planning and education assignments while other settings (e.g. public libraries) saw it to be of primary importance for special interests.

As far as age levels were concerned, agents' responses were limited to what they had experienced in their own setting. Use by individuals was most often favored by libraries in the non-school sector and by alternative schools in the public education sector. Programming for groups was strongest in alternative and junior high schools, with limited interest shown by community services in the non-school sector. Overall, it can be said that the Learnxs Directory has been more often seen as useful for planning group programs in school-related activities.

Alternative schools would seem to be the best proving ground for the implementation of the community resource learning concept in public education. These schools are small, intimate, and oriented towards exploring greater cooperation with home and community and to enriching the learning process. It is significant that the most consistent and varied use of the Directory was found in these settings.

THE INFORMATION-SHARING AND RETRIEVAL SYSTEM

Because of limited facilities and of overlap with the Learning Resources Exchange phase, it was decided to incorporate the Information-sharing and Retrieval System into the Learnxs Project. During the spring and summer of 1974, the Toronto Board of Education provided mainframe computer time and staff assistance to allow for the indexing of the Learnxs Directory and to investigate the use of microfiche.

Through a summer employment grant from the Ministry of Education, a survey was done of existing computer indexing systems. A "keyword retrieval system" was selected, and fifty entries from the Directory were used to test the system. The result was relatively satisfactory as this system would meet one of the long-term goals of Learnxs – to make the information in the Directory immediately accessible to direct requests at a computer terminal. However, the system was not user-oriented, would require a trained interpreter/counselor to access information, and would be quite expensive to operate. It was decided not to pursue a computer-assisted system until adequate financial support was available. (This would not be a problem with today's personal computers and software packages.)

SUBWAY ACADEMY

In May 1973, the Subway Academy proposal was incorporated into a report to the Toronto Board of Education from the Director of Education. Approval was given "in principle" for the establishment of a program for 60 students, using three portable classrooms at Eastern High School of Commerce (near the Donlands Subway Station).

The program would utilize administrative and clerical services of the host school but encourage curriculum and program development to be a shared responsibility of students, teacher-facilitators and parents. Students would pursue credits through independent study using community resources from the Learnxs Directory, attend classes in regular schools along the subway line on a contract-learning basis, integrate work experience into their program, or try a combination of these three approaches.

On September 4, 1973, Subway Academy began operation with three teacher-facilitators and 52 students (*Orbit*, "Profile of a School/22," 1973). It has proven to be one of the most successful of the alternative secondary schools. In 1976, when enrolment reached a hundred, Subway Academy II was established on the west side of the city.

LEARNXS FOUNDATION

The need was particularly pressing for the further implementation of the Learning Resources Exchange and the Information-Sharing and Retrieval System which required funding support other than through the Toronto Board of Education. Therefore, it was proposed that a nonprofit community organization, known as the Learnxs Foundation, be established with the following objectives:

- to solicit funds from private and public sources for the purpose of providing short-term funding for innovative programs within the Toronto system;
- to accumulate sufficient capital to begin making grants to innovative programs from earned interest;
- to encourage each program to document its developmental process by providing additional research funds;
- to assist schools and community groups in developing program proposals to be supported through alternate sources of funding.

(A detailed description of the Learnxs Foundation proposal is contained in Chapter 9.)

Once the decision had been made to maintain phases one and two of the Learnxs proposal as a community education project separate from the Toronto Board but drawing upon its facilities and services, there was a need to establish an external funding base. Potential funders of community projects (such as government, charitable foundations, and business and industry) usually require that the recipient have at least a charitable registration number to ensure that the donor qualifies for tax exempt status. It is also often a distinct advantage for the receiving organization to have a charter of incorporation.

There have been examples in the United States and Canada of municipalities establishing charitable foundations to raise money to assist in the support of worthy projects that could not be funded exclusively through the tax base. These foundations could often qualify to receive private funds which were unavailable to the public body. This was the rationale behind the establishment of the Learnxs Foundation as a community organization which was legally independent but was required "to apply the resources of the Corporation by gift or grant to the Board of Education for the City of Toronto or its successors and to other organizations and groups working in cooperation with the said Board of Education or its successors for the development and advancement of preschool, elementary, secondary and adult educational programmes, particularly of an innovative or experimental nature."

Again the Learnxs Foundation reflected this sense of interdependence in that the Learnxs Project could solicit funds (or goods and services) through the Foundation, but the Foundation could also be used to receive funding to support worthy projects "of an innovative or experimental nature" which were identified by the Toronto Board or a related group.

LEARNXS AS AN INNOVATIVE PROCESS

Learnxs is unique in the study of demonstration projects because it does not operate within one particular formal organization, such as the Toronto Board of Education, but rather as a change mechanism relating to several different organization and service sectors. It began with the premise that the use of community resources in education is a valid approach to learning for both individuals and groups. However, the process of organizing a demonstration project to test this premise resulted in a type of interdependence which emerged between Learnxs, as a small community-based nongovernmental organization, and the Toronto Board of Education, as a large, publicly supported arm of municipal government.

This cooperative relationship between the two organizations has created a mechanism for continuing innovation in a time of austerity. In other words, in promoting a certain end, a means was created which ultimately may be more important than the end itself.

The Learnxs method was not modeled on existing structures of organizational or institutional behaviour. It was developed as a support system to relate to the informational needs of nonformal learners who may inhabit formal institutions and organizations but still maintain their own nonformal style. To this end, Learnxs represents a departure from existing theories or innovation in public education in the following ways:

- It attempts to serve the nonformal learning needs of people at all age levels.
- It does not confine itself to one service sector (i.e. schools) but equally attempts to relate to other service organizations (i.e. libraries, recreation and social agencies).
- It is "people-centered," co-existing with traditional structures while operating on a different plane and relating to a different set of needs.
- It explores the use of different media resources to identify, source and disseminate information (print, telephone, computer).
- It is supported by alternate funding sources through the creation of a nonprofit organization which is community-based (i.e. Learnxs Foundation).
- It uses its contact with nonformal learners and program planners as a forum from which to evolve other concepts.
- It stresses shared decision-making and community involvement in all facets of its operation.

LEARNXS AS A DEMONSTRATION PROJECT

The demonstration project has not traditionally enjoyed a position of respect in public education or in the human services field in general. Because these projects have often been identified with short-term funding from external sources, there has been a tendency to dismiss their usefulness as a legitimate way of influencing social change and program development. This has been particularly true of job creation schemes, such as the federal Local Initiatives Program (or its successor Canada Works) and the student employment programs of the province of Ontario. Generally, these programs have been initiated out of community interests and dedicated to the identification of local needs and the creation of alternative service patterns. They have often been resented by the public service sector for creating expectations of new services and for identifying gaps in existing service patterns which municipal government may later be asked to fill. As a result, they have been viewed by many public administrators as a nuisance which must be tolerated but neither appreciated nor encouraged.

Such has not been the case, however, among private and voluntary service organizations, who have tended to use these projects to supplement their relatively meager budgets and to serve as an informal research and development source to guide their future programming. This method of organic planning has been a form of "action-research." Information gained through surveys to identify needs and assess user attitudes has been translated into new program directions through the creation of new resources or the reallocation of existing ones. The relatively small size and limited scope of operation of these organizations has enhanced this sense of flexibility and responsiveness.

This has not been the tradition in the public service sector, where a tiny fraction of the overall budget may be devoted to research and development and most of it allocated to maintaining and extending existing service patterns. This has often led to a lack of responsiveness to community needs and to program rigidity. The situation is further exacerbated in a time of declining revenues and fiscal restraint when energies may be directed toward retrenchment and systems maintenance, resulting in organizational stagnation.

It is in this type of climate where the value of the demonstration project as an action-research method to encourage internal growth, external responsiveness, and mutual cooperation among public and private organizations becomes apparent. The Learnxs Project has focused on "community-resource learning" as an area of need which was originally identified in educational theory but has more recently surfaced in government policies and community interests. Because of financial restraints and other program priorities, the Toronto Board of Education was not able to allocate resources to respond to this need. The creation of Learnxs as a community-based demonstration project using an action-research design represented an alternative approach to the solution of this problem.

Learnxs began with the hypothesis that the creation of a directory of community resources, to be utilized by schools and other service organizations, could be a way to demonstrate the relative importance of that portion of community education theory known as "community-resource learning." As a result, the demonstration project incorporated an action-research design to test this hypothesis. This was accomplished by initiating a new type of relationship between two organizations – one in the private sector and the other in the public education sector of municipal government.

A strength of this design is the creative problem-solving and flexibility which is integral to the process. It is my opinion that the establishment of a demonstration project can result in a special focus of energies and resources which normally are completely unrelated. This form of energy-sharing and creative communication can also result in a variety of "spin-off activities" and other outcomes which may ultimately eclipse the original intent of the exercise. For example, the Learnxs Foundation has sponsored other demonstration projects, as follows:

- *Project 121* – selected volunteers were trained to work with children with learning difficulties.
- *Community Learning Resources Consultant* – a person was employed to work with schools and community groups in developing community resource learning projects.
- *School Community Organization to Revitalize Education (SCORE)* – community resources were used to improve inner-city education.
- *Toronto Urban Studies Center* – a program to assist students and teachers to better understand and participate in urban living.
- *Student Employment Experience Center Project (SEEC)* – a job creation and remedial education project for Leaving School Early students (14- and 15-year-olds) through the establishment of cottage industries to develop employment skills.
- *Youth Ventures* – a program for 16–19-year-old dropouts based on the SEEC model described above.

Another important outcome of the Learnxs Project has been the establishment of *Learnxs Press* (1976) as a nonprofit publishing and distribution house for innovative materials in community education.

The Learnxs Project has also influenced the development by the Ontario Ministry of Education of a new supplement to the H.S.–1 curriculum entitled *The Cooperative Utilization of Community Resources for Diploma Credit Courses*. The writing of this document has paralleled the Learnxs process, and its principal author has been an ongoing supporter of the Learnxs concept. This supplement legitimizes community-resource learning at the secondary school level both philosophically and practically by allowing up to two-thirds of class time in any subject area to be spent learning in the community. This document should have a profound impact on secondary school programs in Ontario in the years to come.

LEARNXS AND EDUCATIONAL REFORM

Existing studies of learning patterns among adults (Tough, 1971; Fair, 1975) have clearly indicated that 80 per cent or more of their learning is of an nonformal, self-directed nature. That is, they rely upon their own personal contacts with individuals and groups as well as their access to various types of learning materials. There is also a strong indication that similar patterns of nonformal learning may exist for youth and children (Tough, 1971).

If this form of non-institutional learning is so pervasive, is there a need to actively support its growth and development? It is my opinion that our traditional method of institutional schooling has been largely devoted to the creation of learning dependencies rather than enhancing the natural tendency of students to be nonformal, independent learners. This reliance on patterns of dependent learning (i.e. student dependent upon teacher for content) may have seriously inhibited whatever innate abilities teachers have to be encouragers and facilitators of student learning. If the function of the brain is to organize individual experience, the development of inquiry skills among teachers and students is essential to maximize their potentials as nonformal lifelong learners.

A major prerequisite of nonformal learning is access to new sources of information and skills. The creation of a catalog of learning resources (and other types of information systems) will increase the access of nonformal learners to a greater variety of learning options. These people, places, objects and media materials represent a learning process in themselves, each contact tending to identify other sources as the inquiry becomes more extensive.

Schools, libraries, and other social and recreational agencies represent a major socializing influence on our society. The people who operate these institutional settings should be made more aware of nonformal learning theory and practice. More opportunities should be found to modify existing curricula and programs so as to sharpen inquiry skills and enhance the flow of information about learning resources in the community. If these resources can become a legitimate part of the formal (as well as the nonformal) learning process, the true potential of lifelong learning may begin to be realized.

The Learnxs Directory represents a valid model to achieve this goal. Students and other learners can be involved in the process of identifying, recording, and cataloging learning resources as a community project. This process in itself is a learning experience which develops inquiry skills and increases the flow of information among community members. The end product forms an informational network which can be updated regularly and used as a resource for individual learning and programming for interest groups. It is my opinion, however, that more research needs to be done on this model to assess further its potential as a renewable information system in a variety of settings involving both print and electronic applications (e.g.

microcomputers). In addition, more research should also be done on the nonformal learning patterns of children and youth.

The establishment of a private charitable foundation, as a non-governmental body which develops cooperative interdependence with a large governmental organization, can be an important source of support for demonstration projects in a period of austerity and fiscal restraint. Through the pooling of public and private resources, it may still be possible to ensure a sense of creative activity and program excellence at a time when public organizations are struggling to maintain themselves.

A private foundation attached to a public body can also serve as a vehicle for committed persons from the public body and the community at large to participate in joint problem-solving and collective action. Additional research could be done, however, on the potential effect that this organizational interdependence might have on public decision-making.

In summary, Learnxs was developed around the hypothesis that community resources could be better utilized to enhance learning among individuals and groups. The results of the study support this hypothesis both in the availability and use of community resources for learning and in the development of a process model for a demonstration project in community education. As we enter a new era in our history, which some have described as the "conserver society," these findings seem not only important but also vital to the future of public education (Shuttleworth, 1981).

THE POLITICS OF INNOVATION

One theory of innovation in public education is proposed by Ernest R. House (1976) who lists a framework of nine factors to determine whether an innovation will be accepted and used. If the Learnxs method is compared to this framework, the following similarities and differences emerge:

1 "Innovation diffusion depends on face-to-face, personal contact."

By its very nature, the Learning Exchange System, in attempting to compile a catalog of people willing to share their interests and skills with others, encouraged personal contact. The cataloging process involved extensive contacts with potential contributors in the system. Part of the service offered, in the beginning, to agents of the Directory was a personal visit and demonstration of how it could be used as an aid to individual learning and program planning. The staff also made presentations to groups of teachers, principals, librarians, recreationists and social service workers. There was, indeed, a recognition that one of the best ways to spread the word is through the grapevine within communities of interest.

2 "Two of the major determinants of face-to-face personal contact – and hence of innovative diffusion – are transportation routes and organizational structure."

Learnxs was first conceived to be a source of information about learning resources for individuals within the east section of the City of Toronto but was later extended to cover the whole city. Interest in the idea, however, spread throughout Metropolitan Toronto and beyond. Those factors which seemed to have the most influence on this growth were direct mailing and word-of-mouth publicity.

The prime objective of the Learnxs Project had been to encourage the use of the Directory and data base by as many people as possible within the Metro Toronto region. Although there had also been some interest in seeing this approach repeated in other areas, this had been a secondary consideration. Therefore, any concern about spreading the idea along geographical lines from center to center did not apply (i.e. from one organization or school board to another).

3 "The superintendent (and his top staff) play a key role in introducing innovations into their districts, since they have the most outside contact."

House refers to two types of superintendent: place-bound (i.e. one who stays in one place and rises through the ranks); and career-bound (i.e. one who is brought in from the outside, is less affected by traditional roles and is more liable to innovate to build a reputation).

The Director of Education in Toronto at the time that the Learning Exchange System proposal was drafted was very much a "place-bound superintendent" in that he had spent his entire career with the Toronto Board (except for a brief period with the Metro School Board). However, he had long been considered a progressive educator and he was under considerable pressure to act as an innovator by a reform-minded group of trustees.

4 "The politics of the central office staff play a key role in promoting or inhibiting innovation within the district."

I was hired by the Director as a "change agent" to develop new programs in the area of school–community relationships. In this regard, I had access to the Director and a sense of his commitment to support innovative projects. Other central office staff were generally not supportive of school–community initiatives although they too were feeling pressure from the trustees. The fact that I was given responsibility to establish a Cooperative Education Work Group, with a membership of Board staff and community representatives which would report directly to the trustees, allowed the Learnxs project to avoid being blocked by central office politics.

5 "The successful implementation of an innovation ultimately depends on whether an internal advocacy group is formed around it."

House describes the advocacy group as "a small group of people who enthusiastically protect and propagate the innovation." In the case of the Learning Exchange System, there were really three groups that assumed an advocacy role. The first was the Cooperative Education Work Group which initiated the proposal and presented it to the trustees of the Toronto Board. The second was the Learnxs Task Group which developed ongoing policy for the Project and aided in its promotion beyond the realm of schools and formal education. The third and most influential group was the Learnxs Foundation, whose membership of Board administrators, trustees and community representatives oversaw the financing and material support for the Project.

6 "The teacher has very limited access to new ideas and innovations."

The primary sources of contact which the Learnxs Project had with teachers were through principals, vice-principals, library-resource teachers or curriculum consultants. Because Learnxs materials had to be purchased, it required someone with access to a budget for supplies or library books to agree to their acquisition. In the same respect, if those people did not understand or support the concept, teachers would most often never be informed about Learnxs. Those teachers who did acquire the materials usually found out about them from colleagues, acquaintances or through media coverage.

7 "There are few tangible incentives for a teacher to engage in innovation."

The principal sets the tone for the way learning will be defined within a given school. If a classroom teacher wishes to encourage independent study or the use of informal learning resources, it is most difficult without a feeling of understanding and support from the principal. This is particularly essential as the principal is an evaluator of the teacher's performance and a most important source of recommendation for career advancement. Those teachers who choose "to go their own way" where the educational climate is not supportive of this form of innovation may inhibit rather than advance their chances for promotion.

In terms of job satisfaction, traditional classroom practice has been the group instruction method. To experiment with a different, more individualized, approach to learning could result in criticism and alienation from more traditional colleagues. It would seem that incentives, which might exist for the classroom teacher, would more often be of the negative rather than the positive variety.

8   "What is rational for the teacher may not be rational for the administrator or reformer and vice versa."

An innovation, such as the Learning Exchange System, may place the administrator in a real quandary. If he supports the concept, he may find himself running against the tide of professional acceptance and public opinion. Many administrators may attempt to remain in the middle of the road by seeming to be open to innovation but being very careful not to offend the traditionalists. Most often this results in an impossible compromise.

Another important consideration is how the innovation is funded. The use of external sources may enhance the flexibility of the project but never result in any real commitment on the part of the organization. This allows the administrator to support the concept as long as someone else is footing the bill but to back away conveniently when external assistance decreases.

9   "Innovation can be enhanced by increasing interpersonal contact and by restructuring incentives within the school district. (Or it can be decreased by the opposite.)"

House maintains that change ultimately comes about through "face-to-face" contact. An organization with a greater sense of openness to external influences is more liable to support the initiation and ongoing maintenance of an innovation.

By its very nature, Learnxs represented a communications network of information and ideas to open up individuals and organizations to change. Besides being an innovation in its own right, it had the potential to be a change-agent for those who used it. As simply an information system coming from external sources, however, it lacked a sense of official recognition and prestige which might have served as an incentive for people to use it.

The House factors provide an overview of innovation and change within one type of organization known as a School Board. Because the Learning Exchange System had its origins within such an organization, many of his observations are quite appropriate in the beginning. The problem lies in the fact that, when you move beyond a single organization or group of individuals and begin to relate across organizational structures, his premises no longer are as relevant. However, they may serve as a starting point to begin to develop a new framework for innovations in community education which crosses organizational lines.

William W. Biddle and Loureide J. Biddle (1965) define community as "whatever sense of common good people can achieve." Their approach to social change involves a "community development process." Community development is

a process of social action in which the people of a community organize themselves for planning and action; define their common and individual needs and problems; execute these plans with a maximum reliance on community resources; and supplement these resources when necessary with services and materials from governmental and non-governmental agencies outside the community.

According to Biddle and Biddle, the *community development process* refers to

a progression of events that is planned by the participants to serve goals they progressively choose. The events point to changes in a group and in individuals that can be termed growth in social sensitivity and competence.

They maintain that the encouragement of initiative does not occur on an unplanned basis. It has to do with a group of people who discover the process, organize it and make it work. They refer to this social entity as a *nucleus*. This is the group that "thinks out the steps to be taken, plans the actions and reflects upon the events to learn from them."

Membership in a nucleus is "voluntary and open to all who will give time to meetings, to study, to discussion, to planning and to criticism of ideas, actions and themselves."

According to these definitions, Learnxs would qualify as a community development process in that it did involve a progression of events planned by the participants to serve goals which they progressively chose. However, instead of one nucleus, Learnxs had a succession of small groups which thought out the steps to be taken, planned the action and reflected upon the events to learn from them. The first nucleus group was the *Subcommittee on School Community Learning Resources* which conceived the idea and drafted the proposal. The second was the *Cooperative Education Work Group* which legitimized the proposal and planned a strategy for its initiation. The third nucleus group was the *Learnxs Task Group* which planned and guided its implementation and evaluated its progress. The fourth nucleus group has been the *Learnxs Foundation* which eventually became the parent body to the Project by providing an ongoing source of funds and support through goods and services.

Responsibility for the process may rest upon just one person or upon several. Biddle and Biddle refer to the role of the *community developer* as a special type of change agent who "encourages indigenous participant growth." In the context of the Learnxs process, I assumed the role of the "community developer."

In general, Biddle and Biddle offer an insight into social change as a group process from a community perspective. Their major stages of Exploratory, Organizational, Discussional, Action, New Projects and Continuation might be utilized in building a new process model for the Learnxs Project.

Therefore, it is proposed to relate Everett Rogers' general theory of diffusion of ideas (1962) and House's theories of innovative acceptance within public education (1976) as background to a group process model derived from community development. It is intended that a new theoretical framework will emerge to examine Learnxs as a process model for *the interdependency of governmental and nongovernmental organizations in community education.*

ORGANIZATIONAL INTERDEPENDENCE

This model represents an adoption of Biddle and Biddle's "outline for the process flow of a basic nucleus." However, it deals with the process of creating a bond of interdependency between governmental and non-governmental organizations in the interests of common overall goals. The major stages are as follows.

Stage One – Identification

A particular need or problem is identified which relates to both public education (i.e. governmental) and community interests (i.e. non-governmental) sectors. A group of public educators and community people would meet informally to further define the need. (This could be initiated from either the public education or community interest side.) Out of these informal meetings a sense of commitment to alleviate the need or solve the problem emerges. A joint "work group" of committed persons with a variety of interests and skills is established.

Stage Two – Exploration

One or more persons within the work group assume the role of "encourager or community developer." Surveys (e.g. interviews, questionnaires, informal meetings, data search) are undertaken to clarify needs, collect ideas and further identify potential resources (e.g. influence leaders, volunteer workers, seconded personnel, funds, goods and services, etc.)

among organizations and individuals within the public education and community sectors. Proposed alternatives and volunteers are examined and needs, ideas and potential resources are documented.

Stage Three – Formulation

The "first draft" of the project proposal, including an implementation schedule and evaluative design, is prepared for discussion within the work group. As a result of these discussions, the first draft is revised (usually more than once). Through consultation with selected influence leaders in public education and the community at large, a "tentative proposal" is prepared which is submitted to the work group for consideration. The work group then approves a "final proposal" as a basis of submission to support sources.

Stage Four – Application

The work group approaches a variety of possible "enablers" in both the governmental and nongovernmental sectors to create a support environment and to assess their degree of potential involvement (e.g. Boards of Education, Municipal Councils, Federal and Provincial Governments, Foundations, Service Clubs, Community Organizations, etc.). On the basis of this survey, the final proposal is restructured to reflect different types of emphasis and application procedures. Formal applications are submitted to both single and shared-funding sources and other means of support (i.e. goods and services).

Stage Five – Promotion

Informal promotional activity is undertaken to organize support for the applications among decision-makers and influence leaders. This promotional activity might also be formalized through the establishment of (or referral to) an ongoing support organization which could take the form of a nonprofit charitable foundation with the legal status required to receive funds (and/or goods and services) and issue tax-exempt receipts to donors. Smaller grants received might be used to form the basis (i.e. up-front money) of new applications to other sources which only provide support through matching funds.

Stage Six – Implementation

An adequate level of support (i.e. both short- and/or longer-term) is received to begin to implement the final proposal. At this point the original work group would disband to be replaced by a task group (or steering committee) of influence-leaders and resource persons who would guide, support and evaluate the implementation of the proposal as an ongoing project.

Stage Seven – Evaluation

Evaluation of the project (according to its original objectives) through the evaluation design and/or participant observation would be undertaken. This could result in the reassessment and redefinition of the original objectives and sources of support for the project (i.e. action-research design).

Stage Eight – Continuation

As a result of the evaluation procedures and/or spin-off activities from the original project, new needs might be identified and the process model as described above would *repeat* itself.

The next section will examine the development of the Learnxs process in relation to this *process model for interdependency of governmental and nongovernmental organizations in community education.*

EVALUATING THE PROCESS

Stage One of the process model refers to the origin or identification of the need. The Learning Exchange System was an outgrowth of an expressed need for greater relevancy in curriculum and program to combat a rising incidence of secondary school students leaving school before graduation. These general concerns were embodied in the work of the Toronto Board's Special Task Force on Education. Individuals and groups, such as the Metropolitan Toronto Labor Council, met with the Special Task Force and expressed a need for more education related to life-experience. As a result of these expressed needs, the final report of the Task Force proposed the establishment of a Cooperative Education Work Group, made up of Toronto Board staff and community representatives, to study the problem and make specific recommendations. Therefore, the Learnxs process, in terms of its origin, would qualify under Stage One of the process model. The need identified *curriculum related to life-experience*, had been recognized by community or nongovernmental interests as well as by the Toronto Board of Education as an organization of government.

Learnxs followed *Stage Two* of the model by undertaking a more intensive exploration of needs and the preparation of an inventory of ideas and potential resources. I operated as the *community developer or encourager* to the work group process. This role involved the encouragement of the flow of information and communications, both orally and through print materials, among Work Group members to enhance their participation and commitment to the process.

As there were two different areas of need identified, two subgroups (subcommittees) were established to report back to the main Work Group. The Subcommittee on School Community Learning Resources was really a consultative survey where interested Work Group members were joined by a number of external resource people (e.g. Metro Toronto Transportation Review, Ontario Institute for Studies in Education, Faculty of Library Science) to further clarify needs, share ideas and identify resources. In addition, supporting data in such areas as the dropout rate was compiled and a variety of individual contacts made to feed information into the exploratory process.

Consultation within the Subcommittee on Community Learning Resources resulted in *Stage Three*, the formulation of a draft proposal for a Learning Exchange System. This *first draft* was then submitted to the Cooperative Education Work Group. Discussion within the Work Group caused a modification and expansion of the body of this initial draft to form a *tentative proposal*. This new document was submitted to the Work Group and subsequently approved as the *final proposal*.

Stage Four of the process model involves the soliciting of support for the proposal among a variety of possible *enablers*. The Learnxs proposal was discussed informally with the Director of Education and staff of the Toronto Board and officials of the Ministry of Education and the federal Department of Manpower. As a result of these inquiries, an application, in the form of a report from the Director of Education, was prepared and presented to the Toronto Board to establish Subway Academy as phase three of the Learnxs proposal. A second application was prepared and submitted to the Experience '73 student employment program of the Ministry of Education to implement the Learning Resources Exchange as phase one of the proposal. A third application went to the Local Initiatives Program to fund the Resource Bank for Community Learning which allowed for the publishing and distribution of Edition I of the Directory.

Stage Five involves the lobbying of support for the applications among decision-makers and influence leaders. In the case of Learnxs, the Director of Education supported the Subway Academy section of the proposal by permitting a report to be written on his behalf to the Board. He also gave leadership in influencing staff to support the application should it be approved. Individual trustees were approached to better inform them about the report and to gain their support when it was considered first by the

School Programs Committee and later by the full Board. Further discussions were undertaken with the Ministry of Education concerning their policies on independent study and the use of community resources and relating these to the Student's Participating in Community Education grants program.

As an ongoing source of promotion and support for the Learnxs process, a report was prepared on behalf of the Director of Education to establish a nonprofit, charitable community-based foundation. Membership consisted of three staff members nominated by the Director of Education, three trustees nominated by the Chairman of the Board and three community representatives nominated by the Social Planning Council of Metropolitan Toronto. The intent of this nongovernmental community organization was to support innovative and experimental programs in community education (such as Learnxs) by soliciting, receiving and administering funds (and goods and services) not available to the Toronto Board of Education as a governmental organization. This report was subsequently approved by the Toronto Board.

Stage Six of the process model involves the implementation of the proposal after support has been received. The Learnxs process replaced the original work group with two *task groups*. The first task group was responsible for the Learning Resources Exchange and Information-Sharing and Retrieval System phases of the proposal. The second task group was established to guide the implementation of the Subway Academy phase of the proposal. Each task group consisted of interested and committed persons from the community as well as Toronto Board of Education staff.

Stage Seven calls for an ongoing evaluative procedure to be undertaken to assess the future growth and development of the project. The Learnxs process had five main sources of evaluation:

1 The use of the Directory (phase one) was subjected to an ongoing series of user surveys to determine how it was being used and how it could be improved.
2 The Learnxs Task Group was responsible for guiding and evaluating the progress of phases one and two of the original proposal.
3 The Subway Academy Task Group was responsible for guiding and evaluating phase three of the Learnxs proposal.
4 The funding and other sources of support used by the Learnxs project have exercised an indirect form of evaluation on the project in that without their confidence it would never have continued.
5 In the same respect, the consumers of the Learnxs service had to continue to support its growth and development to ensure its future.

Stage Eight relates to the new needs and spin-off activities identified in the evaluation procedure which might result in the stages of the process model being repeated. Again this was the experience of Learnxs as a demonstration project, particularly in the area of spin-off activities where new proposals were drafted and applications for support submitted. Examples of these would be as follows:

1 Each succeeding edition of the Directory required a new application for short-term funding which meant a repeat of at least Stages Four to Eight of the process model.
2 The Toronto Learning Center as an Integrated Service within the Education Center Building proposal was an outgrowth of the Information-Sharing and Retrieval System phases. It was later adopted by the Toronto Board as the *Community Information and Learning Exchange* and established in the main foyer of Education Center building.
3 Learnxs Press was a spin-off from the Learnxs Directory and Supplements which has allowed the Learnxs concept to continue as an integral part of a nonprofit publishing venture.

Therefore, the process model for the interdependency of governmental and nongovernmental organizations in community education, as defined earlier in this chapter, has been a valid theoretical framework for evaluating Learnxs as an innovative process.

Institutional schooling will probably continue to be the predominant means of formal education, at least to the end of this century. But there must be a recognition that technological change (such as the home computer), the information explosion, and the spiraling costs of traditional educational methods in an economy with a decreasing sense of financial commitment to human services will eventually lead to a radical redefinition of the role of public education in our society. It is essential that educators begin to direct their efforts to creating their own futures instead of falling victim to political and economic expediency.

Unfortunately, not enough is currently being done to prepare students, teachers and parents to cope with these changes. Learnxs has attempted to demonstrate the viability of an approach to learning which stresses the right of the individual to grow and develop using all available resources. The alternatives movement in public education from which Learnxs originates has attempted to help people to acquire the information and skills necessary to live with change in the belief that to create the future is to begin to solve the problems of today (Shuttleworth, 1978). The next chapter will explore sources of support for educational innovation in a context of social and economic renewal.

11 Resources for renewal

HOLISTIC ALTERNATIVES

The previous chapter described a project to identify and use community resources to enhance learning opportunities. It also described a process of local needs assessment and resource mobilization to resolve problems and encourage innovation. It has become increasingly apparent that social and economic renewal in the post-industrial era will require such a commitment to cooperation and creativity.

Education and training have a key role to play in this process of renewal. While science, technology and engineering expertise must combine with community enterprise to stimulate local employment and global competitiveness, education and training can provide the skills, information and attitudes necessary to survive in this transition to a new economic age.

These difficult times have also spawned an extensive array of holistic alternatives which encourage both social and economic outcomes. They are most often based on the assumption that needs and resources can be interrelated to find solutions, build self-reliance and reduce industrial-age dependencies.

Such holistic alternatives may represent the cutting-edge to the future. For example in the 1970s the so-called "hippies or counter-culture people" began the back-to-nature crusade which spawned the environmental movement. The implications of this movement are still shaking the earth as we scramble to "reduce, recycle and reuse." But without scientific research and development and the mass media, we would probably know little about the greenhouse effect, acid rain or toxic perils.

There is a danger, however, that just as most industrial-age thinkers and educators saw the counter-culture as a threat to their "established order," new-wave holistic alternatives may suffer a similar fate. Previous chapters have detailed a variety of school-to-work and economic development initiatives which have been responses to the changing times. The following is a sampling of alternative approaches and societal trends which may provide new insights into education and economic futures.

THE COMMUNITY SELF-SURVEY

The social and economic needs of a community can be assessed as part of a "community audit or survey" to gather information concerning the strengths, weaknesses, interests and attitudes of citizens, organizations or commerce. This "informational sounding" may be used as a basis for planning programs, services, economic strategies or just developing a better understanding of community needs.

The *Community Survey Handbook*, prepared by the Alberta Department of Advanced Education and Manpower, provides one insight into how a community may "survey itself" to assess local social and economic needs.

The community survey involves citizens directly in the process so that they became more aware and concerned about the community and more enthusiastic and responsive in addressing its needs. The survey has two main purposes:

• to gather information;
• to stimulate citizen interest in community affairs.

In planning a survey a group of concerned citizens, the *Initiating Group*, must first decide the purpose or "why" the survey is being undertaken. For example, it could be related to such topics as educational upgrading, leisure activities, employment training, business and industry profiles, environmental issues etc., or a combination of these. Next the group must decide the objectives, or "what" is to be accomplished including the particular types of information required to achieve each objective and the framework to collect the data.

The decisions reached regarding the purpose and objectives lead to the following considerations:

• methodology – how it will be done;
• time-line – when it will be done;
• resources – finding personnel and materials required.

Next a *Sponsoring Group* is required to take major responsibility for the overall organization, planning and implementation of the survey. They establish and maintain community cooperation by contacting key "influence leaders," other concerned citizens, community groups and organizations to discuss the objectives, methodology and focus of the survey. The Sponsoring Group might also be responsible for marketing the proposal to potential funding sources.

A *Steering Committee* develops a specific survey plan and an implementation schedule. Subcommittees might also be formed to pursue particular tasks (e.g. developing instrument, data collection, tabulating data etc.). An alternative would be to employ a project director (funds permitting) to coordinate tasks aided by fieldworkers.

The "instrument" (questionnaire or interview schedule) is constructed to reflect the questions solicited from the influence leaders by the Sponsoring Group. Questions would be ranked according to order of importance, frequency of response, length of the instrument and time restrictions.

The questioning format should ensure that the opinions and attitudes of people are reflected. Questions should be clear, concise and only contain one major idea. A decision has to be made whether there will be a closed format (i.e. questions not to be multiple-choice), open-ended or a combination of the two. A closed format obviously is an aid to tabulation but important sources of subjective opinion might be missed.

A pretest of the instrument is essential (e.g. 20–30 respondents) to ensure that questions or instructions are relevant to the objectives of the survey and the needs of the respondents. As a result of the pretest, the instrument may be revised to improve clarity and reduce ambiguity.

Some method of sampling must now be devised. For example the total survey population could be every citizen, every household, every employer, all the citizen organizations, all the service agencies or some combination of the above. Most often, however, some form of sampling is used. The two basic methods of selecting a sample are "arbitrary selection" or "random selection." Random selection is preferable for a community survey because every member of the population has "an equal and/or known chance of being included in the sample."

The first step in drawing a sample is to define the area to be studied according to the specific purpose of the survey. A list of households can be obtained from a city directory, electoral list or telephone directory. Similarly a listing of employers would be available from the city planning department or board of trade. Many municipalities now have an information center which lists community service agencies and citizen organizations.

Small towns and rural areas may represent a particular challenge. If a list of addresses is not available, a complete tour of the area may be necessary to mark households and employers on a map.

The sample size depends on the number of potential respondents in the area and the objectives of the study. All respondents are then numbered and a decision made as to the sample size. For example every person, household, employer or agency might complete the survey. Usually it is desirable to obtain a sample size to estimate a percentage figure which is within plus or minus 5 per cent of the responses to the instrument. If the whole population is surveyed a correct conclusion may be derived from the results 95 per cent of the time. To isolate a smaller, yet still valid, sample of the total potential respondents, a table of random numbers or a computer sampling system might be employed (e.g. a fraction of the total population becomes the sample).

Methods of collecting data are dependent upon the size of the sample and the time and resources available. The following methods are commonly used:

- Mailed questionnaires – respondents receive a letter of introduction, a questionnaire and a return envelope. While this is the easiest way to collect information, the return rate of the mailed questionnaire seldom exceeds 50 per cent.
- Telephone surveys – the sample, based on telephone directory listings, may be biased in that households without telephones and unlisted numbers are excluded. Other concerns relate to people refusing to be interviewed or not at home.
- Personal distribution and collection – the respondent is contacted personally by the volunteer or fieldworker who explains the survey, provides instructions and the time for pickup of the completed questionnaire. As a result additional survey information can often be collected and a higher response rate obtained.
- Personal interview (or interview schedule) – the interviewer records information directly, resulting in higher-quality data and a much better return rate. However, the interviewer must be carefully trained to ensure a consistent application of the instrument. Because this is usually a more expensive procedure, the size of sample is often smaller.

Information obtained is then tabulated, categorized and transferred to tables and charts for analysis.This has been traditionally done by hand, however, computer programs are now available to read and tabulate results of a closed or open format.

One of the main objectives of a community survey is to provide information about needs and resources to influence decision-making. A broad distribution of information gained is extremely important. Alternatives for dissemination are as follows:

- Summarized findings are presented to all persons involved in implementing the survey including influence leaders and participating community organizations.
- A "town meeting" might be convened with all organizations and the public at large invited to attend.

- The local media (e.g. newspaper, radio, television) would be solicited to broadcast survey findings;
- A series of presentations would be organized at meetings of community organizations, chambers of commerce, labor unions, service clubs etc., with groups encouraged to use survey results to influence program planning.
- Short summaries of results (2 to 4 pages) would be mass distributed to all community residents or households.

A case study of such a community survey was presented in Chapter 9, in which the *York Community Economic Development Committee*, comprising the key governmental, social and economic forces in the City of York, developed and implemented a community survey, among employers, with the following objectives (York Community Economic Development Committee, 1986):

1 To examine the attitudes of local industries in order to determine whether they were generally satisfied with their location in the City of York.
2 To determine what changes, if any, industry would like to see in the City of York.
3 To obtain an industrial profile of York, particularly industry needs, and the potential for further industrial development in the City.

The questionnaire used in the survey included three basic types of questions:

- *Profile questions* to provide general information about the respondents, for example, type of industry, number of employees, length of occupancy.
- *Substance questions* to provide empirical data, for example the extent to which business is done with other firms in their area, number of employees using public transit and whether it is difficult to find suitable employees when needed.
- *Subjective questions* to identify the respondents' opinions concerning a variety of issues related to the state of industry in the City of York.

The study population comprised all of those industries listed in the *1983 City of York Industrial Directory*. It was decided, to save time and avoid potentially skewed results, to reduce the size of subgroups which were not industrial in nature. A random sample of the subgroups (Contractors, Auto Body Shops and Auto and Miscellaneous Repair) was chosen and inserted into the total sample for representation. A total of 255 potential respondents, therefore, made up the sample.

The survey questions were open-ended and precoded to allow for a variety of comments concerning:

* the state of industry in the City of York;
* the needs of industrialists;
* the industrial level of satisfaction with their location in York.

The initial method of delivery adopted by researchers was a face-to-face interview by appointment. However, during the pretest, the researchers found that obtaining appointments with appropriate personnel was difficult. As a result the appointment aspect was dropped and the interviewer simply appeared at the door to conduct the survey.

In conducting the final survey the "face-to-face" method was supplemented with the addition of a "drop-off, call-back" option when a specific managerial person was unavailable. A copy of the survey was left, with a covering letter outlining the significance of the survey and advising that the interviewer would call back to pick up the completed questionnaire.

The results of all surveys were coded and entered onto a disk. The data was then run through the computer at York University using the "Statistical Analysis Systems" package. Totals for each response were obtained and numerous cross-tabulations were made.

A total of 123 completed questionnaires was received, representing a return rate of 49 per cent based on the original sample of 255 potential respondents. The overall results of the survey are included in Chapter 9. Of particular importance, however, is the response to the questions concerning whether firms could benefit from training or retraining of staff. Forty-eight per cent of the companies surveyed felt they could benefit from such training. When asked what form this training should take, almost everyone indicated that training would have to be done "in such a way as not to affect their business." "On-the-job" or "in-house" training, night schools or government grants were suggested ways to accomplish this objective. More specifically, employers indicated that "machine shop training, technical sketch reading, office administration, computer training and upgrading were areas where training could be beneficial" (York Community Economic Development Committee, 1986).

EDUCATION IN THE WORKPLACE

During the recession of 1981–82 the first management employees to be laid off among medium-sized firms were often training officers, followed by research and development personnel. It is ironic that at a time when cries from all sides focus on the need for more skill training and research and development to remain competitive, that decision-makers see these positions as superfluous. The old industrial axiom that "when things get tough you have to get lean and mean" seems as prevalent as ever. Perhaps it would be more relevant, however, to reflect on another saying "short-term gain equals long-term pain."

Many employers surveyed in the York Community Economic Development Committee survey, as quoted above, expressed a need for upgrading employee skills provided that it was not disruptive of the production process (i.e. "keep your eye on the bottom line"). The report of the Committee proposed that the resource-sharing and joint-venturing, that had created the project in the first place, be further expanded to address training needs in local business and industry.

As previously described, in Chapter 9, a new approach to workplace education and skill training evolved which was built on the foundation of needs identified and cooperation realized from the project. The Board of Education for the City of York joined forces with the Learning Enrichment Foundation (LEF) to create the *Microtron Center*. Vacant space on the ground floor of a local secondary school was recycled to provide accommodation for training in word and numerical processing, desk-top publishing and microelectronic assembly and repair.

During its first two years of operation, as a demonstration project, the Center was staffed by the Learning Enrichment Foundation but is now operated by the Board's Community Services Office. Training was provided to employees of the Board of Education, business and industry and community service agencies during the day, in the evenings and on Saturdays. The facility also served citizens of York and small businesses through general interest courses and advice regarding hardware and software acquisitions and use. Industrial partners in the process were Commodore Business Machines, Comspec Communications and Corel Systems.

To make the training even more accessible to employers the *Microtron Bus* was developed. An old "million-miler" school bus, previously owned by Humber College and then used by the Learning Enrichment Foundation for bus-driver training, was converted into a mobile training vehicle.

Using technology developed by a local boat-building firm a new outer shell was added and, with seats removed, eight work stations, cabinetry, heating, air-conditioning and an electrical generator were installed. With a driver/trainer employed by LEF, the Bus delivered computer training services directly to industries, hospitals, social agencies and public housing estates. Conversion costs and operating expenses for the bus project were assumed by the original sponsors of the Microtron Center plus user fees.

A most important element in the "education in the workplace" strategy, however, has been the *Adult Day School (ADS)* as described in Chapter 9.

The original Academic and Life Skills (ALS) coach concept (as described in Chapter 8) was incorporated into ADS in two ways:

1 The *Education for the Workplace* department in which regular teachers were assigned to workplace based training sites. Educational upgrading and language skills, were provided on a withdrawal basis, to complement training programs operated by LEF, Humber College and other training agencies (e.g. renovation and construction, computer skills, furniture upholstery, industrial sewing, healthcare aides, childcare assistants, food services and catering etc.) in response to employer needs.

2 The *Alternative Studies* department, an outgrowth of the original LEF *Action for Literacy in York (ALY)* project which provided independent study for home-bound individuals, has extended its services into the workplace. The *Adopt-an-Industry* program places teachers directly into the workplace to assess and deliver education and training skills to employees.

The availability of these services and the resulting sense of economic partnership have been cited as reasons for employers to remain in the City of York. The fact that teachers are gaining direct experience on the cutting-edge of manufacturing, service provisions and training has also enriched their knowledge-base, instructional skills and relevancy to the workplace.

THE FULL SERVICE INCUBATOR

Small-business incubators (as described in Chapter 7) have had an outstanding rate of success in assisting new enterprises to become established and prosper. A survey of 120 US and Canadian incubators conducted by the National Business Incubator Association in 1990 discovered that 22 per cent of tenants leave "the womb" each year, creating free-standing businesses and new jobs for their communities. In 1989 the incubators studied graduated 270 businesses representing 1,850 new jobs.

Other studies have shown that four out of five companies that go through an incubator process still exist after five years. By comparison four out of five companies that start up on their own tend to fail (Zeidenberg, 1990).

As described in Chapter 9, the York Business Opportunities Center (YBOC) has been another asset derived from the community economic development process in the City of York. YBOC is unique in the incubator world in that it provides a full range of "wrap-around" services to tenants or other companies who use YBOC. The *Tenant Program* has been the core service whereby new small businesses are leased space, usually between

500 and 2,000 square feet, in a vacant warehouse (27,000 square feet) which was converted by the Learning Enrichment Foundation (LEF) renovation and construction trainees. Rental rates are substantially below current market value. Both full-time and part-time tenants are provided with a number of services as part of their tenancy such as:

* typing, word-processing and computer skills provided by Adult Day School staff and advanced business students:
* shared reception, messaging and facsimile services;
* a workplace childcare facility;
* on-site networking, collective problem-solving and shared marketing and sourcing among tenants;
* the use of a conference room for business meetings;
* a fully stocked and maintained self-help business resource center;
* on-site business consultants to assist in preparing a business plan or prospectus;
* a referral network to access professional services and venture capital sources;
* assistance in recruiting and training staff through LEF employment and training programs and the Adult Day School.

The on-site workplace childcare center is provided for resident entrepreneurs to ease the problem that may occur when childcare needs conflict with the heavy demands of an entrepreneurial career. Tenants are able to devote quality time to their business knowing their children are being cared for in a quality-conscious on-site childcare facility.

Another important benefit tenants receive is the services of on-site business consultants who assist in the areas of enterprise planning, market research, advertising, public relations and product development. A network of outside professionals broadens the resource base and matches the right consultants to the tenants' specific needs.

Outside business clients receive specially tailored workshops, seminars and on-site consulting. They can also access office services through the *Business Address Package*. Other outreach programs include:

* Small Business Owner Development Program;
* Enterprise Planning System;
* "How to Start a Business" seminars.

To quote the LEF *Partners in Progress* publication:

> YBOC is more than just a place to rent space. It is an experience designed to give a new business the supportive environment it needs to make their entrepreneurial dream a reality. Over the years all of YBOC's

objectives have been achieved. We have created a dynamic, entrepreneurial environment for small growing companies. Their growth has had a positive impact on the local community.

(Learning Enrichment Foundation, 1990a)

The "bottom-line" of any business enterprise, however, is its productivity. During the period from March 31, 1987 to March 31, 1991, YBOC reported the following benefits:

- Businesses assisted
  - – Full-time/part-time tenant program   50
  - – Skills development programs   215
  - – Business counseling   1,320
  - – Total number of businesses assisted   1,585
- Jobs created by full-time and part-time tenants
  - – Full-time jobs   155
  - – Part-time jobs   75
  - – Total jobs created   230
- Aggregate sales of full-time and part-time tenants $12,442,013

WOMEN ENTREPRENEURS

The fastest growing sector of small enterprise development in North America has been among women. In 1977 a US Census Bureau Survey of women-owned businesses reported that such businesses made up 7.1 per cent of all firms. From 1977 to 1980 the number of female-operated, nonfarm sole proprietorships increased by 33 per cent as compared to 11 per cent for men (Gould and Lyman, 1984).

More recent studies indicate women have failure rates of only 1 out of 5 as opposed to their male counterparts' record of 4 out of 5. Women now own more than 40 per cent of all retail stores in the United States and 35 per cent of all service companies (Atwood, 1990).

In Canada, the Federal Business Development Bank reports that after five years, twice as many businesses started by women are going strong as compared to those started by men and it takes only two years for women to boast a 2 to 1 success rate over men. The number of women-led firms grew five times more quickly than their male-owned counterparts from 1981 to 1986. The most outstanding growth has been in the business and personal services sector. While the growth rate in such businesses owned by men was nearly 22 per cent, growth of those owned by women was more than double at 47 per cent (Brehl, 1990; Hilborn, 1990). About one-third of independent businesses in Canada are now owned by women and that is expected to rise 50 per cent by the year 2000 (Brennan, 1989). Some characteristics of, and factors influencing, this successful breed of women entrepreneurs are (Brehl, 1990; Hilborn, 1990):

- Women plan their businesses more carefully, starting with the initial business plan and continuing through day-to-day operations.
- There is often less pressure on women because their business is a secondary source of income for the family – people perform better without excessive pressure.
- It allows them to raise a family while earning a salary more easily than if they work for someone else.
- Forty per cent of female entrepreneurs are between the ages of 35 and 40.
- Nearly one out of three have postsecondary education and more than 50 per cent are involved in the service sector.

Some of the constraints on their successful entrepreneurial efforts are (Gould and Lyman, 1984):

- no central source of information and referral;
- isolation and a lack of self-confidence;
- lack of appropriate and affordable training programs;
- the need for support systems, such as childcare and a network of other women entrepreneurs.

One example of a community economic development organization which has targeted the needs of women is the Women's Economic Development Company (WEDCO) in Minnesota. As a business advisory agency, WEDCO is run "for women, by women." Located midway between Minneapolis and St. Paul, WEDCO works with a cross-section of clients, from the affluent to the very poor, emphasizing small-business start-ups.

Participants, grouped into monthly meetings of about 20 people each, explore the "pros and cons" of self-employment. They have the opportunity to meet women like themselves and to learn from each other.

Once a client has developed a definite business idea, she attends an individual counseling session to learn what WEDCO can do to help and what alternative services there are available. If the client chooses to stay with WEDCO a simple contract is signed.

To assist in developing a business plan, clients go through a series of counseling sessions. Each session includes an individual sheet of questions to be discussed by the counselor and client. A completed questionnaire is brought to the next interview which may involve a different member of the WEDCO team specializing in such areas as finance or market research.

Individual counseling sessions are supplemented by training modules consisting of three two-hour sessions. They are held in the evening for groups of four women at a time and are rerun every month (e.g. finance, employment/personnel matters, bookkeeping and marketing). Training manuals for both service businesses and manufacturing enterprises supplement the courses. Fees for counseling and training sessions are on a sliding scale depending upon the client's ability to pay.

WEDCO has persuaded local banks to adopt a standard format for business plans.

> Average bank loans for WEDCO clients have been $15,000–20,000. These are normally unsecured with repayments starting after two months. To date there have been no defaults, and for anyone refused by the bank, WEDCO has its own fund as a last resort.
>
> (Grayson, 1986)

The Learning Enrichment Foundation (LEF) has been another example of a community economic development organization which has particularly recognized the self-employment potentials of women. Training programs have made a special effort to recruit women in nontraditional roles (e.g. renovation and construction, carpentry). The York Business Opportunities Center provides wrap-around services such as childcare, networking, referral services and training programs particularly geared to the needs of women entrepreneurs. LEF itself is a role model of a very successful not-for-profit enterprise led primarily by women.

The Adult Day School (ADS) has always had a tradition of life skills across the curriculum which has been extremely responsive to women's needs and aspirations. Tutorial outreach, adopt-an-industry and entrepreneurial studies are other ADS programs which particularly target the self-employment potentials of women.

INTERGENERATIONAL CARING

Fortune magazine reports that women will represent two-thirds of the employees hired in the United States in the 1990s and 80 per cent of them will, at some time, have children. Moreover, half the women with children less than a year old already work full-time, a 100 per cent increase since 1970. By 1995, two-thirds of the twenty million American children under five will have a working mother (Smith, 1991). Unfortunately, women will not achieve their full potential as productive workforce participants unless affordable high-quality childcare is available.

However, another form of familial care is already on the horizon. Childcare concerns may soon be matched by parent-care needs as more and more workers become responsible for their aging parents. The financial and emotional burdens of eldercare can quickly drain both the energies and the bank accounts of working adults.

This promises to be a major concern in the United States, where twenty-nine million Americans are aged 65 or older. By 2030, their ranks will reach 65 million, almost a quarter of the population. We know that a large minority of the elderly require assistance with daily activities as follows:

- 17 per cent of 65–74-year-olds;
- 28 per cent of 75–84-year-olds;
- 49 per cent of those over 85.

Less than half of those who need such assistance get it (Smith, 1991).

The exploding need for sources of "intergenerational caring" may represent new employment opportunities, provided a skilled para-professional workforce is available in the community. While early childhood educators and healthcare professionals are the front-line of service provision for children and elders, there is a demonstrated need for ancillary support and maintenance personnel. Unemployed youth and redundant workers may represent an economical alternative in the emerging dilemma of how to provide high-quality community-based care at a price that the average family (and the tax-paying public) can afford.

It is a particular problem for smaller communities that lack the social service infrastructure that most large urban centers take for granted. Where the public sector cannot provide, or afford, such services, local entrepreneurial initiatives may bridge the gap. Community economic development activities might encourage cooperative enterprises, as well as not-for-profit and profit-oriented ventures, through the provision of skill-training for the unemployed.

For example, in the City of York the Learning Enrichment Foundation, in partnership with the Adult Day School, has developed and implemented a series of such initiatives in response to the employment needs of a very disadvantaged population.

Childcare Assistant Training is a 26-week program, sponsored by the federal government for unemployed people who are interested in working with children but have encountered barriers which make it difficult for them to achieve employment. They may require English as a second language (ESL) instruction or academic upgrading before they can be considered for jobs in the childcare field.

Trainees attend theory classes, are given individual tutorials and work under close supervision in LEF Childcare Centers, kindergarten programs and childcare/drop-in centers. They benefit not only from the on-site program but also from the supportive environment created for them by the placement supervisors. Life-skills counseling includes discussions on how to overcome employment barriers, assistance with résumé writing, job-search skills and employment preparation and maintenance. "Role playing" allows trainees to examine specific situations such as "how to handle a job interview." ESL and academic upgrading is provided in the workplace by teachers from the Board of Education for the City of York.

Participants receive an hourly wage equivalent to the provincial minimum wage for their 40 hours of work per week during the training period. After graduation, trainees may choose to continue their studies to achieve a diploma in Early Childhood Education from a community college or seek employment as a Childcare Assistant. Graduates often continue to maintain contact with the program to receive remedial assistance, as needed, to secure full-time employment (Learning Enrichment Foundation, 1990b).

LEF also originally initiated the *Health Care Aide* (HCA) training program for employment-disadvantaged adults. These are individuals who lack the academic qualifications to gain admittance to a community college program but have had practical experience in the healthcare field. After a successful federally-sponsored pilot project operated by the Foundation, the program became part of the Adult Day School's Education for the Workplace Department.

Trainees receive healthcare theory and academic upgrading from ADS teachers who are also qualified nurses. Field experience is gained in local hospitals, chronic care facilities and seniors' residences where trainees learn the fundamentals of institutional care as well as practical skills which could be related to an entrepreneurial career in home-support for the elderly. The program has been so successful that a Registered Nurses' Assistant (RNA) program was added in 1990 for HCA graduates and other unemployed persons.

Another community economic development process in response to the needs of senior citizens was undertaken in 1991 as a joint venture of ADS and the Community Services Office of the Board of Education. As related in the City of York Schools newsletter:

> They both had different goals – Ms. Denise Cross' goal was to meet the educational needs of her Business Studies class at the Adult Day School and Mrs. Rose DiVincenzo's goal was to meet the program needs of [Silverthorn Place] a new seniors' residence in York. Both collaborated to design a project that turned out to be an exciting learning experience for the students as well as a valuable intergenerational exchange with the seniors.
>
> Ms. Cross' entrepreneurship course includes a market research assignment that the students are responsible for completing. The seniors

had indicated an interest in some courses. To accomplish both goals, it was decided that the students would administer a survey to determine the education needs of the Silverthorn residents. From this survey, the Board could determine what courses to offer.

With the support of Mrs. DiVincenzo, the students were guided through the preparation, application, tabulation and interpretation of the survey. The students visited Silverthorn Place to administer the survey and conduct personal interviews. It was a great experience for the students and for Mrs. DiVincenzo as she is participating in the City of York's first Teacher Apprenticeship Program, but the testimonies of the students and seniors express it best.

From the seniors:

- "It's a wonderful idea. We need education for seniors in this place – its great to learn new things and meet new people."
- "Its a darn good thing to have the Board of Education think about seniors too."
- "Sometimes we're lonely – having the students here today has taken away some of that loneliness."

From the students:

- "The whole process was fun and exciting and very informative as well. It helped me to understand seniors more. In an educational sense, it gave us real-life experience on a survey project. Now we can go out and do our own surveys with confidence."
- "Doing a real-life survey sinks in a lot more. It's a much better way to learn. I could have read a text book six times and not understood it as well."
- "It's good practice for students to do a real-life survey. Now I'm not scared of becoming old. I got a lot of encouragement from these seniors. They have lots of energy and enthusiasm that I never knew they had."

For Ms. Cross' Adult Day School Business Studies students, this was student-centered learning at its best. For the seniors at Silverthorn Place, they will join over 1,000 other seniors this January as York Board students. Everyone wins!

(York Board of Education, 1991–92)

Intergenerational caring, whether for children, the elderly or the disabled, represents a new employment frontier which promises to both create jobs and provide an alternative to costly institutionalization. As the number of people in the population who are actually working continues to decline, there is a desperate need to find new innovative service strategies which benefit all our citizens.

COMPUTER LITERACY

As advances in microcomputer technology and accompanying software continue to have an impact on our daily life, a fundamental skill for future employment is computer literacy. Elementary and secondary schools have been introducing personal computers into the curriculum as teaching aids and as a focus for skill-training since the 1970s.

As previously described, the Microtron Center in the City of York (based on the ITEC model in the UK) was created to train personnel for the school board and local employers, adult learners and citizens of the community at large to be computer literate. The Microtron Bus allowed the Center to operate an outreach service to the workplace and low-income housing estates.

The Adult Day School, through its Business Skills Department, provides employment training in computer applications to immigrants, refugees and other unemployed persons. The Alternative Studies Department uses "lap-top" computers to serve the needs of "home-bound" learners and provides skill-training in the workplace.

A challenge, however, to both the Learning Enrichment Foundation and the Adult Day School has been the use of computer technology to assist students of English as a second language and basic literacy. For example, LEF's *Job Opportunities for You Employment Counseling Center (JOY)* serves youth, immigrants and social assistance recipients in their search for employment, employment training, or educational upgrading. Services are offered in as many as 26 languages since JOY's staff reflect the diverse cultural mix of the community it serves. Childcare is provided free for clients visiting the Center.

The Adult Day School operates a *Computer Assisted Language Instruction Unit (CALI)* at JOY, where computers are used to facilitate studies in English as a second language, literacy, numeracy or academic upgrading. In the process clients begin to acquire computer skills which are so essential for future training and employment opportunities.

Such a service has been particularly important for participants in the *African Immigrant Bridging Program* also located at JOY. This federal-government-funded program provides life-skills counseling, assistance with settlement issues, job-readiness training and employment assessment and placement, as well as language and academic upgrading utilizing CALI (Learning Enrichment Foundation, 1990b).

On the horizon, however, are more exciting innovations using *local area networks (LAN)* in which 8 to 10 personal computers are linked to a file-server to deliver such software packages as the following.

The Principle of the Alphabet Literacy System (PALS)

This system was developed by IBM for low-level adolescent and adult readers below the fifth grade level. Utilizing interactive video-disc touch screen technology, non-readers learn to use 44 letter–sound combinations. They see the symbols on the screen, hear the words, and practice writing them in a work journal and on the screen. The system is self-paced so the students can review their progress regularly. By the end of the program (90 to 100 hours) they can spell most of the words they can see.

To demonstrate the effectiveness and versatility of the PALS system, IBM formed a partnership with the LaSalle Street Cycle – a community development organization serving the Cabrini-Green public housing project in Chicago. Forty adult learners are bused regularly to the IBM Building's *Adult Learning Center*, where professional instructors and IBM volunteer-tutors utilize PALS and other IBM educational courseware to provide free upgrading in reading, mathematics, science, critical thinking and keyboarding skills. To quote David Cox, Literacy Programs Manager at IBM:

> This is something that must be done. There is such a thing as corporate responsibility. If that responsibility does not include teaching those who share the community with you to read, if it doesn't include helping to make them employable, then I don't know what it would include. And I don't know what it would say about us.
>
> (*Chicago*, 1990)

A pilot PALS program in British Columbia produced remarkable results, with students improving their literacy levels while working on the system one hour a day for 20 weeks. PALS takes the adult learner to about the grade 4 level where they then can continue on a system such as Pathfinder as described below (Lambe, 1991).

The Autoskill Component Reading Subskills program

Originally developed in Ottawa, Canada, this is a highly structured computer-based system to combat adult illiteracy. All students begin with a detailed computer assessment of their reading abilities. The program generates a personal profile which helps the instructor and the student understand the kinds of difficulties the student is having in reading. It also provides information for monitoring student progress graphically.

Autoskill has been used extensively with students of all age and ability levels. The program has been evaluated in elementary and secondary schools, community colleges, among disadvantaged and minority adults, in correctional institutions and in the workplace. In general, it has been reported to be four times more effective than conventional reading instruction as indicated by gains on independent tests of reading comprehension.

Pathfinder Learning System

This is a computer-managed competency-based, "mastery-learning" system. It provides self-paced, individualized instruction, through an IBM local area network, serving disadvantaged older adolescents and adults. An extensive "wrap-around" library of multi-media educational resources includes texts, kits, workbooks, videos, cassettes and instructional software. The curriculum, based on provincial or state guidelines, includes modules in reading and writing, mathematics, the social sciences, general science and employment/life skills up to the level of a high school diploma.

The program was originally designed in Toronto as part of the nonprofit Youth Employment Skills (YES) Canada Inc. project to give academic upgrading to 16–24-year-old school-leavers. To date Pathfinder has been established in 71 locations including high schools, community colleges, workplace settings, adult literacy programs, dropout and re-entry programs, correctional institutions and native upgrading programs. To quote George Power, interim president of Holland College in Prince Edward Island:

> To me it's a very powerful tool for managing student learning . . . . It's a state of the art learning opportunity for adult learners in this area.
>
> (Lambe, 1991)

The Almena Method

A prerequisite for computer-assisted learning is keyboarding skills. The *Almena Method* teaches the entire keyboard at once rather than one key at a time. Students learn to locate, without looking, all the letters of the alphabet, using correct finger positioning. According to the developers, children as young as seven years of age can learn the correct finger position and locate the appropriate keys by touch. Typically, a student will be able to touch-type at a rate of 10 words per minute after two full days of training.

The Almena Method is not a computer-dependent system. It is based on a 20-minute video demonstration followed by teacher-supported individual practice. A variety of software packages are available to assist students with skill development after the initial training (York Board of Education, 1990).

It should be stressed, however, that computer-assisted instructional technology complements, but does not replace, the teacher. As a teaching aid, it allows teachers to better individualize their programs and support learner needs. It offers a hands-on process in which students continue to service the material, at their own pace, until the information and skills are mastered. The role of the teacher, or learning facilitator, remains crucial to assess needs, reinforce accomplishments and build self-esteem.

ENVIRONMENTAL INITIATIVES

It has been said that the 1990s will be the "decade of the environment." A growing recognition that abusing the air, land and water will eventually destroy humanity has swept the world. Waste management and environmental protection also represent new potential sources of employment in both local communities and in the invention and production of new recycling and energy diversification technologies for the global marketplace (Ehrlich and Ehrlich, 1991).

As previously described, in Chapter 7, *Youth Ventures Developments of Metropolitan Toronto* did research and development on three environmentally-related initiatives to create sources of employment for disadvantaged young people.

Hydroponic units

City Farmer Hydroponic Gardens was designed to be an innovative and integrated enterprise to construct, operate and market produce from a test facility greenhouse and demonstrate, assemble and sell hydroponic gardens to the home and apartment market. A greenhouse facility of 14,000 square feet was to be constructed on the rooftop of a school, utilizing waste heat from the building (using heat exchangers) to ensure a year-round operation.

A prototype hydroponic unit would grow fresh vegetables, herbs and spices to be sold to the restaurant industry on a contract basis. The existing technology would be used as a demonstration model in the marketing of smaller 8-foot units to be manufactured for house and apartment installations.

As a not-for-profit business, the enterprise would utilize federal job-creation funding as venture capital in the three-year start-up phase. A suitable location (a rooftop playground at Eastdale Collegiate) would be donated by the Toronto Board of Education as well as assistance with design, engineering, construction and operating costs. City Farmer

Hydroponic Gardens would be incorporated as a not-for-profit corporation directed by a board comprised of representatives from the two sponsoring bodies (Youth Ventures and the Toronto Board of Education) knowledgeable business and community interests, the greenhouse manager and one worker. Any profit generated by the enterprise would be recycled back into the company or into a related community enterprise.

Hydroponic gardening is an intensive, carefully controlled form of agriculture in which plants are grown in liquid nutrients instead of soil. Given ideal temperature, light, humidity, oxygen, carbon dioxide and nutrient conditions, it is claimed to be ten times as intensive as growing tomatoes in soil, five times as intensive as growing cucumbers in soil and two and one-half times as intensive as growing lettuce in soil. Canada must import almost 50 per cent of its tomatoes, 30 per cent of other vegetables and has no year-round source of fresh herbs, leaf plants and seasonings used in salads and specialized cuisine. Having a dependable year-round access to such crops would ensure freshness and reduce travel and energy costs.

The City Farmer project would have employed five persons including a greenhouse manager, marketing manager and three laborers. The laborers, in particular, would be recruited from the ranks of disadvantaged unemployed youth in the area. The project might also have been a demonstration for environmental studies courses in neighboring elementary and secondary schools. Unfortunately, concerns that the project might not be self-sustaining and the limited potential for job creation resulted in City Farmer not being selected for funding by the federal government (Love, 1980).

Other forms of urban farming

Other, more conventional, urban farming projects elsewhere have met with greater success, however. The *Camden Garden Centre* covers just under one acre of once derelict land in the heart of inner London. Originally established as an employment/training project by the Borough of Camden, the garden center began with market research conducted by the London Business School. It concluded that a garden center would be an ideal enterprise in an area with a shortage of supply of garden and indoor plants. The availability of waste land and the skill-training needs of local unemployed youth were other positive features of the proposal.

Venture capital for the project was provided through a £100,000 bank loan guaranteed by the Wellcome Foundation. During less than two years of operation a revenue of £320,000 was achieved with a projected growth rate of 30 per cent per year.

A unique design has been incorporated with plants stored "upwards" along narrow paths with trellises, poles and other vertical structures to make good use of the limited space. A sunken garden and greenhouse display spring bulbs, bedding and rockery plants, aromatic alpine shrubs and trees. Racks of books, gardening tools, seeds, bagged compost and indoor plants complete the showing.

Almost 60 per cent of sales occur on spring weekends, with summer and autumn providing much reduced revenue. During the winter, plants are ordered and delivered while the Center is being prepared for the spring rush. The site is in a constant state of change to insure every inch of space is used to maximum advantage.

Staffing consists of two full-time managers, including a qualified horticulturalist and his assistant, a part-time administrator/bookkeeper and a part-time delivery driver. Six or seven trainees work at the Center full-time, with more brought in during peak periods. After three years they hope to achieve City and Guild qualifications. Not only should they have learned about running a garden center but a series of enterprising skills which can be applied to any business venture (Nash, 1985).

The South Bronx area of New York City has long had a reputation for desolation and urban decay. *GLIE Farms Inc. (GF)* was established in 1982 as a profit-making joint venture of the South Bronx 2000 Local Development Corporation Inc. and Group Live-in Experience Community Youth Program Inc., two not-for-profit community economic development organizations. Focusing on vacant land and an unemployed labor force, GF went into the production of high-value crops grown under glass for sale in the metropolitan area.

Initially GF specialized in bedding plants, vegetables and herbs supplied to New York's major restaurants. To this GF added a line of exotic vegetables and wild berries brought in from outside. In addition to delivering, GF decided to operate a mail order service.

Because of increased product demand, GF decided to expand beyond the limits of its original site. A $1.2 million loan from the Port Authority of New York enabled the construction of a purpose-built greenhouse of 14,000 square feet, incorporating computer-controlled heating and hydroponics.

In its first year of operation (1982), GF broke even on gross sales of $250,000. By 1984 sales had expanded to $500,000. With expansion into the new site, GF projected sales of $20 million by the end of the decade. In 1985 GF employed 27 full-time and three part-time workers drawn from the ranks of the unemployed in South Bronx. Despite the fact that this disadvantaged workforce is considered by many to be undependable, GF has experienced a turnover rate of less than 2 per cent.

The success of the venture seems to lie in the quality of its initial market research, fine-tuning of the product line, avoidance of middlemen and the ability to meet the quality control and service demands of its customers. In so doing GLIE Farms Inc. has carved out "an expanding and profitable commercial niche for itself" (Stares, 1985).

In order to create jobs for redundant employees Nippon Steel has converted one of its closed plants in northern Japan to house a new business – *mushroom growing*. Excess heat from a blast furnace still in operation is channeled through steam pipes to create a warm, moist climate ideal for cultivating mushrooms. Production is estimated at 60 tons per year with a projected profit in year two.

Through the flexibility of workers, unions and management, one-third of the former steel-workers accepted early retirement. The remainder found employment in this new agricultural industry. Thus the local economy was maintained and a surplus plant "recycled" to an alternative productive use (*Guardian*, 1985).

Wood recycling

Another Youth Ventures demonstration project was the recycling of waste wood as a source of fuel. A feasibility study discovered that the volume of waste wood discarded yearly in Metropolitan Toronto approaches 70,000 tons. This included industrial pallets, packaging from glass, furniture and appliance manufacturing and various waste from wood processing and tree maintenance. In fact 140 million industrial pallets (or skids) are discarded each year in the United States:

> Cut to firewood length (16 inches) these pallets would make an incredible pile four feet high and 12,066 miles long, or from New York to Los Angeles over four times . . . . Unfortunately, the vast majority of pallets are currently still buried, burned or dumped into the ocean, wasting valuable resources and damaging our environment. However, considering how well suited they are for fuel and the ever-increasing cost of heating oil and natural gas, pallets may soon become a respected source of fuelwood.
>
> (Wallin, 1980)

To explore the feasibility of collecting, processing and marketing discarded pallets as fuelwood, Youth Ventures established *York Wood Works* in 1982 as a one-year demonstration project utilizing job creation funding through the federal government's Canada Community Development Project. An abandoned warehouse became the site of an enterprise employing nine workers who collected discarded industrial pallets from local factories. Nails were removed and the hardwood cut into 16-inch lengths for sale as firewood to households in the community.

The use of more refined versions of biomass, in the form of wood waste or any other cellulose (plant) derived material, may have a very promising future in the energy-through-waste management field. *Woodex International Limited*, a subsidiary of Shell Canada Limited, has constructed three plants in Ontario and Quebec to process 315 tonnes per day (or 105,000 tonnes per year) of wood waste into palletized fuel as an alternative heating source to coal, oil or natural gas. The small pellets may be burned in stoker-fired equipment or pulverized for suspension burning. Woodex is being used successfully in industrial, commercial and domestic applications. Because the pellets have essentially no sulphur content, the sulphur dioxide and particulate emissions are negligible.

The workforce for a Woodex plant operating 24 hours per day would be 21 people. While plants, to date, have utilized waste from the lumber and pulp and paper industries, a facility to process wood and other plant waste from a municipal area would also seem to be feasible. In fact a smaller test unit has already been built in Japan to process waste from the demolition of wooden houses (Tellier, 1982).

An even more exciting innovation is on the horizon, however. Biomass-powered gas turbines, derived from jet aircraft engines, have been tested which generate electric power twice as efficiently as conventional coal, gas or nuclear power plants at approximately half the cost per kilowatt hour. Using the principle of co-generation feeding into the electricity grid, small biomass-fired gas turbines could then be located wherever a source of cellulose waste exists (e.g. forest products or waste disposal sites). Eventually excess cropland and substandard soil could be converted into "energy farms" raising hybrid poplar trees or other rapid-growth biomass to feed the gas turbine power plants. Most important, the clean-burning biomass would eliminate carbon dioxide emissions, and thus help to ease the greenhouse effect (*Futurist*, 1991).

The third area of exploration in the original Youth Ventures feasibility study was the recycling of waste paper from local offices, industries and households. Besides providing employment opportunities for that sector of the population most severely hit by high unemployment, Youth Ventures Recycling Inc. offered substantial benefits to the community through environmental protection and conservation. Approximately seventeen trees are required to produce one ton of paper. By the end of its third year of operation, Youth Ventures Recycling recovered more than 6,300 tons of paper and saved about 98,000 trees. In addition the fuel required to collect and process waste paper represents only 66 per cent of that needed to transport logs from forests to paper mills. Paper recovery also reduces the strain on our shrinking landfill reserves and diminishes water pollution generated by paper manufactured from virgin timber.

CREATIVE ENDEAVORS

Another feasibility study conducted through the Youth Ventures process was a *Visitors' Guide Service*. It was found that there was a strong demand for trained tourist guides to receive the 20 million visitors who arrive in Metropolitan Toronto annually. It is estimated that tourism contributes more than a billion dollars to the Metro Toronto economy each year, while the New York City area receives more than 20 billion dollars. Most European cities have a well-established professional guide service but no such program exists in Toronto or most other North American cities.

The development of a visitors' guide service would require the creation of an in-depth information base concerning points of historic, cultural, artistic, environmental, commercial and civic interest. A survey among incoming tour companies and visitor reception agencies to assess the need for trained multilingual guides to assist tourists and visitors would also be undertaken. Such a service could represent an ongoing source of employment for young people, recent immigrants or older redundant workers. It might also be a source of entrepreneurial opportunity for cooperative enterprise, as well as nonprofit or commercial ventures.

Economists have traditionally not seen the visual and performing arts as contributors to employment creation and the Gross National Product. Creative endeavors such as cinema, television, musical recordings, literary works, painting, sculpture, theater, concerts and athletics create millions of jobs and recycle billions of dollars within western economies each year. The fact that SONY, the high-tech electronics giant, has recently purchased Columbia Pictures, while the Walt Disney enterprises continue to expand their empire of fantasy and profitability demonstrates the importance of creative expression to the economy.

Where once a man of wealth might go to a safety deposit box to examine the paper symbols of his success he may now just look at his walls to admire his appreciating investment. In fact, works of artistic capital have risen several times faster than financial capital during the decade of the 1980s. The custodians of artistic wealth whether in galleries, museums, public or private collections now have responsibilities comparable to that of a very large banker as well as being caretakers of our cultural heritage.

But what of industrial products? While we value utility and efficiency in the products we purchase, design has almost as important a role to play. Italy has been a prime example of a nation which pulled itself out of the ashes of World War II to achieve one of the highest rates of economic growth in the western industrial world. This has not been a result of the successes of its many governments or labor/management cooperation but rather Italy's age-old commitment to artistic design which produces automobiles, garments and objects of utility which are truly beautiful to behold. Once more, as described in Chapter 2, a large part of the Italian success story continues to be the contributions of small enterprises.

To quote the renowned economist John Kenneth Galbraith:

> An important weakness of the modern industrial economy is traceable to the unsolved problem of great organization to the immobility and frequent inefficiency of the modern great private and public bureaucracy and its tendency to measure intelligence by whatever is being done and excellence by what most resembles what is already there. Association with the arts preserves a smaller, more flexible form of enterprise . . . . It is on the artistic tradition not less than on engineering and scientific excellence that economic security and progress depend. Those communities that are the richest in artistic tradition are also those that are most progressive in their economic performance and, I think, most resilient and secure in their economic structure.
>
> (Galbraith, 1983)

WORKER OWNERSHIP

As described in Chapter 7, the *Mondragon* movement has been particularly successful in developing worker-owned cooperatives in northern Spain. Cooperatives are businesses owned by their members. Members may use the businesses as consumers, work in the business as workers or produce goods for the company to process as producers. Members in any one of these three different kinds of cooperatives may fully understand their role as joint owners and shareholders in a business set up to benefit themselves (Gleeson, 1980). As reported in Chapter 4, Sweden has pioneered skill-training programs for school-leavers based on a cooperative enterprise model. But how do we prepare students for cooperative entrepreneurship before they leave school? *The Cooperative Resource Center (CRC)* at the Ontario Institute for Studies in Education has worked with teachers at both the elementary and secondary level to heighten their awareness of the potential role of cooperatives as a means of local enterprise development:

> Cooperatives play a vital and unique role in the economy of small and large communities. They are democratically structured businesses which are locally owned and operated by community members who directly benefit not only from the services provided, but also from their participation and involvement in enterprise management. Cooperatives have been organized to provide a myriad of services including banking,

insurance, health care, day care, agricultural marketing, retail, media production and many others.

(Lang, 1991)

CRC has developed a *Cooperative Youth Entrepreneurship Project* with the following objectives:

- To involve groups of young people working together towards a common goal, thereby affording them the opportunity to develop cooperative skills and social support in the learning process.
- To offer students an experience with a model for economic development which favors democratic values such as equity, equality, mutual self-help and participation.
- To offer students exposure to a different business model, different from single proprietorships, partnerships or private or public corporations, thereby broadening their awareness and giving them greater choice when making career/business decisions.
- To relate to other local co-ops and credit unions as part of a process of economic development which involves the sharing of resources and expertise.
- To create and manage a cooperative business to gain a sense of their own potential as community leaders, and as "social agents" shaping their economic and social destinies for the benefit of themselves and their local communities.
- To provide an opportunity for students to create work within their own communities as opposed to leaving to find work outside.

The Co-op Youth Entrepreneurs Project consists of five basic components (Lang, 1991):

1 Information and access to learning resources on cooperatives.
2 Expert consultation with students in small business development/ start-up using a co-op model.
3 Cooperative skill development sessions.
4 Matching of community resources with classroom needs through identi- fication of local co-ops which can provide expertise and/or assistance.
5 Possibility of small amounts of start-up funds for business ideas.

But what of the fate of older redundant workers whose jobs are lost owing to industrial restructuring? One innovative approach to this problem has been the *Philadelphia Association for Cooperative Enterprise (PACE)*. This nonprofit organization provides regional technical assistance to employee-owned enterprises. Founded in 1976, PACE is modeled on Mondragon in that it focuses its services on a geographic region.

When the A & P supermarket chain began shutting down stores in Philadelphia in 1982, the United Food and Commercial Workers Union (UFCW) saw the concept of worker ownership as a possible option for saving the jobs of its members. They approached PACE to provide assistance in strategic planning. As a result a network of six O & O (for "Owned & Operated") worker-owned Supermarkets was established in the Philadelphia area. The ultimate goal of the network was "to attain control over a large section of the food retailing market in order to promote community economic development and working conditions sensitive to the needs of the poor, working people, women and minorities" (Kreiner, 1987).

With the successful opening of the supermarkets, PACE has concentrated on food-related businesses drawing upon the following resources:

- *Union support* – PACE maintains a close working relationship with the United Food and Commercial Workers Union to source workers for new ventures, facilities for worker training and credit union resources for worker-equity loans.
- *Government and institutional support* – PACE has developed working relationships with state and city departments of commerce, quasi-governmental lending institutions, other lending institutions interested in worker-ownership and community development plus conventional lending sources.
- *Food industry support* – grocery wholesalers have provided a wide range of development assistance, including site evaluation, reviewing architectural drawings, preparing specifications for major systems, preparing floor plans, identifying equipment packages and developing relationships with engineers and other technicians.
- *Voluntary sector support* – to complement the limited resources of the credit union, PACE created the Interfaith Revolving Loan Fund (IRLF) in conjunction with the Philadelphia Catholic Archdiocese, the Philadelphia Episcopal Diocese and a broad range of church and foundation supporters to raise more than $1 million dollars for below-market loans, equity and debt financing.

It was anticipated that O & O stores would serve as the core of a more comprehensive food delivery system which would provide a protected market for more capital-intensive food production or processing enterprises. As a result, PACE began identifying food production or processing industries most conducive to worker-ownership. Market support, common problem-solving and economics of scale were seen as factors which encouraged PACE to continue this community economic development process in the food industry (Kreiner, 1987).

Unfortunately, the O & O experiment does not have a happy ending. By 1989, of the original six stores, only one was still in business. The others had succumbed to a combination of a shortage of ongoing investment capital, problems of wholesale supply and stiff competition from the larger chains. However, over the seven years of operation 200 jobs were maintained which otherwise would have been lost. The workers took pride in ownership and demonstrated the potential of employee ownership (Lindenfeld, 1990).

Recent research undertaken by the Canadian Employment and Immigration Commission (CEIC) has concluded that worker buy-outs should not be used primarily to rescue industries which are already in serious decline. Worker ownership should involve a gradual transition by successful unionized businesses with one of the following characteristics:

- the owners are retiring without a successor;
- they are larger companies which may be the targets of leveraged buy-out by outsiders;
- they are new start-ups on a limited basis in specific industries.

To ensure the success of the worker buy-out it was found that these conditions should prevail (*Making Waves*, 1991):

1 Maximum worker control through a collectively-held intermediary which allows block voting of worker holdings.
2 Adherence to cooperative principles, including one worker/one vote and allocation of surplus on the basis of labor participation.
3 Transfer of ownership gradually or all at once.
4 Little or no out-of-pocket investment of workers should be required. Nor will individual workers' contributions be taxable until cash is actually received.
5 The use of corporate assets to secure financing.
6 Nonworker, nonparticipating equity should be secured to assure that transactions are not overly leveraged.
7 Loans are to be repaid in a tax-advantaged fashion.

How strong is the movement towards employee ownership? Joseph Blasi reports:

> new research shows that if all worker-owned (US) stock is counted, employees have more than $150 billion-worth and control an average 12 per cent of the 1,000 largest US corporations. Employee ownership is reaching a critical mass that may soon affect how companies are run. This decade, worker-owners will be demanding input into corporate decisions in exchange for the use of their "patient capital."
>
> (Blasi, 1991)

SOCIAL INVESTMENT

A strength of both PACE and Mondragon has been their ability to create their own sources of financial security to support enterprise development. Because traditional sources of finance have been unwilling or unable to support community economic development, a number of different alternatives are being explored to provide venture capital for new enterprises. These new vehicles for social investment focus funds and expertise on technical assistance and careful venture monitoring, utilizing the talents of professional portfolio managers.

Churches in the United States have been in the vanguard of the movement towards social investment in support of new or young, sometimes unconventional, small-business ventures. For example, in 1973 the Protestant Episcopal Church and the United Church for Homeland Ministries committed equity capital to assist the *Illinois Neighborhood Development Corporation (INDC)* to purchase the *South Shore Bank (SSB)*. This, in turn, helped INDC to revitalize the South Shore, a run-down, predominantly black, lakefront area in Chicago. Numerous other church groups also maintained low-interest "development deposits" at SSB to help cover its high operating costs (Rolland, 1984).

During the period from 1973 to 1986, South Shore provided $63 million in new development loans while earning a better return on equity than most more conventional banks. With the reestablishment of a viable market economy many people have been willing to invest their time and money in the rehabilitation of older rental housing and create new businesses. To quote the INDC:

> Within the private sector lie the skills and capital necessary to rebuild urban neighborhoods. Essential elements for neighborhood development include local capacity to attract available resources; entrepreneurship for creatively combining debt, equity and skills from diverse sources; ability to attract private capital and foster community confidence and local control of money sources. Because banks are well-capitalized, self-sustaining, knowledgeable and trusted by area residents, banks can provide crucial support in any fight against neighborhood deterioration. But banks are prohibited by law from initiating development projects or investing equity capital . . . . SSB & INDC have demonstrated that dramatic lasting community renewal can be accomplished when the capital, credit, talent and power of a regulated commercial bank are combined with the investment initiatives of three non-bank development corporations.

Besides SSB, INDC owns and operates:

- *City Lands Corporation* – a real estate development company;
- *The Neighborhood Fund* – a venture capital company;
- *The Neighborhood Institute* – a not-for-profit organization that engages in remedial education, job training, creation and placement as well as cooperative housing development.

The South Shore Bank has demonstrated that neighborhood development loans to inner-city and minority group members are usually repaid as scheduled without incurring losses that are appreciably higher than those on more conventional loans. Although the costs of running a neighborhood bank tend to be higher, SSB has produced a surplus of over $1 million on a turnover of $63 million during its first 13 years of operation.

The INDC experience in social investment for economic development has resulted in the following conclusion:

> Community renewal can only occur if a local enabling institution provides financial resources and builds the confidence needed to induce the investment of savings of the local community. A local bank can best fulfil the role of encouraging local investment through the proactive offering of usable credit to local people. But at the same time the local bank can change the orientation of external investors and create conditions which will encourage more outside resources to flow into the community.
>
> (Eversley, 1987)

Another outstanding example of social investment in action has been the *Grameen Bank* in the desperately poor third-world nation of Bangladesh. Dr. Mohammed Yunus, a US-educated professor of economics, at the University of Chittagong, became disillusioned with traditional models of economic development. Yunus recalls:

> I began to try to learn economics from the lives of people. Among many things I noticed was a woman making bamboo stools, and having to borrow from the local trader to buy the bamboo. The same trader would buy the finished stools and give her a very low price. I made a list of 42 such people in the village – and I needed about $30 for all those 42 people.

As an experiment, Yunus went to a conventional bank to secure a loan, but was told that it was bank policy not to lend money to the poor. He finally persuaded them to give loans to the poor people in the village, using himself as a guarantor. The villagers, free of moneylenders charging usurious interest, were successful and began to save and reinvest. When he was still not able to convince the skeptical bankers, Yunus decided to set up his own bank.

Beginning with start-up capital from such organizations as the Ford Foundation, Yunus created the Grameen Bank. To date more than one million people have joined the bank's 900 branches serving 23,500 communities. Ninety-two per cent are landless, illiterate women who receive tiny loans to finance such enterprises as sewing, livestock raising and furniture making. All of this in a conservative Muslim society in which women are usually never allowed even to touch money.

In addition to offering loans at market rates, the bank runs literacy programs, schools and other social services. Using a system where groups of five people provide support for one another, Grameen has enjoyed an astounding repayment rate of 98 per cent as compared with some conventional banks in Bangladesh who get only 10 per cent of their money back (Miller, 1991). The Grameen experience has now become a model for anti-poverty programs in Africa, Latin America, Europe and North America.

The essence of the Grameen system has been *revolving loan funds (RLF)* whereby financing is made available to fill gaps left by the private financial market. The loans are called "revolving" because as they are repaid into the fund's capital base, repayments are used to make additional loans to other businesses. A study of RLFs undertaken in the United States by the Mt. Auburn Associates covering the period from 1982 to 1986 produced the following data:

- 32 per cent of RLFs were operated by economic development districts and multi-governmental agencies; 30 per cent by private nonprofits, 9 per cent by state governments; 16 per cent by city and town governments and 25 per cent by quasi-public institutions;
- the primary target of 46 per cent of the RLFs was manufacturing; 5 per cent targeted women and minority firms; and 8 per cent targeted firms in distressed areas;
- 61 per cent of the borrowers had less than 10 employees; 96 per cent less than 100 employees;
- 38 per cent of the borrowers were start-ups; 13 per cent established companies experiencing operating losses; 23 per cent established companies breaking even; and 26 per cent established companies with healthy profits;
- 14 per cent of the borrowers were women and 20 per cent minorities;
- 50 per cent of the borrowers were in manufacturing; 18 per cent in retail; and 17 per cent in services;
- 49 per cent of the loans were for less than $50,000; only 26 per cent were for over $100,000;
- 97 per cent of the loans were at fixed rates with the average interest rate charged three points below prime.

In general, the study concluded that "revolving loan funds" can provide communities with an effective tool for filling gaps in the local supply of business capital and, consequently, creating and retaining local jobs. RLFs serve firms that are most likely to be shut out of the private capital market, provide the types of financing that are most difficult to obtain and tend to finance firms with relatively high local employment impacts.

To be successful an RLF needs to develop realistic goals and a well-designed strategy based on a thorough understanding of the community's economy and financial market. An RLF that is willing to take higher risks than conventional financing is likely to produce greater economic benefits for the community. Higher-risk lending, however, must be accompanied by a capacity to monitor borrowers closely and provide effective management assistance when necessary (Mt. Auburn Associates, 1987).

A European example of a high risk venture capital fund is to be found in *Samenar* (meaning "to sow" in the local Occitan language), an agency concerned with the provision of seed money to support small enterprises in the southern French Alps. Building on a strong sense of local identity (not unlike Mondragon), Samenar managed to get local authorities, chambers of commerce and regional councils to contribute capital to establish a revolving loan fund. Their commitment covered a cross-section of political beliefs ranging from communist to socialist to right-wing. All agreed to share funding "as long as it helps to finance productive and creative initiatives for employment." The bank Crédit Agricole was a partner right from the start and the success of Samenar has persuaded other banks to participate in the fund. In its first two years of operation, Samenar invested in ten enterprises, including: SECIA – an electronics firm; Source du Cal Saint-Jean – a spring water distributor; Faissalle – a rusk-making firm; and a high-tech manufacturing company producing "molecules" used in pharmacy, chemistry and biology. During this period Samenar has not suffered a single business failure.

Because Samenar was originally the creation of a group of local entrepreneurs who pressed local government for assistance, they have been able to combine the strengths of the public and private sectors. Because the fund serves a range of municipalities in the region, representing varying political beliefs, the process has not become "politicized." Skeptics, including other local governments and conventional lending institutions, are now "beating a path" to Samenar's door (Kuenstler, 1986).

A credit union is really a money co-op made up of a group of people with a common bond who pool their money, make low-cost loans to each other and share any excess income. Therefore, a credit union, like any cooperative, is literally owned and operated by its members/customers.

One share in a credit union entitles you to one vote; 5,000 shares still entitles you to one vote, so no one group or individual can take control.

Credit unions, by their very nature, would be expected to be more conscious of the social and economic needs of the community. This is not always true, however, for in North America it appears that many credit unions act as if "they really would want to be banks."

An exception to this trend has been the *Bread & Roses Credit Union.* Bread & Roses was founded in 1978 by a group of 20 Metropolitan Toronto social action organizations. Bread & Roses offers two types of deposit accounts to its members: "bread" accounts pay a fixed rate of interest on the minimum monthly balance compounded semi-annually while "roses" accounts pay no interest. Interest earned on funds in roses accounts is used to reduce the amount of interest charged to small enterprises and not-for-profit business ventures which provide both social and economic benefits to the local community (Masters, 1980). By 1991 Bread & Roses had a membership of 1,300, with assets of $5 million (Bread & Roses Credit Union, 1991).

The Canadian province of Newfoundland and Labrador has provided another source of innovation to the social investment movement. *Development Savings Bonds (DSB)* are issued by the *Newfoundland & Labrador Development Corporation (NLDC)* and guaranteed by the provincial government. These five-year bonds are available in multiples of $100 (to a maximum of $100,000) and pay interest each year. They are on sale to provincial residents at all banks, trust companies, credit unions, investment dealers and through a payroll deduction plan. They pay a competitive rate of interest according to current market conditions but the rate has always been higher than Canada Savings Bonds. DSBs can be cashed- in, on any November 16 prior to maturity, can be used as collateral for a loan and can be sold or given to another person.

Money from the sale of DSBs stays in Newfoundland and Labrador to help build the province. Funds are used by NLDC, a community economic development organization formed in 1973, to assist small and medium-sized businesses through financial programs, technical and business support services. By helping businesses ranging from fishing to retailing, from manufacturing to tourism, NLDC creates jobs in the province with the highest rates of unemployment in Canada (more than 20 per cent). During the period from 1973 to 1989, NLDC approved loans of $92 million to 290 enterprises. Development Savings Bonds raise in excess of $21 million per year and each offering is typically sold out in eight days (NLDC, 1989).

BARTER TRADING

Bartering is a type of informal economy which is as old as civilization itself. Before the introduction of currency and coinage, communities depended upon mutual aid whereby goods and services were exchanged, resulting in neighborly interdependence and community self-reliance. A novel form of bartering services has emerged in the 1980s, known as "skills exchange." It can operate on a very small scale between neighbors or become complex in an urban community. It consists of people "providing a number of hours of skilled work to other members of the exchange in return for an equal number of hours of others' skilled work." In a capital-poor community, this informal economic exchange can contribute a source of employment, self-esteem and community well-being (Ross and Usher, 1986).

A unique approach to barter trading has emerged, in the Comax Valley on Vancouver Island, British Columbia, known as the *Local Exchange Trading System (LETS)*. Like many areas of Canada, the economy of Vancouver Island has much in common with the third world as it is heavily dependent upon natural resources. As exports of lumber disappear so do the money, jobs and self-respect of people used to "paying their own way." Because money is in short supply, even locally produced goods and services cannot be exchanged among its members.

In 1983 the people of the Comax Valley decided to do something about their situation through LETS – a computer-based barter system. To quote Michael Linton, the founder of the system:

Joe cuts firewood. Peter is a welder, and he wants wood but has no money. Joe doesn't want any welding. That's usually where it stops.

However, if Joe and Peter are members of the LETSystem, then Joe delivers the wood, and Peter picks up the phone. He dials the LETSystem office and says – "Hi, this is Peter, No. 48, please acknowledge Joe, No. 83, $75 green for firewood."

Joe's account balance increases and Peter's decreases by $75. In turn Joe employs the carpenter, the carpenter has a haircut, gets some clothes made, buys food from the farmer. The farmer now has a way to pay for a welder, so Peter gets to work again.

Margaret needs the brakes fixed on her car. She is billed for parts and taxes in federal dollars, which represent the essential outgoing costs involved, and pays the balance in green dollars.

And so it goes. The unit of exchange, the green dollar, remains where it is generated, providing a continually available source of liquidity. The ultimate resource of the community, the productive time of its members, need never be limited by lack of money.

(Racey, 1985)

LETS was established as a not-for-profit organization with a trustee who acts as an agent for the accountholders in the system. An information exchange and recording system are maintained so members can keep track of their transactions. The LETS agency uses a computer program and the telephone to update accounts. An imaginary currency, "green dollars," is related in value to the appropriate legal tender (i.e. federal dollars). All accounts start at zero but no money is actually received or issued. On the authority of an accountholder, a credit may be transferred from one account to another. Accountholders are also aware of each other's balance and turnover. Administrative costs are met through internal deductions from accounts on a cost-of-service basis.

Transactions may take place either totally in green dollars, or in part green and part federal dollars. Members receive a monthly print-out of "offers" and "requests." An astonishing variety of goods and services have been traded including masonry, carpentry, plumbing, auto repair, appliance repair, word-processing services, guitar repairs, photography, book-keeping, babysitting, well divining, sign painting, janitorial services, firewood, cooking and baking, farm produce, puppet shows, portrait painting, language lessons, navigation, wine-making, Tai-Chi, scuba diving, and childbirth education (Racey, 1985).

Success in the Comax Valley has resulted in LETSystems being established across Canada, in Australia, New Zealand and the United States. To quote a coordinator of the Toronto system:

> People who hear the LETS story generally want to sign up for it eagerly. Some are slow to take the first step of making the phone call. Others want to participate, but wonder what they really have to offer. But once they begin trying it out, it becomes a lot of fun. People find they suddenly have access to consumer goods and services that normally wouldn't fit in their budget.
>
> (Stanfield, 1991)

GLOBAL VENTURING

Canada is currently experiencing a nationalistic "buy Canadian" campaign in an effort to stimulate the economy. While this may represent a feeling of some comfort to local retailers who are concerned about "cross-border" shopping in the United States, what does this "shop at home" theme really mean in a global economy?

Unfortunately, few consumer goods today can be said to be completely made from indigenous materials, crafted by homegrown workers at local manufacturing plants and marketed by domestically inspired manufacturing strategies. For example a man's dress shirt marked "Made in Canada" may have the following history:

- designed in *Italy*;
- financed in the *U.S.A.*;
- assembled in *Hong Kong* (by *Vietnamese* refugees);
- with material from *China*;
- shipped by *Air France*;
- sold from a retail chain controlled by *UK* investors.

Let's try heavy equipment. The town of Greece, a suburb of Rochester, New York, recently voted to buy a John Deere dirt excavator, instead of a cheaper used Komatsu model, for purely nationalistic reasons. It was later discovered that both were products of American–Japanese joint ventures but the Komatsu was actually made in the USA while the John Deere model originated in Japan (Aarsteinsen, 1992).

The multinational interdependency of today's goods and services and the movement towards free trade blocks in Europe, North America and Southeast Asia has a strong message for local enterprise – "Produce locally but sell globally." Fortunately the electronic age has opened world markets to small businesses who never before had a chance "to walk on the world stage."

Facsimile machines, computer modems, and strategic alliances have reduced traditional dependencies on big business or big government to carry the economy. These new means of telecommunication have allowed relatively small producers of goods and services to establish their own trading networks with other such enterprises anywhere in the world in order to source and supply raw materials, technologies and expertise. As a result new small enterprise alliances are being activated which are based more on mutual respect, cooperation and resource-sharing, than traditional patterns of multinational clout and corporate muscle. This new style of joint-venturing ensures a rapid diffusion of knowledge, design, engineering expertise and market accessibility never before available to the small-business sector.

FINDING A NICHE

This chapter has showcased a series of holistic alternatives which are contributing to social and economic renewal. Common elements of these initiatives have been a focus on the needs of the community and the resources to develop small entrepreneurial ventures, not-for-profit and cooperative enterprises which can create employment, while contributing wealth to stimulate the local economy. Research, education and training are often integral components of this community economic development process.

A community self-survey may help to highlight gaps in goods and services. This knowledge may identify a "niche" which can be filled through the creation of an innovation or a small enterprise to address the need. The resulting product or service, while satisfying a local requirement, may also be exportable to other areas as part of a marketing strategy to increase production and expand employment.

For example, a stockpile of discarded automobile tires could focus the efforts of science and engineering expertise to invent a solution to the immediate problem. A recycling initiative might create employment but also develop a new technology which could be marketed to other communities, regions or nations faced with the same problem. The initial entrepreneurial venture now becomes the basis of a new environmental industry with global trading potential creating more jobs and a new economic niche for the community. This inward/outward visioning may be the essence of the "entrepreneurial city state" of the future.

By locating these new enterprises in the nurturing milieu of a small-business incubator, we further enhance their potential for success and create a climate where joint-venturing and marketing cooperatives can emerge and flourish. By incorporating training, childcare and other support services into this environment, we ensure that skills will be continuously upgraded and the familial needs of workers supported.

Intergenerational caring or "kin-care" is another expanding area of employment opportunity. In particular, eldercare in which older adults are assisted in remaining in their own homes, as opposed to institutional placement, represents a new service opportunity which is currently not being met in most western countries.

Computer literacy remains a basic requirement for future jobs in almost any field of employment. The software capabilities now exist to use the computer as a "mastery-learning" tool in educational upgrading at the same time as one is developing word-processing and design skills. The visual and performing arts which have long been relegated to being just a leisure-time pursuit are now being recognized as an economic engine generating both jobs and the creative skills so essential for survival in the global marketplace. As previously mentioned, environmental industries may be the new frontier of employment as we struggle to save the planet from toxic destruction.

How are we to find the organizational skills and financial resources for developing postindustrial enterprises? Worker ownership and cooperatives are certainly alternative styles of operation which appear to be on the rise in both goods-producing and service venues. The fact that profits are reinvested directly into the enterprise, and the destiny of the operation remains in the hands of the workers, may provide new ways of coping with industrial restructuring and employment dislocation.

The successes of social investment strategies through community-controlled banks, credit unions and revolving loan funds have become powerful instruments to stimulate entrepreneurship and local economic development. We appear to be rediscovering the barter system using computer technology to exchange skills and commodities.

Improvements in telecommunications offer small enterprises the opportunity "to walk on the world stage" by linking up with their counterparts in other countries to form new trading networks not dominated by large multinational industrial-age corporations. A common element to be found in most of these new-age endeavors has been the rise of the not-for-profit or *third sector*. Its ability to bridge the gap between the governmental and commercial for-profit sectors as part of a process of community economic development has been a 1980s phenomena of profound importance. Survival in the post-industrial age will require us to become more in tune with local needs and to mobilize resources for community betterment. The industrial-age spiral of ever-increasing wealth and prosperity no longer exists. We must learn to be better problem-solvers and resource-sharers as we learn to live with less in the shadow of a new millennium.

The final chapter will survey what "future-thinkers" have to say about the social and economic challenges of the twenty-first century. It will conclude with a projection of what community education and economic development could look like in the 1990s and beyond.

12 Creating tomorrow

FUTURESCAN

Social and economic theorists have had a lot to say about life in the twenty-first century. Not surprisingly, there is a diversity of opinion about the nature of needs and resources in the new age. The following is a sampling of beliefs.

Alvin Toffler

Alvin Toffler, author of *Powershift*, contends that companies must strengthen their organizations and let their employees be more creative if they are to survive. Those that encourage a bureaucratic style of thinking and limit the creativity of workers will be left behind in the emerging business environment. They must establish communication links from the bottom of the company to the top and use these links to react quickly to opportunities.

Companies should abandon the idea of "mass society" in which everyone wants the same kind of product. "Now we are seeing the increasing customization of distribution – niche marketing" (Adolph, 1989).

John Naisbitt and Patricia Aburdene

John Naisbitt and Patricia Aburdene, in their book *Megatrends 2000*, see economics becoming more important than ideologies, leading to less emphasis on war and military armament and more concern for global free trade. At the same time, the arts will take on an increasing importance as more people patronize theaters, concerts, museums and art galleries. A drive to preserve the uniqueness of language and culture will result in a drive to maintain national, religious and racial identities. The ongoing privatization and "contracting out" of goods and services in both government and the private sector will provide new opportunities for emerging entrepreneurial enterprises and employee ownership. The massive economic shift to the Pacific Rim will require countries to invest more in education, training, research and development to remain competitive. The majority of new jobs created will be filled by women, making such benefits as childcare, eldercare, maternity leave, flexible full-time/part-time work and home businesses so important. Finally there will be a new respect for the individual as the foundation of society, using technologies (e.g. computers, cellular phones and fax machines) to empower and reward individual initiative (Naisbitt and Aburdene, 1990).

William Van Dusen Wishard

William Van Dusen Wishard, a special assistant to the US Deputy Secretary of Commerce, in an article entitled *The 21st Century Economy* maintains that the primary force driving the world economy today is the flood of new knowledge from research laboratories which contribute to a doubling of the world's body of scientific knowledge every decade. This research results in new technology which becomes obsolete in five to seven years, while in electronics it is two to three years. Modern telecommunications ensures that research findings and technological innovation are soon integrated into worldwide production.

Manufacturing, as a percentage of the US Gross National Product has remained roughly the same from 1950 to 1986 (about 21 per cent). In fact manufacturing production rose 40 per cent between 1975 and 1985 yet there were 5 million fewer workers employed in blue-collar jobs. Therefore manufacturing itself is not declining, it is the employment in manufacturing which is decreasing – from 25 per cent of the workforce in 1980 to under 10 per cent by the year 2000.

But the production and trading of goods and services does not represent the majority of wealth created in the world each day. In fact the annual movement of money, whether through foreign exchange transactions or the investing and reinvesting of private pension funds, represents about 19 times the wealth that producing and trading goods and services does (e.g. $38 trillion vs $2 trillion). Any firm operating in the international economy is in two businesses at the same time – producing goods and services and managing money.

As economic activity shifts away from heavy industry towards services and high technology, a new type of corporate leadership is emerging. The "organization man" is giving way to a management style which believes in merit, is willing to take risks, decreases middle management, believes strongly in personality and intuition and displays personal vision . . . . In an information era, people are more valuable than capital. The new leadership is totally international, and its marketplace is the world.

(Wishard, 1987)

Robert B. Reich

Robert B. Reich, author of *The Work of Nations*, recognizes three different, but related, skills that will drive "high-value businesses" operating in a global marketplace:

1 *Problem-solving* skills required to put things together in unique ways (be they alloys, molecules, semi-conductor chips, software codes, movie scripts, or pension portfolios).
2 *Problem-identifying* skills required to help customers understand their needs and how these needs can best be met by customized products.
3 *Strategic-brokering* skills to link problem-solvers and problem-identifiers by understanding enough about specific technologies and markets to see the potential for a new product, raise whatever money is necessary to launch the project and assemble the right personnel to solve and identify problems.

To quote Reich:

The idea of 'goods' as something distinct from 'services' has become meaningless, because so much of the value provided by a successful enterprise – in fact, the only value that cannot be easily replicated worldwide – entails services: the specialized research, engineering, design, and production services necessary to solve problems; the specialized sales, marketing and consulting services necessary to identify problems; and the specialized strategic, financial and management services necessary to broker the first two. High-value enterprises are in the business of providing such services.

(Reich, 1991)

Richard Lipsey

Richard Lipsey of the *Canadian Institute for Advanced Research* believes that technological change is what drives growth in the economy and in fact is "the major engine for economic improvement." Ideas matter and technological change is "the history of ideas – new ways of doing things, new ideas for making new products or new ways of making existing products." New ideas allow you to take the same amount of labor and capital and use them differently. This may lead to a new world of economic growth and higher living standards while adjusting to environmental concerns and improving the standard of living in developing countries.

A growing economy which generates new sources of employment requires two capacities:

1   The instructions and designs for putting raw materials together.
2   The organization or manufacturing to produce the final product.

This new concept of economic growth replaces the old neoclassical conventional theory of selfish, greedy individuals aggressively competing with one another. Lipsey sees governments, employers and "totally new kinds of institutions" joining together to build the new economy (Crane, 1991).

Charles Handy

Charles Handy, in his book *The Age of Unreason*, envisions the world of tomorrow as a place where the only constant is change. Discontinuous change without logic, reason or prediction demands "upside-down, inside-out and backward thinking."

The age of discontinuity will require a new breed of "upside-down thinkers" to cope with a twenty-first-century world in which manufacturing jobs will have declined to no more than 10 per cent. Seventy per cent of all jobs in Europe and 80 per cent of those in the United States will require mental rather than manual skills. At least half these jobs will require higher education and/or professional certification. Knowledge and creativity, not muscle power, will be the order of the day.

Handy sees new-age organizations as being made up of four different types of people like the leaves of a shamrock.

1   The *professional core* consists of managers, professionals and technicians – the keepers of the organization's knowledge.
2   *Outside contractors* assemble products or broker services connecting the customer to the supplier.
3   *Part-timers* including home-workers, retirees or people who prefer part-time employment.
4   The *customer*, who is increasingly doing the company's work (e.g. pumping our own gas, clearing away our own food in the fast-food restaurant).

Handy also speaks of "triple I" organizations combining intelligence, information and ideas. In the agrarian age wealth meant owning land. The industrial age rewarded the ability to make things. Today's wealth is equated on our ability to possess knowledge and use it.

The Age of Unreason will require managers who encourage workers to think for themselves and constantly upgrade their skills. As a result:

– changing will be synonymous with learning.
– effective organizations will require intelligent people.
– careers will be shorter and more varied.

Upside-down learners will require upside-down schools in which courses are more aligned to the real world by solving real problems. They will learn more because they'll see the purpose behind what they're doing (Handy, 1990).

Tom Peters

Tom Peters, author of *Thriving on Chaos*, advises the successful leaders of tomorrow to develop flexible organizations that can learn to live with continuous change in a chaotic world by (Peters, 1987):

1 Being responsive to customer trends by listening carefully to their needs and responding rapidly to produce new goods and services which stress quality and value for the money.
2 Encouraging fast-paced innovation through small incremental improvements, field-tested pilots and the ability to risk making a mistake in order to learn how to succeed.
3 Developing partnerships among management, workers, distributors, suppliers and customers which focus on the quest for better products and services by encouraging risk-taking and a sense of ownership in the enterprise.
4 Demonstrating a love for change and a clear vision for the future which inspires confidence and dissolves barriers to progress.
5 Setting realistic, yet challenging, goals which enhance success, encourage the sharing of information and maintain a sense of creativity and integrity in the organization.

Faith Popcorn

Faith Popcorn, in her *Popcorn Report*, speaks of the "Decency Decade" in which companies will have to "sell what they are, as well as what they make." By listening to consumer needs they can humanize their goods or services, prove that their products are not harmful and demonstrate that they are doing their part for the earth and the people who live on it. She sees the consumers of the 1990s to be much more concerned with: quality of life rather than material opulence; with feeling secure, entertained and serviced at home; with small extravagances; with personalized "one-of-a-kind" products; with a reconnecting to our childhood memories (down-aging); with "wellness" and self-healthcare; product quality and truthful advertising; with services which combine functions and preserve more quality time for ourselves (e.g. Videotown Launderette in New York City combines a tanning room, exercise bike, copying and fax machines, video rentals, popcorn – and laundry facilities); and with investing in products and services which exemplify the three critical Es – environment, education and ethics (Popcorn, 1991).

David Jamieson and Julie O'Mara

David Jamieson and Julie O'Mara, in their book *Managing Workforce 2000*, describe the diverse needs of the employees of the twenty-first century. Their "flex-management" system stresses:

1 Working with individual differences and providing choices.
2 Involving employees in decisions and sharing information.
3 Enabling workers to strike a balance between work and home commitments.
4 Helping them cope with problems that might otherwise keep them from being productive.

They see the diverse employment patterns of the future as being influenced by the following demographic trends (Jamieson and O'Mara, 1991):

- An *aging population* (median age of 40) will mean different motivational incentives, management, practices and competition for entry-level jobs.
- More *women in the workforce* (50 per cent of employees) will require new recruitment and retention strategies, child-related and eldercare needs as well as more part-time flexible and home-based jobs.
- Increasing *cultural and visible minorities* will mean new challenges in providing awareness training, English-as-a-second-language skills, remedial education and affirmative action.
- *Education gaps* will see a wide disparity between the highly educated and the functional illiterate dropouts, requiring sensitivity to the aspirations of the former while providing upgrading and skill training for the latter.
- *Disabled workers* will have to be recruited, requiring provisions for workplace access, adjusted work schedules and co-worker sensitivity.

- *Differing values* will mean that some workers will cling to traditional values; some will espouse new-age ideals, others will be family-oriented or loyal to their profession but not necessarily to the firm.

Bowles, Gordon and Weisskopf

The vision of the 1990s and beyond is not always encouraging, however. According to Bowles, Gordon and Weisskopf, in *After the Waste Land*, the US conservative economic policies of the 1980s have resulted in the building of a "garrison state."

They see a proliferation of what they call "guard labor" and "threat labor." *Guard labor* enforces rules that govern economic life by providing surveillance and security to enforce rules that workers often perceive as invasive and oppressive. For example:

- *Workplace supervisors* monitor and discipline workers to extract more intensive labor.
- *Domestic guards* including police, judicial and corrections employees and private security personnel protect against rule violations and deal with violators.
- *International guards* include the armed forces, civil defense employees and producers of military and domestic security equipment.

The authors estimate that guard labor employs 25 million in the US alone. *Threat Labor* refers to the threat of job dismissal which is used to intimidate and control employed workers in conflict-laden workplaces by imposing a labor threat made up of the unemployed, discouraged workers (who have given up working) and prisoners in correctional institutions. Threat labor consisted of 11.5 million people in the US in 1987. Thus guard and threat labor together accounted for almost 37 million individuals.

Bowles, Gordon and Weisskopf (1990) see the garrison state growing steadily in recessionary times as structural unemployment, part-time work and low-paying service jobs become the only alternative for displaced industrial-age workers. The result is an ever-diminishing middle class and a polarization between the wealthy and the impoverished which has long been a characteristic of third-world totalitarian regimes.

SKILLING TO SURVIVE

What are the skills that workers of the twenty-first century will require to get and keep a job and be valued citizens of the community? The American Society for Training and Development (ASTI) surveyed employers for a set of skills which are basic for success in the workplace. They found that besides the traditional three Rs – reading, writing and arithmetic, an additional 13 skills are essential (Witt, 1989):

- Foundation skills
  - Knowing how to learn
- Competence skills
  - Reading
  - Writing
  - Computation (mathematics)
- Communication skills
  - Listening
  - Speaking
- Adaptability skills
  - Creative thinking
  - Problem-solving
- Personal management skills
  - Self-esteem
  - Goal setting/motivation
  - Personal/career development
- Group effectiveness skills
  - Interpersonal skills
  - Negotiation
  - Teamwork
- Influence skills
  - Organizational effectiveness
  - Leadership

Willard Daggett, as Director of Occupational Education Instruction for the State of New York, lists the following skills for employability (Daggett, 1989):

- basics – reading; writing and mathematics;
- keyboarding;
- data manipulation;
- concepts, principles and systems of technology;
- resource management;
- problem-solving/decision-making;
- economics of work;
- human relations;
- applied math and science;
- career planning.

The Quest National Center in Columbus Ohio has produced a program entitled *Skills for Adolescence* which is sweeping North America. It was developed in cooperation with Lions Club International – the largest service organization in the world. Aimed at grades 6 to 8 (age 12–14), Skills for Adolescence is a semester-long program that offers detailed lesson plans and a full complement of curricular materials, including a textbook for students, a guide for parents, and a series of parent seminars.

One of the major goals of the program is for students "to discuss aspects of early adolescence in order to gain a greater understanding of the changes they are beginning to experience." Titles of the units of instruction are as follows:

- Entering the Teen Years: The Challenge Ahead;
- Building Self-Confidence Through Better Communication;
- Learning About Emotions: Developing Competence in Self-Assessment and Self-Discipline;
- Friends: Improving Peer Relationships;
- Strengthening Family Relationships;
- Developing Critical Thinking Skills for Decision Making;
- Setting Goals for Healthy Living;
- Summing Up; Developing One's Potential.

A study on the effectiveness of the program, involving 300 students in grades 7 and 8 in experimental and control groups, found those who participated in Skills for Adolescence (Gerler, 1986):

1 Improved their attitudes toward school and their teachers.
2 Felt more comfortable accepting responsibility and were more able to avoid peer pressure.

As a result of the success of the adolescent program the strategy has now been extended to incorporate *Skills for Growing*, a program for kindergarten to grade 5 which brings together parents, educators and members of the community to teach children important life and citizenship skills within a caring and consistent environment. The five main components mirror the different aspects of the child's world (Lions–Quest, n.d.):

- *Classroom Curriculum* – complements the standard curriculum by offering a variety of ways to teach and reinforce social and academic skills in the areas of language arts, social studies, health and guidance.
- *Positive School Climate* – offers different ways to improve school climate by involving the school and community in positive activities and events related to program goals and curriculum themes.
- *Parents as Partners* – encourages parents to play a vital role on planning teams, carrying out activities at home with children and attending meetings about key parenting issues.
- *Community Involvement* – provides specific opportunities for involve-

ment including students participating in community service projects and members of the community having direct input into the program.

• *Training and Follow-up Support* – whereby the school's Implementation Team, consisting of administrators, teachers, support staff, parents and community members, is training in the program components and hands-on experience with innovative teaching techniques and materials.

The "back to the basics" movement in public education during the 1970s and 1980s decried student deficiencies in English and mathematics. Standardized testing was introduced as a "quality control" mechanism to identify weaknesses and ensure that remedial action was taking place. Test scores became the all-important indicator of success in schooling in many jurisdictions.

The far-eastern nations of Japan, Korea and Taiwan always seem to have better scores in mathematics and science, and the cry goes up that their success as manufacturers must be as a result of their better educational systems. Seldom has there been an analysis of cultural differences, teaching techniques (e.g. rote vs. didactic) and societal values which may contribute to success in the "test score olympics." The bottom line seems to be "Do European and North America nations really want to adopt these behaviors and lifestyles to win the test score olympics? Particularly when we aren't sure that 'academic achievement at any cost' is the reason for industrial success."

Ironically, these same nations with the high scores are commissioning consultants from the US to help them to develop an education system which provides students with *greater* self-esteem, self-reliance, creativity and entrepreneurship and *less* dependency and structure. While the US has the highest rating in the first set of skills, they seem to lag far behind in the test scores. Obviously, this imbalance raises the question "What is the role of education to be in the post-industrial era?"

It is comforting to see that both the American Society for Training and Development and the State of New York propose a "skill package" which is balanced between the more abstract academic-achiever skills and the more concrete, affective, human service-oriented abilities.

Lions–Quest represents a "repackaging" of the original visions of Dewey (1915) Olsen (1945) and Irwin and Russell (1971), as described in Chapter 5. Their concept of "community school" sees the school as an extension of the community it serves with a mandate to build self-esteem, encourage problem-solving and prepare students to be productive and caring citizens of the community. These would also seem to be survival skills for the twenty-first century.

EDUCATION FOR A NEW MILLENNIUM

What have we learned from our experiences in the 1980s in relating education to the world of work? What do new technologies and economic development strategies have to tell us about the nature of work in the post-industrial era? How can the beliefs of futurists, such as those described above, inform us about educational directions in the 1990s and beyond?

The previous chapters have provided an inventory of experiences, strategies and beliefs concerning the role of public education in a world which is no longer dominated by industrial-age dependencies. A new economic environment, which stresses smaller, creative enterprises within a global perspective, appears to be our vision for the future. A post-industrial era, dominated by automated production, advanced telecommunications and the facility to source raw materials and finished goods anywhere in the world provides a challenge to educators preparing youth and redundant workers for employability. Does institutional schooling have the capacity to cope with these demands?

We are a culture that is "addicted to work." Our identities, traditionally for males and increasingly for females, are tied to vocational pursuits. Our status in society is often dependent upon the goods or services we produce. In both the agricultural and industrial ages, we could gain the skills on-the-job, which would lead to financial security and a sense of identity – Joe the farmer, Pete the autoworker. Even our last names in the past often denoted occupational heritage (Taylor, Baker, Smith etc.). But we can no longer guarantee our children a "job for life" if they "stay in school and play the game." The North American dream that our children will do better in life than their parents no longer has relevance. The discarded workers from the "rust-belt" may never work again. What will this mean to our social, psychological and economic well-being?

If schools are the major socializing agents in society, how are they to function in the 1990s and beyond? How can entrepreneurial initiative, cooperative problem-solving and creative expression become a mainstay of the curriculum? How can teachers, seen by many as role-models, exemplify these virtues? How can we reduce industrial-age dependencies in organizations which still celebrate their exclusionary powers in sorting the achievers from the discards? How can "gate-keepers" afflicted by the "edifice-complex" and obsessed by the need to preserve the status quo be reborn as "emancipators of learning"?

Social science research is helping us to better understand personality types, particularly in relation to career patterns. The *Myers-Briggs Type Indicator (MBTI)* explains the subtleties in the contrasting behaviors of 16 personality types based on the theories of Carl Jung (Myers and Myers, 1980), e.g.

- extraversion vs. introversion;
- sensing versus intuition;
- thinking versus feeling;
- judging versus perceiving.

Don Lowry has refined and popularized the MBTI research into *True Colors*, "an effective tool to help individuals build self-esteem by understanding their behaviors, skills, needs and motivations." He organizes the 16 personality types into four basic colors (Lowry, 1988):

- *Gold* persons are realistic, matter-of-fact and more curious about new products than they are about new ideas and theories. They are very good at following procedures and in detailing rules and regulations. They prefer work environments in which duties and authorities are well-defined and where they can be rewarded through hard work, loyalty and following the rules. They are usually neat and orderly at work and companies value them as responsible and dependable employees. Their interest in thoroughness, pragmatism, punctuality and efficiency leads them to occupations in which these preferences are appreciated.
- *Greens* are the most reluctant of all the color types to do things in a traditional manner. They are always on the lookout for new projects, new activities and new procedures. This accounts for their tendency to become entrepreneurs and to work for themselves. Greens can succeed in a variety of occupations as long as the job does not involve too much humdrum routine. They tend to lose interest once their work is no longer challenging and they may fail to follow through, often to the discomfort of colleagues. As an employee, the Green person might work against the system just for the fun of being one-up. However, this type can contribute immensely in a work atmosphere that allows independence and expression of ingenuity.
- *Blue* persons have a remarkable latitude in career choices and they succeed in many fields. They are imaginative, enthusiastic, and can do almost anything which is of interest to them. At work, they are at ease with colleagues and others enjoy their presence. They are highly creative in dealing with people and are outstanding at inspiring group spirit and getting people together. Blues are likely to lose interest in their job once people or projects become routine. They prefer a family-like, friendly, personalized, and warm work environment. They dislike jobs which require painstaking detail and follow-through over a period of time. They prefer people-oriented careers and job opportunities which allow creativity and variety in day-to-day operations.
- *Orange* men and women are action oriented. They are highly resourceful and can sell a product, an idea, or a project in a way no other color type

can. However, their lack of interest in administrative details and follow through makes them the target of blame and criticism within an organization. When striking out on their own, they must have someone to follow-through if they are to be successful. When the Orange need for excitement and their promotional talents are used to constructive ends, any institution is fortunate to have them as employees. However, if these energies are not channeled correctly, destructive and anti-social activities will result. Confining rules and regulations and day-to-day routines are deadly to Orange. They seek excitement in a job above all else.

What do these four basic personality types have to tell us about education? Perhaps it is not surprising that 56 per cent of teachers and administrators are Gold whereas 43 per cent of the general population in the US is that type.

There are 8 per cent of teachers who qualify as Green versus 12 per cent of the general population. Thirty-two per cent of teachers are Blue while the general population has 12 per cent who are that personality type. Finally only 2 per cent of teachers (mostly industrial arts) are Orange while the general population consists of 33 per cent.

Judging from these statistics, it would appear that most schools are staffed and administered by persons who are the most resistant to change, and least receptive to taking risks (56 per cent) while the majority of students (57 per cent) are just the opposite. The concern becomes particularly acute when at least 45 per cent (Orange and Green) require a nontraditional, flexible, entrepreneurial learning environment, which it appears will be so important in preparing for twenty-first-century employment, while the educational enterprise is being lead by authoritative "gate-keepers" (Gold).

BACK TO THE FUTURE

It would appear that the social and economic needs of the twenty-first century may have a lot in common with the learning styles, service patterns and creative enterprises of the nineteenth century. Advanced technologies such as computer application, robotics and bio-engineering may result in most goods and information production requiring a minimum participation by human labor. Similarly, if primary resources and manufactured products continue to be sourced in developing countries, employment opportunities in the western world will be drastically reduced and modestly remunerated.

What will be the employment patterns of the future in a post-industrial age where jobs are still synonymous with identity? How can we improve our reading and computation skills while heightening our technological literacy? How can we ensure that discarded youth and redundant workers will not be left out of this process of finding vocational identity and technological acculturation?

I believe the top 20 per cent of our school populations will continue to excel as abstract achievers filling our scientific, executive and professional rolls. However, we can no longer afford to sacrifice the more than 60 per cent who have not benefited from higher education. Their lack of self-esteem and occupational identity are resulting in the disillusionment, despair and destructive behavior characteristic of the under-classes of the "garrison state." A growing army of idle, despondent youth and redundant workers are turning many of our cities into violent, drug-infested battlegrounds.

To prevent this destruction of human potential, we must radically change the way we prepare our young people for the world of work. The primary years of schooling (as described in Chapter 6) should focus on the spatial concrete learning needs of our children to enable them to build self-esteem rather than being forced to compete in a world of abstraction in which the majority will fail. The nineteenth-century agrarian age provided a set of manageable skills in which everyone had a chance to participate and their contributions were valued. While we can't go back to tilling the soil and tending our flocks, there are many hands-on activities related to craft, design and technological skills, community service and cooperative entrepreneurship which can contribute a sense of personal well-being and creative accomplishment while building a foundation of self-esteem and positive identity. These are obviously prerequisites of more abstract achievement as well as being fundamental skills of the post-industrial age.

Adolescents must not be excluded from the world of community problem-solving and decision-making so important for new-age survival. The challenges of inventing new products and services, both individually and as part of a working group, will provide opportunities for hands-on expression, self-reliance and the feeling of creating one's own destiny instead of being a casualty of fate. Environmental protection, eldercare and artistic endeavors are but a few "niche" areas which may begin to replace traditional industrial employment. Computer literacy will join reading and mathematics as fundamental skills but they must also have some concrete application to real-life enterprises and cooperative ventures.

Traditional institutional industrial-age schooling for youth should evolve into smaller more entrepreneurial "learning cooperatives." Teachers and students working together, often in noninstitutional settings, would form "quality circles" to master academic and technological skills which have direct application to the community's social and economic needs.

Most important, everyone should have an opportunity to contribute to the collective enterprise, gaining a sense of identity and personal well-being.

Community economic development represents an effective means to "reskill" the workforce while creating new sources of employment to offset industrial-age dislocation. The community as a whole gains a feeling of empowerment which overcomes corporate and governmental dependencies. The use of the "third sector" as a potent economic force which combines governmental, commercial and voluntary resources in a unified process of community betterment is also a "window of opportunity" on the twenty-first century.

How are existing teachers and administrators to cope with these non-institutional learning alternatives? The Adult Day School and the Learning Enrichment Foundation in the City of York have tried to demonstrate the potential of combining education, training and economic development. This has been a joint venture which has survived, and even flourished, during the decade of the 1980s. Traditional institutional dependencies have given way to a new process of consumer-responsiveness and cooperative problem-solving. These have not been people who worshiped "bricks and mortar" but those who learned to put the learner/trainee/entrepreneur at the center of the economic enterprise. To date thousands of persons have found jobs or acquired skills through this process. As a result it has been recognized as an exemplary project on the "world stage."

I have sometimes referred to the Adult Day School as being staffed by "born-again teachers." In its ten years of operation, ADS has demonstrated that it is possible to remove people from industrial-age dependencies so as to liberate the sense of nurturing, creativity and learner-responsiveness which brought many persons into the profession in the first place. While the gate-keepers still dominate most institutional settings, I believe that educational alternatives such as the Adult Day School and the Learning Enrichment Foundation are helping us to find our way as we reach for the challenges of the twenty-first century.

Finally, there will be no real progress until we change the "culture of dependency" which got us through the industrial era but is so out of place in the "knowledge society." As our primary socializing influence, public schooling must lead the way in changing values and life styles while creating the future. A new breed of teachers must be recruited who have an entrepreneurial world-view while recognizing the importance of hands-on learning and direct service to the community. These people should not be institutionally trained but prepared in the "skunk-works" real-life environment made famous by Peters and Waterman.

Just as all workers have to be retrained, existing teachers and administrators must emerge from their "institutional wombs" to learn about "life-on-the-cutting-edge" where dependency is a disability not a virtue. The discarded must be active and valued contributors to play in the new millennium if for no other reason than that the economy needs their purchasing power, concrete skills and visioning to survive. Public education still has a vital role to play in this process of renewal. Let us cast aside our chains of industrial-age dependency and institutional bondage and GET ON WITH THE JOB.

References

PREFACE

Flanigan, J. (1991) "GM cutbacks mark end of era for middle class," *The Toronto Star*, December 23.

Maynard, M. (1991) "Goal: save $5 billion by mid-decade," *USA Today*, December 19.

OECD (1989) *Towards an Enterprising Culture*, Paris: CERI.

—— (1992) *Partners in Education: The New Partnership between Business & School*: Paris: CERI.

Shuttleworth, D. E. (1978) "The Learning Exchange System (LEARNXS): analysis of a demonstration project in community education," Toronto: University of Toronto, unpublished Ph.D. thesis.

Tough A. (1977) "Major learning efforts; recent research and future directions," *Adult Education*, 28(4) Summer.

Whyte, W. H., Jr. (1956) *The Organization Man*, New York: Simon & Schuster.

CHAPTER 1

Daggett, W. (1989) "The changing nature of work – a challenge to education," speech in Kansas.

Dewey, J. (1915) *School and Society*, Chicago: University of Chicago Press.

Donner, A. (1983), "Education helps in recession," , *Toronto Star*, March 25.

Drucker, P. (1985) *Innovation and Entrepreneurship*, London: Heinemann.

Economic Council of Canada (1990), *Good Jobs, Bad Jobs*, Ottawa: ECC.

Henchey, N. (1983) *Education for the 21st Century: Canadian Imperatives*, Ottawa: Canadian Teachers Federation.

Kirsh, S. (1983) *Unemployment – Its Impact on Body and Soul*, Toronto: Canadian Mental Health Association.

Levine, H. (1983) "Future work mostly menial: US study", *Toronto Star*, March 23.

OECD (1989) *Employment Rates for 15–19 Year Olds 1986/87*, Paris: CERI.

Perelman, L. J. (1986) "Learning our lesson," *The Futurist*, March–April.

Peters, P. J. and Waterman, R. H. (1982) *In Search of Excellence*, New York: Harper & Row.

Phillips, C. E. (1957) *The Development of Education in Canada*, Toronto: Gage.

Statistics Canada (1986) Census Data, Ottawa: Statscan.

Toffler, A. (1980) *The Third Wave*, New York: William Morrow.

CHAPTER 2

Bargellini, S. (1980) *Firenze come un'avventura*, Florence: EDIFIR.
Canadian Press (1992) "Jobs shift to small firms," *Globe & Mail*, March 20.
Drucker, P. (1989) *The New Realities*, New York: Harper & Row.
Halal, W. E. and Nikitin, A. I. (1990) "Democratic free enterprise," *The Futurist*, Nov.–Dec.
Hatch, C. R. (1986) "Industrial rebirth in Italy's flexible production networks,", *The Entrepreneurial Economy*, Washington, D.C.
Hirsch, M. (1990) "The strength of corporate Japan is built on small workshops," *Toronto Star*, December 17.
MacInnis, J. (1985) "Charities don't need more stringent controls," *Toronto Star*, December 13.
OECD (1989) *Towards an Enterprising Culture*, Paris: CERI.
Ross, D. (1990) "How valuable is volunteering?" *Perceptions*, Ottawa, 14(4).
Sanders, P. and LaRoe, M. (1983) *Quality Circles for Schools*, Talahassee, FL.
Schumacher, E. F. (1974) *Small is Beautiful*, London: Sphere Books.

CHAPTER 3

ACCESS Inc. (1986), *Be Your Own Boss*, Washington, DC: Access Inc.
Alberta Education (1987) *Career & Life Management 20: Senior High School Curriculum Guide, Interim 1987*, Edmonton: Alberta Education.
Barnes, B. & O'Connor, J. (1987) *Manual for Cooperative Work Study Programs*, Toronto: Guidance Center, University of Toronto.
Benedict, R. R. (1988) "Enterprise High: where students profit from education," *The Entrepreneurial Economy*, May.
Clark, D. M. (1989) "Partnerships of business education a flop," *Adult and Continuing Education Today*, October 23.
Coleman, B. (1984) "Enterprise High," *Inc*, September.
DeLargy, P. (1987) *Real Enterprises*, Athens, Georgia: REAL Enterprises.
Glendinning, B. (1987a) "What is J.A.?" *CEAA Informer*, June.
—— (1987b) "Project Business," *CEAA Informer*, June.
Hoyt, K. B. (1986) "A career education perspective on business–education partnerships," *Community Education Journal*, July.
Industry–Education Council (1987) *Linking Learning With Earning*, Hamilton–Wentworth, Ont: IEC.
—— (1987) *Partnerships in Education*, Hamilton–Wentworth, Ont: IEC.
Marshall, W. (1983) "Tomorrow's school today," *Educational Horizons*, 62(1).
McREL (1990) *Rural Schools & Community Development*, Aurora, CO: McREL.
Mini-Enterprise in Schools Project and Community Service Volunteers Advisory Service (1990), *Enterprise Education in the National Curriculum*, London: CSV.
National Center for Research in Vocational Education (1981) *Program for Acquiring Competence in Entrepreneurship (PACE)*, Columbus: Ohio State University.
OECD (1989) *Towards an Enterprising Culture*, Paris: CERI.
—— (1992) *Partners in Business: The New Partnership Between Business and Schools*, Paris: CERI.
—— (1990) *Human Resources Development: Education, Training and Labor Market Developments and Issues*, Paris: CERI.

O'Connor, J. (1987) *Designing and Introducing an Enterprise Skills Curriculum Project in Ireland*, Paris: OECD (internal document).

Ontario Ministry of Education (1990) *Entrepreneurial Studies*, Toronto.

Perry, N. J. (1988) "The education crises: what business can do," *Fortune*, July 4.

Sher, J. (1977) *Education in Rural America*, Colorado: Westview Press.

Stone, N. (1991) "Does Business have any business in education?" *Harvard Business Review*, March–April.

The Training Agency (1989) *What is TVEI?*, London: TVEI Unit.

—— (1990) *This is TVEI*, Sheffield: TVEI Enquiry Point.

CHAPTER 4

Barber, L. W. and McClellan, M. C. (1987) "Looking at America's dropouts: who are they?" *Phi Delta Kappan*, December.

Danzberger, J., Lefkowitz, B. and Hahn, A. (1987) *Dropouts in America: Enough Is Known for Action*, Washington DC: Institute for Educational Leadership.

Hahn, A. (1987) "Reaching out to America's dropouts: what to do?" *Phi Delta Kappan*, December.

Jensen, M. T. (1990) "Denmark: production schools" (unpublished article).

Justiz, M. J. and Kameen, M. C. (1987) "Business offers a hand to education," *Phi Delta Kappan*, January.

Levine, S. (1980) *The Psychological and Social Effects of Youth Unemployment*, Toronto: Child in the City Project – University of Toronto.

OECD (1986) *Facets of the Transition to Adulthood*, Paris: CERI.

—— (1989) *Towards an Enterprising Culture*, Paris: CERI.

Raynes, P. (1986) "Muscling in on unemployment," *Initiatives*, December.

Roberts, J. (1987) "Striding ahead in the North East," *Employment Gazette*, September.

Turner, D. (1985) "Learning to be enterprising: the CITY model," *Initiatives*, August.

—— (1986) "New ways of promoting enterprise," *Initiatives*, February.

Wallin, E. (1988) "Enterprise and enterprise skills: some Swedish examples and a rationale," Paris: OECD (internal document).

Wilburn, N. (1988) "CREATE in Action," *Initiatives*, February.

CHAPTER 5

Boyer, E. (1990) "Service linking school to life," in J. C. Kendall, *Combining Service & Learning*, Vol. I, Raleigh, NC: NSIEE.

Briscoe, J. (1991) "Citizenship, service, and school reform in Pennsylvania: PennSERVE," *Phi Delta Kappan*, June.

Brison, D. W. (1972) "Restructuring the school system," in M. Byrne and J. Quarter, *"Must Schools Fail?"* Toronto: McClelland & Stewart.

—— (1973–74) *Peterborough Alternative Education Project*, Toronto: Ontario Ministry of Education.

Conrad D. and Hedin, D. (1990) "Youth program models," in J. C. Kendall, *Combining Service & Learning*, Vol. II, Raleigh, NC: National Society for Internships and Experiential Education.

—— (1991) "School-based community service: what we know from research and theory," *Phi Delta Kappan*, June.

Counts, G. S. (1932) *Dare the Schools Build a New Social Order?*, New York: John Day.

Dewey, J. (1915) *School and Society*, Chicago: University of Chicago Press.

Dickson, A. (1973) "A curricular approach to community service," *Today's Education*, Sept.–Oct.

—— (1980) "Community service and the curriculum" (unpublished).

Dickson, A. and Dickson, M. (1976) *A Chance to Serve*, London: Dobson Books.

Education Commission of the States (1985) *Reconnecting Youth: The Next Stage of Reform*, Denver: Education Commission of the States.

Goodlad, J. D. (1984) *A Place Called School*, New York: McGraw-Hill.

Hanna, P. R. (1937) *Youth Serves the Community*, New York: D. Appleton Century.

Irwin, M. and Russell, W. (1971) *The Community Is the Classroom*, Midland, MI: Pendell.

Kendall, J. C. (1990) *Combining Service and Learning*, Vol. I, Raleigh, NC: NSIEE.

Kielsmeier, J. C. and Cairn, R. W. (1988) "Minnesota Governor's youth service recognition," *Program Guidelines*, May.

Kilpatrick, W. H. (1918) "The project method," *Teachers College Record*, September.

Lewis, B. (1991) *The Kid's Guide to Social Action*, Minneapolis: Free Spirit Publishing.

Mang, L. (1979) *Community as Classroom*, Toronto: Learnxs Press.

Nathan, J. (1991) "A restructured school," in R. W. Cavin, and J. C. Kielsmeier, *Growing Hope*, Roseville, MN: National Youth Leadership Council.

Nathan, J. and Kielsmeier, J. C. (1991) "The sleeping giant of school reform," *Phi Delta Kappan*, June.

Newmann, F.M. (1975) *Education for Citizen Action: Challenge for Secondary Curriculum*, Berkeley, CA: McCutchan.

Olsen, E. G. (1945) *School & Community*, New York: Prentice Hall.

Parsons, C. (1991) "SerVermont; the little initiative that could," *Phi Delta Kappan*, June.

Scott, S. (1991) "School-wide focus on service learning," in R. W. Cairn, and J. C. Kielsmeier, *Growing Hope: A Sourcebook on Integrating Youth Service into the School Curriculum*, Roseville, MN: National Youth Leadership Council.

Shuttleworth, D. E. (1968) *Volunteers Unlimited*, Toronto: North York Board of Education.

Silcox, H. (1991) "Citizenship, service and school reform in Pennsylvania: Abraham Lincoln High School," *Phi Delta Kappan*, June.

Wigginton, E. (1985) *Sometimes a Shining Moment: Twenty Years at Foxfire*, Garden City, NY: Anchor/Doubleday.

William P. Grant Foundation (1988) *The Forgotten Half: Non-College Youth in America*, Washington, DC: W. P. Grant Foundation.

CHAPTER 6

Board of Education for City of York (1990) *Technology in City of York Schools*, City of York, Ont.: Board of Education.

Clandfield, D. and Sivell, J. (1990) *Co-operative Learning and Social Change*, Toronto: OISE Press.

Conrad, D. (1991) "Situations & Alternatives assignment application of Mazlow's hierarchy of needs," in R. W. Cairn and J. C. Kielsmeier, *Growing Hope*, Roseville, MN: NYLC.

Crossett, B. (1983) "Using both halves of the brain to teach the whole child," *Social Education*, April.

Day, G. (1989) "Some hands-on solutions to problems," *Toronto Star*, December 5.

Department of Education and Science (1983) *Science in Primary Schools: A Discussion Paper*, London: HMI Science Committee.

—— (1985) *Problem Solving: Science and Technology in Primary Schools*, London: The Engineering Council and the Standing Conference on Schools" Science and Technology.

Dewey, J. (1916) *Democracy and Education*, New York: Macmillan.

Edwards, B. (1979) *Drawing on the Right Side of the Brain*, Los Angeles: J. P. Tarcher.

Evans, P. (1983) *Technology in the Primary School*, National Center for School Technology.

Jones, A. (1990) "A responsive higher education system" in P. Wright (ed.), *Industry and Higher Education*, Oxford: Oxford University Press.

Kearns, D. P. and Doyle, D. P. (1988) *Winning the Brain Race*, San Francisco: ICS Press.

O'Malley, S. (1990) "Innovative program helps students build working skills," *Whig-Standard*, Kingston, Ont.

Ontario Ministry of Education (1980) *Issues and Directions*, Toronto.

—— (1988) *Science Is Happening Here*, Toronto.

—— (1990) *Technological Education – The Way Ahead*, Toronto.

—— (1990) *The Transition Years*, Toronto.

Rennels, M. (1976) "Cerebral symmetry: an urgent concern for education," *Phi Delta Kappan*, March.

Rouse, C. (1990) "Students build a future; literally," *Kingston This Week*, September 22.

Royal Society of Arts (1986) *Education for Capability*, Windsor: NFER–NELSON.

—— (1984) "Capability for all," *Education for Capability Newsletter*, Spring.

Senate of Canada, Special Committee on Youth (1986) *YOUTH: A Plan of Action*, Ottawa: Senate of Canada.

Shuttleworth, D. (1989) "Hands-on, concrete learning: why it's needed now," *Community Education Journal*, Spring.

Slavson, S. R. (1961) *Re-educating the Delinquent*, New York: Collier.

Staley, F. (1980) "Hemisphere brain research," *Joper*, April.

US National Institute of Mental Health (1991) "Day care and school performance," *Toronto Star*.

Ward, D. and Benfield, E. (1985) *Industry in Primary Classrooms*, Salford: Schools Curriculum Industry Project, City of Salford Education Department.

CHAPTER 7

Allen, D. N., Ginsberg, J. E. and Meiburger, S. A. (1984) *Home Grown Entrepreneurship: Pennsylvania Small Business Incubators*, University Park, PA: Institute of Public Administration, Penn. State University.

Drucker, P. (1989) *The New Realities*, New York: Harper and Row.

Hatch, C. R. (1990) "Manufacturing modernization: strategies that don't work, strategies that do," *The Entrepreneurial Economy Review*, Autumn.

Mt. Auburn Associates (1986) "Designing a small business incubator policy," *The Entrepreneurial Economy*, November.

Plosila, W. H. (1990) "Technology development: perspectives on the Third Wave", *The Entrepreneurial Economy Review*, Autumn.

Ross, D. and Friedman, R. E. (1990) "The emerging third wave: new economic development strategies in the "90s," *The Entrepreneurial Economy Review*, Autumn.

Town of Pasadena (1990) *The Venture Center: An Industrial Incubator*, Newfoundland.

Zeidenberg, J. (1990) "Breeding success in vitro," *Profit*, December.

CHAPTER 8

Caja Laboral Popular (1969) *Nuestra Experiencia Cooperativa*, Mondragon: CLP.

Center for Community Economic Development (1975), *Community Economic Development*, Cambridge, MA.

Larranaga, J. (1981) *Don Jose Maria Arizmendiarrieta*, Mondragon: Caja Laboral Popular.

Leroy, M. (1979) *Evaluation of New Dawn Enterprises Ltd.*, Sydney, NS: College of Cape Breton.

MacLeod, G. (1986) *New Age Business*, Ottawa: Canadian Council on Social Development.

Macsween, R. (1991) "New dawn for a depleted island community," *Making Waves*, 2(2), April.

Muszynski, L. (1979) *Jobs Needed, Community Economic Development, A Job and Social Development Strategy for Metropolitan Toronto*, Toronto: Social Planning Council.

Shuttleworth, D. (1983) "What's a nice teacher like you doing in a place like this? Education in the workplace," *Orbit*, Ontario Institute for Studies in Education, February.

Social Planning Council of Metropolitan Toronto (1978), *The Problem Is Jobs, Not People*, Toronto Social Planning Council.

Social Planning Council of Metropolitan Toronto and Learnxs Foundation Inc. (1979) *Youth Ventures – Feasibility Study (1979–80)*, Toronto: CEIC.

—— (1980) *Youth Ventures Submission for Funding (1980–83)*, Toronto: CEIC.

Stein, B. (1973) "How successful are CDCs?" *Review of Black Political Economy*, Spring.

Young, V. and Reich, C. (1974) *Patterns of Dropping Out*, Toronto: Research Dept., Toronto Board of Education.

CHAPTER 9

OECD (1991) *Partners in Education: The New Partnership Between Business and Schools*, Paris: CERI.

Shuttleworth, D. (1978) "The Learning Exchange System (LEARNXS): analysis of a demonstration project in community education," Toronto: University of Toronto, unpublished Ph.D. thesis.

—— (1981) "The Learnxs method: a support system for community – resource learning," *Interchange*, 2(1), Summer.

—— (1986) "Community as classroom: continuing education for community development in the City of York," *Community Services CATALYST*, 26(2), Spring.

—— (1988) "Community as classroom," *Community Education Journal*, July.

—— (1990) "Adopt-an-Industry," *Orbit*, Ontario Institute for Studies in Education, April.

Statistics Canada (1986) Census Data, Ottawa: Statscan.

Toronto Board of Education (1973) *Learnxs: Learning Exchange System*, Toronto.

York Community Economic Development Committee (1986), *Community Report*, City of York, Ontario.

CHAPTER 10

Biddle, W. W. and Biddle, L. J. (1965) *The Community Development Process*, New York: Holt, Rinehart and Winston.

Dewey, J. (1915) *School and Society*, Chicago: University of Chicago Press.

Etobicoke Board of Education (1971) *SEE; School of Experimental Education*, Etobicoke, Ont.

Fair, J. (1975) *"Peers as helpers: personal change in members of self-help groups in metropolitan Toronto,"* Toronto: University of Toronto, unpublished doctoral thesis, OISE.

House, E. (1976) "The micropolitics of innovation: nine propositions," *Phi Delta Kappan*, January.

Illich, I. (1970) *De-schooling Society*, New York: Harper and Row.

Irwin, M. and Russell, W. (1971) *The Community is the Classroom*, Midland, MI. Pendell.

North York Board of Education (1971), *A Feasibility Study for An Alternative and Independent Study Program (AISP)*, North York, Ont.

Olsen, E. (1945) *School and Community*, New York: Prentice Hall.

Ontario Ministry of Education (1968) *Living and Learning*, (Hall–Dennis Report), Toronto.

—— (1972–73) "Secondary school organization and diploma requirements," *Circular H.S.–1*, Toronto.

—— (1975) *The Formative Years*, Toronto.

—— (1977–78) *The Co-operative Utilization of Community Resources for Diploma Credit Courses*, A supplement to H.S.–1, Toronto.

Ontario Ministry of Colleges and Universities, Commission on Post-Secondary Education (1972) *The Learning Society*, Toronto.

Orbit (1973) "Profile of a School/22: *Subway Academy*," *Orbit* 20, December.

Rogers, E. M. (1962) *Diffusion of Innovations*, New York: Free Press.

Shuttleworth, D. (1978) "The Learning Exchange System (Learnxs): analysis of a demonstration project in community education," Toronto: University of Toronto, unpublished PhD. thesis.

—— (1981) "The Learnxs method: a support system for community-resource learning," *Interchange*, 2(1), Summer.

Toronto Board of Education (1971) *People for an Alternative Elementary School and the ALPHA Experience*, Toronto.

—— (1972) *Proposal for CONTACT*, Toronto.

—— (1972) *Final Report of the Special Task Force*, Toronto.

Tough, A. (1971) *The Adult's Learning Projects*, Toronto: OISE Press.

—— (1977) "Major learning efforts: recent research and future directions," *Adult Education* 28(4), Summer.

Yip, D. (1971) "SEED: a preliminary report," Toronto: Toronto Board of Education, Research Dept.

CHAPTER 11

Aarsteinsen, B. (1992) "Why 'Buy Canadian' is a real hard sell," *Toronto Star*, February 8.

Alberta Department of Advanced Education and Manpower, *The Community Survey Handbook*, Edmonton, Alberta.

Atwood, J. (1990) "Women entrepreneurs are an educational opportunity," *Adult and Continuing Education Today*, March.

Blasi, J. (1991) "US employees own 12% of their firms," *Business Week*, July.

Bread and Roses Credit Union (1991) *13th Annual Report*, Toronto.

Brehl, R. (1990) "Women outshine men in small business," *Toronto Star*, October 26.

Brennan, P. (1989) "Small firms do survive study says," *Toronto Star*, October 23.

Chicago (1990) "Training tomorrow's work force," January.

Ehrlich, P. R. and Ehrlich, A. H. (1991) *Healing the Planet*, Reading, MA: Addison–Wesley.

Eversley, J. (1987) "How the do-gooders became bankers," *Initiatives*, June.

The Futurist (1991) "Biomass for cleaner energy," May–June.

Galbraith, J. K. (1983) *Economics and the Arts*, London: Arts Council Lecture.

Gleeson, H. (1980) *A Guide to Co-op Alternatives*, Toronto, Ont.

Gould, S. and Lyman, J. (1984) "Women entrepreneurs at the hub of enterprise development," *The Entrepreneurial Economy*, November.

Grayson, D. (1986) "WEDCO: to date there have been no defaults," *Initiatives*, April.

The Guardian (1985), "Growth from hot air" February.

Hilborn, C. (1990) "Boss ladies lead growth," *Small Business*, April.

Kreiner, S. (1987) "PACE and the O & O supermarkets: an integrated proactive development model," *The Entrepreneurial Economy*, November.

Kuenstler, P. (1986) "Risk capital with a local accent," *Initiatives*, August.

Lambe, S. (1991) "College goes high tech in fighting illiteracy," *Charlottetown Guardian* (PEI) November 4.

Lang, C. (1991) *Co-operative Resources Center*, Toronto: Ontario Institute for Studies in Education.

Learning Enrichment Foundation (1990a) *Partners in Progress*, City of York, Ont.

—— (1990b) *LEF Report*, City of York, Ont.

Lindenfeld, F. (1990) "O & O – The rise and fall of a great idea" *Worker Co-ops*, Spring.

Love, W. G. (1980) *Business Plan for City Farmer Hydroponic Gardens*, Toronto: Youth Ventures Feasibility Study.

Making Waves (1991) "CCE assists Manitoba worker ownership strategy," January.

Masters, P. (1980) "The banks," in *A Guide to Co-op Alternatives*, Toronto.

Miller, J. (1991) "The banker who bucked the odds," *Toronto Star*, December 16.

Mt. Auburn Associates (1987) "Experience with revolving loan funds," *The Entrepreneurial Economy*, October.

Nash, B. (1985) "The GROWTH industry roots in the inner city," *Initiatives*, April.

Newfoundland and Labrador Development Corporation (1989) *Development Savings Bonds 1989 – Agent's Book*, St. Johns, Newfoundland.

Racey, D. (1985) *An Idea for the Times: A future for our Young?* Schumacher, Ont: Underdog Publications.

Riordan, J. (1980) "Development of the fuelwood processing Venture," Toronto: Youth Ventures Feasibility Study.

Rolland, K. (1984) "The 'Second Wave' of church social investments," *The Entrepreneurial Economy*, December.

Ross, D. P. and Usher, P. J. (1986) *From the Roots Up*, Toronto: James Lorimer.

Smith, D. M. (1991) *Kin Care and the American Corporation*, Homewood, IL: Business One Irwin.

Stanfield, B. (1991) "The LETSYSTEM takes off," *Edges*, 4(3).

Stares, R. (1985) "GLIEFARMS", *Initiatives*, April.

Tellier, D. (1982) "What's new in the biomass field?" *Canadian Forest Industries*, January.

Wallin, J. C. (1980) "Pallets – a new source of fuelwood?" *Alternative Sources of Energy* 41.

York Board of Education (1990) *Report re Almena System*, City of York, Ont.

—— (1991–92) "Working together to offer courses for seniors," *City of York Schools*, Winter.

York Community Economic Development Committee (1986) *Community Report*, City of York, Ont.

Youth Ventures Development Corporation (1980) *Youth Ventures Feasibility Study (1979–1980) Submission for Funding (1980–1983)*, Toronto.

Zeidenberg, J. (1990) "Breeding success in Vitro," *Profit*, December.

CHAPTER 12

Adolph, C. (1989) "Toffler's crystal ball warns of worker neglect," *Toronto Star*, February 16.

Bowles S., Gordon D., and Weisskopf, P. (1990) *After the Waste Land*, London: M. E. Sharpe.

Crane, D. (1991) "Building a new economic order," *Toronto Star*, June 2.

Daggett, W. (1989) "The changing nature of work – a challenge to education," Speech in Kansas.

Gerler, E. R., Jr. (1986) "Skills for adolescence: a new program for young teenagers," *Phi Delta Kappan*, February.

Handy, C. (1990) *The Age of Unreason*, Boston, MA: Harvard Business School Press.

Jamieson, D. and O'Mara, J. (1991) *Managing Workforce 2000*, San Francisco: Jossey-Bass.

Lions–Quest (n.d.) *Skills for Growing*, Columbus, OH: Quest International.

Lowry, D. (1988) *True Colors*, Toronto: Guidance Center, Ontario Institute for Studies in Education.

Myers I. B. and Myers, P. B. (1980) *Gifts Differing*, Palo Alto, CA: Consulting Psychologists Press.

Naisbitt, J. and Aburdene, P. (1990) *Megatrends 2000: Ten New Directions for the 1990's*, New York: William Morrow.

Peters, T. (1987) *Thriving on Chaos*, New York: A. A. Knopf.

Popcorn, F. (1991) *The Popcorn Report*, New York: Doubleday.

Reich, R. B. (1991) *The Work of Nations*, New York: A. A. Knopf.

Toffler, A. (1989) *Powershift*, New York: William Morrow.

Wishard, W. (1987) "The 21st century economy," *The Futurist*, May–June.

Witt, M. (1989) "16 skills employers really want," *Getting Hired*, 10(1).

Index